The Slave Trade and the Origins of International Human Rights Law

THE SLAVE TRADE AND THE ORIGINS OF INTERNATIONAL HUMAN RIGHTS LAW

Jenny S. Martinez

OXFORD
UNIVERSITY PRESS

OXFORD
UNIVERSITY PRESS

Oxford University Press, Inc., publishes works that further
Oxford University's objective of excellence
in research, scholarship, and education.

Oxford   New York
Auckland   Cape Town   Dar es Salaam   Hong Kong   Karachi
Kuala Lumpur   Madrid   Melbourne   Mexico City   Nairobi
New Delhi   Shanghai   Taipei   Toronto

With offices in
Argentina   Austria   Brazil   Chile   Czech Republic   France   Greece
Guatemala   Hungary   Italy   Japan   Poland   Portugal   Singapore
South Korea   Switzerland   Thailand   Turkey   Ukraine   Vietnam

Published by Oxford University Press, Inc.
198 Madison Avenue, New York, NY 10016

www.oup.com

Oxford is a registered trademark of Oxford University Press

Library of Congress Cataloging-in-Publication Data
Martinez, Jenny S.
The slave trade and the origins of international human rights law / Jenny Martinez.
    p.   cm.
Includes bibliographical references and index.
ISBN 978-0-19-539162-6 (hardback)
1. Slavery—Law and legislation. 2. Human rights—International cooperation. I. Title.
K3267.M37   2011
341.4'8—dc23   2011016418

1 3 5 7 9 8 6 4 2

Printed in the United States of America
on acid-free paper

Dedicated to Mom, David, Alyse, Patrice, and Nancy

CONTENTS

The Slave Trade and the Origins of International Human Rights Law

CHAPTER 1

Introduction

It was April 1822, and Captain Henry John Leeke was sailing off the coast of Africa on the HMS *Myrmidon*. As always, Leeke scanned the horizon, looking for the contrast of white sails against the brilliant blue waters. The sails might belong to one of his fellow captains in the British Royal Navy. They might belong to an English merchant ship, headed to the British colony at Freetown, Sierra Leone. Or they might belong to an illegal slave ship. In the holds of that ship might be 300, 400, even 600 miserable men, women, and children.

Leeke carried orders directing him to search for and capture ships carrying slaves. British law had banned slave trading since 1807, but more recently Britain had signed treaties with Spain, Portugal, and the Netherlands outlawing the traffic. Leeke, like other British officers stationed in waters where slave traders were known to sail, had copies of the treaties authorizing him to search ships from these nations. Ships that were slave trading in violation of the treaties were subject to seizure and forfeiture. Leeke and his crew stood to profit from the successful capture of an illegal slave ship, for the law allowed them a share of the proceeds from the sale of the forfeited ship and sometimes a bounty for each slave liberated.

When he spotted a suspicious vessel, Leeke would order his men to trim the sails and begin the chase. Even a legitimate merchant ship might flee; from a distance, her crew would not be able to tell that the *Myrmidon* was a navy ship and not a pirate. The captain of a slave ship was certain to try to get away.

The appearance of the *Myrmidon* on the African coast had "completely alarmed the slave captains," who up until then had "trusted in the superiority of their schooners sailing."[1] The slave traders favored fast ships, like the light Baltimore clippers that had been built for use as privateers during the War of 1812 between Britain and the United States.[2] A heavy merchant ship might travel at five knots; the clippers regularly traveled at ten or twelve knots, and some were reported to have reached twenty knots. Many of the Royal Navy's ships were built for rough conditions in the North Atlantic, not speed in tropical waters.[3] But the *Myrmidon*, a sprightly sloop, was fast enough to catch the swiftest slave ships.[4]

Even at the helm of a fast ship like the *Myrmidon*, Leeke might find himself chasing a suspected slaver for hours or even days. When the *Myrmidon* finally pulled within cannon range of the other ship, Leeke knew anything could happen. Leeke had been on the African coast for three years and had stopped dozens of ships. The *Myrmidon*'s twenty guns had a range of more than half a mile and could knock down a ship's mast or put a hole in her hull, but Leeke would not likely risk anything more than a warning shot. If he fired on an innocent vessel, he would be liable for damages in court. But the other ship might take its chances and fire on the *Myrmidon*. Leeke might have to send his men out in the smaller boats that the *Myrmidon* carried for just such a purpose. If the slave vessel resisted, his sailors could fight their way onboard with pistols and cutlasses.

Worst of all, just as Leeke drew near, the other ship might suddenly hoist an American flag. The United States had thus far refused to sign a mutual search treaty with the British, and Leeke was powerless to interfere with a slave ship under American colors. The United States had passed legislation prohibiting the slave trade and declaring it piracy, punishable by death. But the American laws were enforceable solely by the American navy, and only a handful of American navy ships were hunting for slavers in 1822. Any slave captain worth his salt knew about the Americans' indifference. Even if his ship was actually Spanish, Portuguese, or Dutch, a smart slave captain was likely to keep a spare American flag and forged papers just in case the British appeared. The French flag was also a good cover, for the French had likewise prohibited slave trading but refused to grant the British permission to search their ships. If Leeke was willing to run the risk of not only a diplomatic incident but also defending a personal lawsuit, he might board anyway, hoping that a quick inspection of the ship's papers would reveal that the flag was a fraud.

If Leeke were really lucky, the slave ship captain might not be clever or rich enough to have procured a false flag and papers, and the Spanish, Portuguese, or Dutch flag fluttering on the mast would serve as his invitation to search the ship. Sometimes the exercise would end in frustration. If no slaves were on board, the ship was not subject to seizure even if things like manacles and water casks in the hold made it obvious that the intent of the voyage was to pick up slaves. Desperate slave captains had even been known to throw slaves overboard on the approach of a British ship, figuring it was better to lose the cargo than the whole ship.

If Leeke found slaves on board and determined that he had a lawful basis to detain the ship under one of the treaties (which in 1822 contained many technical details about where and when some slave trading was still allowed), he would order his men to disarm the slaver's crew. The Africans would be released from their chains, and the *Myrmidon's* surgeon would attend to the sick. Leeke would then put one or two of his young officers and a light crew of seamen onboard the slaver, and the ship would sail to Freetown, where a highly unusual court awaited their arrival.

In Freetown sat a new international tribunal established to enforce the treaties prohibiting the slave trade. Most people think of international courts as an innovation of the twentieth century, with the Nuremberg trials of the Nazi war criminals at the end of World War II being the first real effort to use international law to prosecute those accused of gross human rights abuses. But more than a century before Nuremberg, international courts in Sierra Leone, Cuba, Brazil, and other places around the Atlantic heard cases related to the slave trade, the original "crime against humanity."

Though all but forgotten today, these slave trade courts were the first international human rights courts. Called the "Mixed Commissions" because they consisted of judges from different countries, the slave trade tribunals sat on a permanent, continuing basis, and they applied international law. The courts explicitly aimed to promote humanitarian objectives. Though the courts were extremely active for only a few years, over the treaties' life span the courts heard more than six hundred cases and freed almost 80,000 slaves found aboard illegal slave trading vessels. During their peak years of operation, the courts heard cases that may have involved as many as one out of every five or six ships involved in the transatlantic slave trade. This book tells the story of these forgotten courts, a story that sheds important light on the origins of our contemporary system of international legal protection for human rights and also provides insight into issues faced by modern international tribunals like the International Criminal Court.

But back to Captain Leeke. On April 15, 1822, Leeke was cruising along with his commanding officer, Commodore Sir Robert Mends. Mends was onboard the squadron's flagship, the HMS *Iphigenia*, a thirty-six-gun frigate somewhat larger than the *Myrmidon*. Though Leeke had been at sea since he joined the navy as a thirteen-year-old in 1803, he was still a young man in one of his first commands. Mends was an experienced officer who had lost his arm fighting in the American Revolution.[5] They already had in their custody one prize, the Portuguese slaver *Esperanca Felix*, which they had caught in the River Lagos a week earlier with 187 slaves on board. They had heard reports of several more ships near the mouth of the River Bonny, a notorious place for loading slaves.

On that day, Leeke and Mends were in luck. They found several ships anchored at the Bonny, a large river, navigable for miles inland, which lies in what is today Nigeria. But to reach the river, a ship had to cross the shoals of the sandbar formed where the river met the ocean. The *Iphigenia* was too large to safely travel through the shallow waters and rough surf near shore, and the *Myrmidon* could only cross the shallow sandbar if conditions were just right. Leeke had taken the *Myrmidon* across the bar on a previous occasion, but the wind and tides would not allow it that day. Instead, Mends and Leeke dispatched some of their bravest young officers and men in small boats to confront the suspected slave ships.

The leader of the expedition that day was Lieutenant George William St. John Mildmay, the third son of a baronet and the senior lieutenant on the *Iphigenia*. Mildmay and his boats crossed the bar soon after daylight. From four miles out, he spotted seven ships lying at anchor—two schooners, four brigs, and one brigantine. Mildmay hoisted the British colors so they would know he was not a pirate but an officer of the Royal Navy. As he approached, the two schooners opened fire without showing their colors.[6]

They were Spanish slave ships, and heavily armed. One of the ships, the *Icanam*, was a large schooner with "ten guns mounted" and a crew of forty-six men with "muskets, pistols, swords and ammunition."[7] Her companion, the *Vecua*, was similarly equipped. The two ships had sailed together some months earlier from Havana, Cuba. Their plan was evidently to bulldoze their way through any opposition. Their owners had assumed that two large ships "so formidably manned and armed" and with such "determined and desperate spirit" could fight off any attackers, whether pirates or naval vessels.[8]

The other vessels at anchor nearby were flying French colors, but three of them joined in the fight. Mildmay's boats advanced, the men rowing "under a heavy fire of round grape and musketry" and "in about 20 minutes from the commencement succeeded in boarding and taking possession of the whole of them."[9] Two of the British sailors were killed and five were wounded. Mildmay would be promoted for his valor in the raid.[10]

The ships held more than a thousand slaves: 300 onboard the *Vecua*, 380 on the *Icanam*, 343 on the French brig *Vigilante*, 218 on the French brig *Petite Betsy*, and 247 on the French brigantine *L'Ursule*.[11] The last, another French brig, had no slaves onboard yet, though it was obvious it was planning to load some soon.

As the defeated Spanish crew fled the *Vecua*, they left behind a surprise for the British. A lighted fuse was hanging over the open magazine hatch where barrels of gunpowder were stored. "[W]hen no hope remained of their preventing her falling into our hands, merely to gratify a diabolical feeling of revenge for their defeat, [the Spanish crew] would have blown up 300 poor fellows ironed in the hold," Mildmay related.[12] One of the British sailors spotted the match and managed to extinguish it just in time.

Because there was no treaty between Britain and France for enforcement of the ban on slave trading, the British had no jurisdiction over the French ships based on their slave dealing. But the British boats had clearly displayed their colors and were obviously exercising a right of legal search. Firing on the approaching British boats was arguably an act of piracy. Mildmay let one of the French ships go with a warning, since that ship had held its fire.[13] But he determined that the other three French ships should be taken to the British vice-admiralty court in Freetown, Sierra Leone, to face piracy charges.[14] Pursuant to the treaty with Spain, the Spanish ships would go before the Court of Mixed Commission.

The ships began the arduous journey to Freetown. The prevailing winds were hostile, and it could take two months to sail north from the

River Bonny to Sierra Leone. Already, a number of the Africans were sick, and the illness seemed likely to spread throughout the crew. Leekes soon realized that the *Esperanca Felix*, a "dull sailing vessel," was not really seaworthy.[15] The voyage to Freetown was long and hazardous enough as it was, and with the *Felix* limping along, it would take so long that the health and safety of everyone onboard all the ships would be endangered. Leeke ordered that the slaves be taken off the *Esperanca Felix* and distributed among the other already overcrowded ships, including his own.[16] He then ordered his men to destroy the *Felix*; although the ship was a pathetic wreck, a slave trader who found it abandoned might be desperate (or greedy) enough to try to load it with another cargo. The remaining ships began making their way to Freetown. Along the way, they encountered a fierce tropical storm—a "tornado" in the words of their reports. The *Icanam* sank, and hundreds of Africans and more than a dozen British sailors onboard drowned. Only a handful of men from the *Icanam* survived to be rescued by the *Myrmidon* some days later "in a state of derangement, from want of food."[17]

The cases of the *Vecua* and *Icanam* were decided by the international Mixed Commission court in July 1822. The court had little difficulty in finding the ships guilty of trading in violation of the treaties between England and Spain. Of course, the *Icanam* had been lost along the way, but the *Vecua* was sold by order of the court and the surviving Africans were freed. As for the French ships which had fired on the British boats, as best the records reveal, one ship was released by the British vice-admiralty court in Sierra Leone, while the others were sent back to England and from there on to France, where they were condemned by a French tribunal at Nantes.[18]

The Mixed Commission court in Sierra Leone also decided the case of the ship *Esperanca Felix*, the other ship that the *Myrmidon* and *Iphigenia* had captured on that cruise, which had been scuttled on the journey. The Portuguese crew of the *Esperanca Felix* tried to excuse their conduct by claiming that they had a royal passport allowing them to trade slaves south of the equator, where the treaty between Britain and Portugal still permitted such dealing as part of a gradual plan for extinguishing the trade. They claimed that adverse currents and winds had forced them north of the equator, where the slave trade was illegal. After questioning the ship's master about the wind and currents, the court decided (in the condescending language of that racist era) to question "the most intelligent of the Negroes."[19] These individuals testified that they had been loaded onboard the ship at Lagos (in what is now Nigeria, well north of the equator) and "had been put on board so short a time before the capture, that they had not eaten onboard."[20] The court believed the Africans' testimony and granted them their freedom.

Between disease and the sinking of the *Icanam*, only 85 of the original 187 Africans from the *Esperanca Felix* made it alive to Freetown.[21] One of the Africans from the *Esperanca Felix* who arrived safely in Freetown onboard the *Myrmidon* was a young boy named Adjai, who vividly remembered his voyage on the *Myrmidon* some decades later. In many ways, Adjai's story was typical of the thousands of individuals from western Africa who found themselves on slave ships. Adjai was born the son of a weaver in a large town of some 3,000 inhabitants in what is now Nigeria. When Adjai was just thirteen years old, warring factions raided his village. As he recalled many years later, the morning he was taken as a slave was paradoxically "one of the most lovely and pleasant I had ever witnessed."[22] Around nine in the morning, "as we were preparing breakfast, an alarm was made that the enemy were approaching."[23] Adjai's father disappeared into the crowd after warning his family to flee, and Adjai never saw him again. In less than half an hour, the town was completely surrounded by an army from the rival tribe. As the soldiers swept through the town, they set the houses on fire, though, Adjai recalled, "There was not much slaughter as the aim was to capture as many as they could."[24] As Adjai fled with his mother, two sisters, and a cousin, they were seized by two of the invaders, who threw nooses around their necks and took them prisoner. They were led out of the town with thousands of other captives, and in the crowd Adjai had his last view of his grandmother. They marched some twenty miles to a larger town, which they reached late at night. In the morning, the soldiers divided the prisoners. Adjai's mother and nine-month-old sister were sent in one direction, while Adjai and his other sister were sent in another. "The anguish of mind felt at this separation can not easily be described," Adjai would write many years later.[25] Soon he was separated from his other sister as well, and he thought of suicide. Adjai changed hands several times before being sold to Portuguese slave dealers, the first white men he had ever seen.

By then some months had passed. Around seven in the evening on a fine April day, they were loaded from canoes onto a large slave ship, the *Esperanca Felix*. But that very day, as Adjai recalled, the ship "was surprised by two men of war, the 'Ephigenia' [*sic*], Captain Sir R. Mends and the 'Myrmidon,' Captain Leeke."[26] Adjai and the other African prisoners were initially afraid of the British, whom the Portuguese had called sea robbers. But the British put the Portuguese in irons and released the Africans. Adjai and his companions had not been fed since being loaded on the slave ship, and "as hunger rendered [them] bold," Adjai and his companions came onto the deck and were given breakfast.[27] After breakfast, the Africans were divided among the ships and, Adjai recounted, "We six boys had the luck of being taken into the 'Myrmidon,' where we were very kindly treated."[28]

Adjai was one of the eighty-five Africans granted certificates of freedom upon the condemnation of the *Esperanca Felix*. Most of the more than 80,000 persons freed by the Mixed Commission faded into obscurity, leaving little trace. Not Adjai. Living in the British settlement at Sierra Leone, he was baptized by a missionary and took the name Samuel Crowther. He began going to school in Freetown, eventually attending Fourah Bay College, the first university in Africa. Later, he traveled to England to complete his education. A devout convert to Christianity, Crowther became a missionary himself. He translated the Bible and several other books into his native language. But that is not the end of his story, nor of Captain Leeke's.

Captain Leeke and Samuel Adjai Crowther met again decades later, on June 24, 1864. On that morning an enormous crowd gathered in Canterbury, England, at the famous cathedral. As one newspaper reported, "The ancient city presented a very animated appearance, as not only did a very large number of the inhabitants and visitors from the immediate neighborhood evince great anxiety to witness the proceedings, but a special train on the London, Chatham, and Dover line brought many from the metropolis."[29] By half past eleven, every corner of the cathedral was filled. Three new bishops were to be ordained that day. One of them was Samuel Adjai Crowther, who became the first African bishop in the Anglican Church and the first Bishop of Niger.[30] Captain Leeke, by then an elderly man, was a guest at the ordination, and when he died his obituary would note that he had saved Crowther and some 3,000 others from slavery during his service on the African coast.[31] Crowther frequently spoke of Leeke's role in his rescue, even after Leeke had passed away.[32]

In another world, the little boy Adjai would have stayed onboard the *Esperanca Felix* until that ship landed in Brazil or Cuba. He would have been sold in a slave market and taken to a plantation for backbreaking labor and early death. But providence, Captain Leeke, and international law had changed his fate.

In the year 1800, slavery was normal. European countries used international law to authorize and justify the ownership of human beings. In the first decade of the nineteenth century, an estimated 609,000 slaves arrived in the New World. Within a relatively short time span, however, things began to change. In 1807, Britain became the first major seafaring country, followed shortly by the United States, to ban its subjects from participation in the slave trade. By the early 1840s, more than twenty nations—including all the Atlantic maritime powers—had signed international treaties committing to the abolition of the trade. By the late 1860s, only a few hundred slaves per year were illegally transported across the Atlantic. And by 1900, slavery itself had been outlawed in every country in the Western Hemisphere.

The abolition of the slave trade has received a great deal of attention from historians, but much less so from international lawyers. Yet the abolition of the transatlantic slave trade remains the most successful episode ever in the history of international human rights law. Slavery and the slave trade are among the few universally acknowledged crimes under international law. Though powerful countries today defend torture—another practice placed strictly off limits by international law—no nation today officially defends slavery. To be sure, modern forms of forced labor remain a significant human rights issue affecting millions of people, but the type of widespread, legalized chattel slavery that was commonplace in the nineteenth century has disappeared.

How did such a dramatic shift occur in disparate societies around the world in less than a century? Changes in the world economy in the nineteenth century certainly created the conditions that made the abolition of slavery more feasible. But the best historical evidence suggests that slavery did not die an accidental death of abandonment in the face of competition from industrial capitalism. Slavery was eradicated, intentionally, by people who had come to believe it was morally wrong. It was eradicated in part by military force, but also by coordinated international legal action—including, surprisingly, international courts.

The history of the suppression of the transatlantic slave trade has implications for a number of contemporary debates about international law. Most legal scholars view international courts and international human rights law largely as post–World War II phenomena. But in fact, the nineteenth-century slavery abolition movement was the first successful international human rights campaign, and international treaties and courts were its central features. Indeed, even the phrase "crimes against humanity"—which came to modern fame based on its use at the

Nuremberg trials of Nazi war criminals—was used in the nineteenth century to describe the slave trade.

The abolition of the slave trade lies at a critical juncture in the history of international law and exemplifies a series of dichotomies and tensions that continue to play out even today, tensions between concepts of natural and universal law and law based solely on the positive enactments of a particular sovereign state; between religious and secular ideas of law and society; between European and non-European societies and cultures; between written treaties and unwritten customary law as the most important source of international legal norms; between national and territorial conceptions of jurisdiction and supranational or even universal jurisdiction. Thoroughly understanding how these tensions developed and were resolved (or left unresolved) in the context of the abolition of the transatlantic slave trade can help us better understand the jurisprudential foundations of modern international human rights law.

Moreover, this episode in the history of international law reveals a more complex interrelationship between state power, moral ideas, and domestic and international legal institutions than many contemporary theories of international law and relations acknowledge. Great Britain, the main instigator of the antislavery treaties, no doubt would not have campaigned so strongly for abolition if it had been truly devastating to its economic and political interests. Yet substantial evidence shows that Britain's abolition policy was motivated by genuine humanitarian concerns and that the policy inflicted significant economic costs on its empire. Of equal significance, Britain used international law as one important tool for persuading other countries to abandon a widespread and profitable practice. Britain was the nineteenth century's greatest naval power, and its initial efforts to suppress the slave trade were military and unilateral, involving seizures of slave vessels by the British navy and condemnation of those ships in British courts. Over time, however, Britain found it could not rely on its military power alone but instead had to utilize that power in conjunction with cooperative legal action to achieve its goals. Over several decades, Britain convinced one country after another to ratify increasingly powerful treaties against the slave trade. At the same time, these international legal mechanisms would have been ineffective without Britain's military and economic power. At critical moments, Britain was forced to deploy its "hard" powers, as well as its domestic laws and courts, to bring reluctant treaty partners back into the legal fold. In short, neither raw coercive power nor international law alone was enough to achieve the abolition of the slave trade. Both were necessary.

Each time and place in history is different, of course, and yet the use of international law to suppress the transatlantic slave trade in the nineteenth century is evocative of contemporary problems in international relations, including efforts to foster democracy and human rights both through the use of force and through legal institutions, including international and domestic courts. The antislavery movement's use of international law and legal institutions as part of a broader social, political, and military strategy can help us better understand the potential role of international law today in bringing about improvements in human rights. In more theoretical terms, the history of the antislavery courts suggests a need for a thicker, more robust account of the relationship between power, ideas, and international law. In short, the forgotten bit of history recounted in this book should change the way we think about international courts and international human rights law—their origins, limits, and potential.

CHAPTER 2

Britain and the Slave Trade

The Rise of Abolitionism

S lavery has existed since ancient times, and for centuries it was considered morally and legally acceptable for some human beings to own other human beings. Slavery took a particularly pernicious form in the Atlantic world between the sixteenth and nineteenth centuries. Millions of inhabitants of western Africa were carried across the Atlantic to plantations in North and South America. International law was surprisingly central to this enterprise. At the beginning of this period, international law was used to justify the slave trade; by the end, international law was used to suppress it. How did this transformation occur?

The indisputable star of the international abolition movement was Great Britain, and so it is there that our story begins. British merchants were early and enthusiastic participants in the slave trade, second only to the Portuguese in volume of slaves shipped. To the extent that average Britons thought of the slave trade at all in 1700, they thought mostly of the riches it brought, both directly and through the fruitful plantations run by slave labor in British colonies. But by the late eighteenth century, attitudes toward the slave trade in Britain began to change. Though disagreeing on many details, historians now largely concur that British abolitionism arose out of a confluence of factors, including economic changes, Enlightenment philosophy, and religious revival movements.[1] Regardless of its precise origins, the abolition movement indisputably became an important force in British politics in the late eighteenth and early nineteenth centuries.

On both sides of the Atlantic, opponents of the slave trade conceptualized the issue in terms of human rights, and spoke as well of a religious and moral obligation to end the practice. Upon introduction of an early and unsuccessful bill to ban the slave trade in 1776, one member of the British Parliament argued that the "[s]lave-trade was contrary to the laws of God, and the rights of men."[2] Speaking in support of legislation to ban the slave trade in 1806, Lord Grenville likewise characterized slavery as contrary to the "rights of nature" whereby "every human being is entitled to the fruit of his own labour."[3] President Thomas Jefferson's message to the U.S. Congress in 1806 supported legislation against the slave trade because it would "withdraw the citizens of the United States from all further participation in those violations of human rights which have been so long continued on the unoffending inhabitants of Africa."[4]

Arguments against slavery and the slave trade were deeply intertwined with ideas of natural law and natural rights.[5] Aristotle famously argued that slavery was part of the natural and right order of the world: "from the hour of their birth, some are marked out for subjection, others for rule."[6] But he also noted that "[o]thers affirm that the rule of a master over slaves is contrary to nature, and that the distinction between slave and freeman exists by law only, and not by nature; and being an interference with nature is therefore unjust."[7]

By Roman times, slavery was governed by the body of law known as the *ius gentium*, the predecessor of the "law of nations" (which in turn is the predecessor of modern international law). This was because slaves were typically foreigners who had been captured in war. The *ius gentium* was considered related to, and in large part based upon, the *ius naturale*, or natural law.[8] Slavery was often given by Roman jurists as an example of one of the few instances in which the *ius naturale* and the *ius gentium* diverged, with slavery being inconsistent with natural law but recognized by the law of nations, a view that was reflected in the influential codification of Roman law by Justinian (483–565 A.D.).[9]

The idea that the law of nations allowed prisoners of war to be enslaved was largely accepted among European writers for the next several centuries. For example, Hugo Grotius (1583–1645), the seventeenth-century Dutch theorist viewed by many as the grandfather of modern international law, considered slavery to be consistent with both natural law and the law of nations. Grotius argued that slavery was an "inducement to captors to refrain from the cruel rigour of putting prisoners to death."[10] A slave, in his words, was one who "might have been put to death, but from motives or interest or humanity had been saved."[11] Grotius noted that, by custom, Christian powers did not generally enslave other Christians: "It has long been a maxim, universally received among the powers of Christendom, that prisoners of war cannot be made slaves." He described this as a tradition based on common religion and praiseworthy as based on a "law of charity."[12] But he did not in any terms condemn the practice of enslaving non-Christians.

As the Enlightenment progressed, however, philosophers began to argue in increasingly strenuous terms that slavery violated natural law. Writing several decades after Grotius, the English philosopher John Locke (1632–1704) argued that man had natural, inalienable rights that preexisted the nation-state and that could be the basis for dissolving it. Among the rights Locke recognized was a man's entitlement to the fruits of his own labor. Locke was critical of slavery, asserting, "Slavery is so vile and miserable an Estate of man, and so directly opposite to the generous Temper and Courage of our Nation; that 'tis hardly to be conceived, that an *Englishman*, much less a *Gentleman*, should plead for't."[13] But Locke still believed that slavery might be an acceptable accommodation in a situation where a man might justly be killed.[14]

By the eighteenth century, the murmuring of philosophical voices against slavery was increasing. Montesquieu (1689–1755) argued that "[t]he state of slavery is in its own nature bad,"[15] though he went on to qualify this judgment at least as to certain circumstances. As to the enslavement of Africans, he noted sarcastically, "It is impossible for us to suppose these creatures to be men, because, allowing them to be men, a suspicion would follow that we ourselves are not Christians."[16] Jean-Jacques Rousseau (1712–1778) weighed in more decisively against slavery. Rousseau rejected the assertion of Grotius and others that individuals could voluntarily submit themselves to slavery.[17] "To renounce one's liberty," he suggested, "is to renounce one's humanity, the rights of humanity and even its duties."[18] Rousseau likewise rejected the supposed origin of slavery in warfare and the sparing of prisoners whom one might kill, stating that "this supposed right to kill the vanquished in no way results from the state of war."[19] In short, he argued, "the right of slavery is invalid, not only because it is illegitimate but also because it is absurd and meaningless. These words, *slavery* and *right*, are contradictory; they are mutually exclusive."[20]

But while the philosophers argued that slavery violated natural law and natural rights, the law of nations still allowed both slavery and the slave trade. Emerich de Vattel (1714–1767), the mostly widely read writer on the law of nations among the founding generation of the United States, was ambivalent toward slavery, though he described it as a "disgrace to humanity."[21] He nevertheless agreed with Grotius and other earlier writers that it was lawful to make prisoners of war into slaves "in cases which give a right to kill them, when they have rendered themselves personally guilty of some crime deserving of death," but not in other cases.[22] But Vattel acknowledged a tension between the institution of slavery and his views of natural law: "If I spare his life, and condemn him to a state so contrary to the nature of man, I still continue with him the state of war" and "[h]e lies under no obligation to me: for, what is life without freedom?"[23]

While slavery and the slave trade were still tolerated by the law of nations in the late eighteenth century, lawyers had begun to argue that slavery was contrary to the law of England. In the first edition of his influential *Commentaries on the Laws of England* in 1765, William Blackstone (1723–80) suggested that "a slave or negro, the moment he lands in England, falls under the protection of the laws and with regard to all natural rights becomes *eo instanti* a freeman," though he backtracked slightly in the 1769 edition of his treatise.[24]

In 1772, in the landmark case of *Somerset v. Stewart*, a British court held that slavery would not be legally recognized within Britain itself.[25] James Somerset, a slave from Virginia, had been brought to England by his master, Charles Stewart, who intended ultimately to return with Somerset to America. Once in England, however, Somerset's situation came to the attention of abolitionists, who helped him file a petition for habeas corpus seeking his release.[26] The arguments in the case were wide ranging and eloquent. Somerset's attorneys discussed the history of slavery, the writings of Aristotle, philosophers including Grotius, Pufendorf, Montesquieu, and Locke, and various English precedents establishing customary rights of liberty. The core of their argument was that slavery was contrary to natural law and to the laws of England, and that the court should grant Somerset his freedom. Their arguments were framed in the language of inalienable human rights. Slavery could not arise from contract, for a man could not consent to "dispose of all the rights vested by nature and society in him and his descendants" without "ceasing to be a man; for these rights immediately flow from, and are essential to, his condition as such; they cannot be taken from him."[27] Nor was slavery justified by capture in war; if a soldier had a duty to spare the enemy in battle by taking him prisoner rather than killing him whenever it was feasible to do so, he also had a duty to restore the prisoner to liberty as soon as possible.

Stewart's attorneys, for their part, argued that under the rules of conflict of laws (the body of law governing legal disputes that transcended territorial boundaries from one jurisdiction to another), Somerset's legal status as a slave should follow him to England. These lawyers also argued that it would be impractically idealistic to find in Somerset's favor, suggesting that a decision in favor of his freedom would result in the liberation of some 14,000 slaves in England valued by their owners at hundreds of thousands of pounds.

The judge assigned to the case, Lord Mansfield, suggested that the parties settle the case out of court, but they would not. When forced to a decision, the judge said he would not be ruled by "compassion" on the one hand or "inconvenience" on the other but rather by the law. The law, he concluded, favored freedom. The opinion stated that slavery was "so odious" and contrary to natural law that it could only be justified by "positive law."[28] While slavery was recognized in other territories, the law of England itself did not allow or approve of it. Thus, despite the practical "inconvenience" that might follow from the decision, the court ordered Somerset's release.[29]

Having succeeded in establishing that any slave who touched British soil would be free, the abolitionists next focused their efforts on banning the transport of slaves from Africa to the New World. The immediate abolition of slavery was deemed politically infeasible because it was too vital to the economies of the West Indian colonies. The slave trade was a somewhat easier target, although it was lucrative for the British merchants who participated in it and a vital source of new slaves for British colonies. For one thing, the slave trade was viewed as the cruelest part of the system. Accounts by sailors and freed slaves of the horrors of the Middle Passage were widely circulated in Britain. Abolitionists also argued that cutting off the supply of fresh slaves would induce owners to treat their existing slaves better and thus reduce horrific mortality rates on plantations; better treatment of slaves, they argued, might even improve productivity.

Abolitionist leaders succeeded in putting the abolition of the slave trade on the political agenda in the late 1780s and early 1790s. Under the leadership of William Wilberforce, a bill for the abolition of the trade passed the House of Commons in 1792 but was blocked in the House of Lords.[30] After this initial progress, however, almost a decade followed in which the movement made little headway. The French Revolution had provoked fear in Britain's ruling classes and led to a crackdown on political agitation; the public meetings and petition campaigns that had propelled abolition onto the parliamentary agenda came to a halt.[31] Though Wilberforce continued to introduce antislavery legislation each year, it received little attention, and other matters, such as the war with France, dominated Britain's political agenda.

In the spring of 1806, the abolitionists finally changed tactics and used the renewed war with France to their advantage. The crucial first step was the passage of the Foreign Slave Trade Act,[32] which prohibited British subjects from participating in the slave trade with the current or former colonies and possessions of France and its allies.[33] Framed as a national security measure rather than a humanitarian one, the act easily passed the House of Commons. Proslavery forces realized the potential importance of the measure by the time it reached the House of Lords, and submitted a petition opposing the act with more than 400 signatures from the key trading center of Manchester. The abolition forces responded within hours with a counterpetition from Manchester bearing more than 2,300 signatures.[34] The House of Lords quickly agreed to the act.[35]

Having gained this wedge, the abolitionists promptly renewed their efforts to achieve a broader ban. Conditions were favorable in more ways than one. First, the petition campaign in support of the Foreign Slave Trade Act had shown that popular support for abolition was both widespread and deep, even in regions where trading interests were strong. Although British voting rights would not be expanded beyond a limited segment of the population for another twenty-five years, strong popular sentiment influenced politics.

The slave trade became an issue in key parliamentary elections in the fall of 1806.[36] By that time, two changes since the 1790s had reduced the perceived threat of foreign competition with British commercial interests in the West Indies: first, the war with France had reduced French power in the West Indies and on the high seas; and second, a Haitian slave revolt had led to the independence of France's most productive sugar colony. And so it happened that, in early 1807, both houses of Parliament finally passed the Act for the Abolition of the Slave Trade.[37] As of May 1, 1807, the law completely prohibited participation in the slave trade by British subjects and the importation of slaves to British possessions. The British navy began to enforce the ban, and the slave trade under the British flag rapidly decreased.[38]

Following passage of the 1807 act, it quickly became clear that it would be in Britain's interest to encourage the suppression of slave trading by other countries as well. If other nations continued to tolerate the trade, the only effect of Britain's ban would be to shift the trade from British-flagged ships to the ships of other nations. In addition, the Caribbean colonies of other nations would continue to receive infusions of new slaves, putting British possessions that could not receive such reinforcements at an economic disadvantage. Thus, the British West Indian planters, who had been the strongest opponents of the 1807 act, quickly became supporters of British efforts to stamp out the slave trade carried out by other nations.

At the time, other countries showed little interest in implementing an effective ban on the trade. Denmark was the first European power to pass legislation against the slave trade in 1792 (with the ban to take effect in 1803), but Denmark was not a particularly powerful country. Though there had been abolition movements in France and the United States, abolitionists were not sufficiently influential in domestic politics in either of those countries in 1807 to force their governments to devote significant resources to the suppression of the slave trade, particularly on the high seas. Like Britain, France initially drew a distinction between slavery in its colonies and slavery on French soil. Long before the much-celebrated decision by the British court in *Somerset*, French admiralty courts had granted numerous petitions for freedom on behalf of slaves who had been brought within the French mainland.[39] In 1794, the revolutionary government in France abolished the slave trade as well as slavery in its colonies.[40] This abolition effort was short lived, however, for the trade was never effectively suppressed, and Napoleon reauthorized slavery in French colonies in 1803.[41]

The United States had prohibited the outfitting of slave ships in American ports in 1794 and enacted legislation completely banning the slave trade under the American flag and into American ports in March 1807.[42] That legislation took effect in 1808, the earliest date allowed by the Constitution.[43] Within a decade, the United States had effectively suppressed slave imports into its own territory.[44] But in the face of sectional divisions between North and South, the United States devoted few resources to enforcing the ban against U.S.-flagged ships on the high seas.[45]

Abolitionist movements had even less power in Spain and Portugal, the other major maritime powers with significant plantation colonies in the New World.[46] Both of those countries permitted the trade to continue unrestricted under their flags, and the slave trade from Africa to Cuba and Brazil flourished.

Initially Britain resorted to unilateral military action to suppress the slave trade. The 1807 Abolition Act was enacted during the Napoleonic Wars, during which Britain claimed the right under the law of nations to search ships on the high seas to determine whether they were enemy ships or, if neutral ships, whether they were violating principles of neutrality by, for example, carrying contraband for the enemy or running a blockade. Although the primary efforts of the British navy were in pursuance of the war effort, Britain also began using this right of search derived from international law as a method to suppress the slave trade. Ships found carrying cargoes of slaves were brought into British vice-admiralty courts around the Atlantic for condemnation as prizes under the law of nations.[47]

The British courts first addressed this issue in the case of the *Amedie*.[48] While sailing under the flag of the United States from Africa to Cuba with a cargo of 105 slaves, the *Amedie* was captured by a British warship in 1808. Though the United States was neutral in the war at that time, its ships were arguably subject to search under the law of nations to ensure that they were not violating neutrality. The British vice-admiralty court in Tortola condemned the ship as a lawful prize, and the court in London affirmed that decision on appeal. The court observed that the British Parliament had clearly "declared the African slave trade . . . contrary to principles of justice and humanity."[49] While noting that the United States had also banned the trade as a matter of domestic law, the court acknowledged that the positive law of nations, either by treaty or custom, did not completely ban the slave trade:

> we cannot legislate for other countries; nor has this country a right to control any foreign legislature that may think proper to dissent from this doctrine and give permission to its subjects to prosecute this trade. We cannot, certainly, compel the subjects of other nations to observe any other than the first and generally received principles of universal law.[50]

Using the same natural law reasoning as the court in *Somerset*, however, the court concluded that it was entitled to presume the slave trade unlawful unless some positive law authorized it. Having found the trade presumptively illegal, the court put on the claimant "the whole burden of proof . . . to shew that by the particular law of his own country he is entitled to carry on this traffic."[51] Even where the claimant was able to demonstrate domestic legal authority, the court intimated that "persons engaged in such a trade cannot, upon principles of universal law, have a right to be heard upon a claim of this nature in any court" and that, in any event, "no claimant can be heard in an application to a court of prize for the restoration of the human beings he carried unjustly to another country for the purpose of disposing of them as slaves."[52] It thus appeared the court might be unwilling to return the prisoners on the ship to the slave dealer's custody in any circumstances. The court upheld the condemnation of the ship and its cargo;[53] the slaves were freed, and the ship itself was awarded as a prize to its captor, as was customary.[54]

Throughout the Napoleonic Wars, Britain continued the practice of seizing foreign slave ships, including American, Spanish, Portuguese, Dutch, and French vessels.[55] Other nations protested Britain's heavy-handed search tactics, in relation to both captured slaves and maritime commerce generally, as exceeding permissible bounds under the law of nations.[56] Indeed, British search and seizure of American ships, though not specifically slave ships, was one of the main bones of contention that led to the War of 1812.[57] But Britain persisted in these unilateral seizures through the end of the wars. As table 2.1 shows, Britain captured a substantial number of foreign slave ships during this period.[58]

In one sense, the end of the Napoleonic Wars in 1814–15 was a peculiar time for Britain to change the direction of its antislavery policies. After all, Britain won the war and, more than that, had established itself as the dominant maritime power. But with the end of hostilities, Britain's

Table 2.1. SLAVE TRADE CASES IN BRITISH VICE-ADMIRALTY COURTS DURING THE NAPOLEONIC WARS

YEAR	NUMBER OF CASES TRIED IN BRITISH ADMIRALTY COURTS	% OF KNOWN VOYAGES TRIED IN BRITISH ADMIRALTY COURTS
1806	4	1
1807	8	2
1808	7	6
1809	5	5
1810	29	15
1811	27	15
1812	26	15
1813	10	7
1814	17	11
1815	33	18
1816	29	12
1817	9	4

unilateral actions became more suspect. The right to search foreign-flagged vessels was linked under the law of nations to a state of warfare, and its scope was controversial even in that context. It was clear that there was no general right of peacetime search, aside from cases of piracy. Although the British courts would not begin to invalidate the peacetime search and seizure of foreign-flagged slaving vessels until 1817, the writing was already on the wall. There was no legal basis under international law for Britain to continue to search and detain other nations' ships. Continuing to do so would provoke outrage and retaliation by other countries, many of which had already insinuated that Britain was not interested in the slave trade at all, but was simply using the humanitarian cause as a cover for its self-interested efforts to dominate maritime commerce.[59]

In July 1816, the British government acknowledged that under international law the peacetime searches were illegal, and the following year British courts began invalidating seizures of slave ships starting with the case of *Le Louis*, issued on December 15, 1817.[60] *Le Louis* involved a French vessel seized in 1816 and condemned by the British vice-admiralty court at Sierra Leone. The condemnation was reversed on appeal in an opinion authored by Sir William Scott.[61] The court found that Britain had no legal authority to search the ship on the high seas.[62] Noting that the customary law of nations provided no generalized right to search in peacetime, the court concluded that, in the absence of a specific treaty between the countries, Britain could not lawfully search or seize a French ship unless it suspected piracy. The court found, first, that the slave trade was not piracy under the general law of nations, and therefore no peacetime right of search attached on that basis. Second, the court held that the 1815 treaty in which France had agreed to ban the slave trade was not sufficient to confer a right of peacetime search. Thus, there was no legal basis for the search and seizure.[63] Gone was the rhetoric about slavery being contrary to natural law and the demand for proof of positive law that allowed such an abhorrent institution. In its place was an emphasis on the formalities of state sovereignty and the need for positive law to justify interference with another nation's affairs. It was clear that if Britain wanted to suppress the slave trade, it would need to persuade other countries to commit to the project and to enter into treaties that would give legal legitimacy to its actions.

The end of the Napoleonic Wars not only made it something of a necessity for Britain to address the slave trade issue on a multilateral basis; it also presented an opportunity for the British government to make the issue a bargaining chip in the series of diplomatic negotiations and realignments that inevitably followed the war. In the years after the Napoleonic Wars, Britain successfully negotiated for clauses related to the slave trade in a number of multilateral and bilateral treaties. Although the multilateral treaties ultimately included only statements of principle against the slave trade with no enforcement mechanisms, several of the bilateral negotiations ultimately resulted in treaties that not only banned the slave trade but also provided for enforcement of the ban in international mixed courts.

The British government faced strong domestic political pressure to make abolition a central feature of the immediate postwar negotiations. When the foreign secretary, Viscount Castlereagh, returned from the initial peace treaty negotiations in France in the summer of 1814, he was greeted with euphoria and praise for having brought the long war to a successful conclusion. These accolades, however, were quickly supplanted by criticism because he agreed to a provision in the treaty that allowed France to renew its participation in the slave trade (participation that had been dampened or eliminated during the war) for five more years.[64] Wilberforce, the leader of the abolition movement in Parliament, immediately described the treaty provision as the "death-warrant of a multitude of innocent victims, men, women and children."[65] Lord Canning pointed out that Castlereagh had opposed the 1807 act abolishing the trade, thereby implying that he had not pursued the issue with sufficient diligence in the peace negotiations.[66]

Abolitionist leaders reached out to the public for support. In what may have been the largest popular petition campaign in Britain's history, more than three-quarters of a million people (out of a national population of approximately 12 million) signed petitions denouncing this provision of the peace treaty with France.[67] Debates over the slavery provision tainted local victory celebrations around the country with pictures of Africans in chains being displayed at some festivals.[68] In his correspondence, the Duke of Wellington commented on the "degree of frenzy" in London about the slave trade, noting, "People in general appear to think that it would suit the policy of this nation to go to war to put an end to that *abominable* traffic."[69] Both the House of Commons and the House of Lords passed resolutions urging that the slave trade issue be brought up at the upcoming Congress of Vienna, where the countries involved in the just-concluded war hoped to transform the initial peace agreement into an arrangement for long-term stability in Europe.[70]

Canning's suspicions about Castlereagh were largely correct: Castlereagh did not view abolition as a proper element of British foreign policy, suggesting in private that it was wrong "to force it upon nations, at the expense of their honour and of the tranquility of the world. Morals were never well taught by the sword."[71] But stung by the public outcry, Castlereagh and Prime Minister Liverpool felt compelled to instruct British negotiators to redouble their efforts to conclude anti-slavery treaties with France, Spain, and Portugal.[72]

Castlereagh directed the Duke of Wellington, who had been sent to Paris, to immediately reopen the issue with the French government. Wellington was instructed to press for immediate abolition of the slave trade by the French, as well as rights of reciprocal search on the high seas to enforce the ban. Recognizing that this proposal would not go over well with the French government, Castlereagh noted, "To soften the exercise of this power, perhaps it might be expedient to require the Sentence of Condemnation to be passed in the Courts of Admiralty of the Country to which the Ship detained belongs."[73]

The French negotiator rebuffed Wellington's initial approach, pointing out that the public sentiment against the trade in France was not as strong as in Great Britain.[74] Castlereagh then sent word to Wellington that he should offer France a material inducement for cooperation on the slavery issue—either a cash payment or an island in the West Indies.[75] This offer, too, was rejected.[76]

While negotiations with France were momentarily stalled, Britain proved more successful in its negotiations with the Netherlands, which in August 1814 formalized by treaty the promise it had made in June 1814 to prohibit the slave trade.[77] Negotiations with the United States ending the War of 1812 also included discussion of the slave trade. The United States, which had already banned the slave trade by statute,[78] was amenable to including a provision on the topic in the peace treaty. Thus, the Treaty of Ghent, signed between Great Britain and the United States on December 24, 1814, declared that "the traffic in slaves is irreconcilable with the principles of humanity and justice," and both nations pledged to "use their best endeavours" to abolish the trade, though the treaty did not include particular mechanisms for enforcing this promise.[79]

Throughout the summer and fall of 1814, the British government tried to obtain similar agreements from Spain and Portugal. Britain's emissary in Madrid, Sir Henry Wellesley, initially sent word that he was not optimistic about obtaining any abolition agreement whatsoever from the Spanish government.[80] Following the British public outcry in reaction to the French treaty, Wellesley told his Spanish counterpart, the Duke of San Carlos, that any treaty they might conclude would not be well received in London unless it included an abolition clause. San Carlos responded that the continuance of the slave trade was essential to the viability of Spain's colonies, and its abolition was inconceivable in the immediate future. Wellesley only managed to secure a provision agreeing to limit the traffic under the Spanish flag to Spanish citizens and to Spanish possessions.[81]

This concession was unsatisfactory to the government in London, which faced continuing pressure to show some progress on the issue. Wellesley thus received instructions to use the cash incentive approach. He offered the Spanish government a loan of 10 million Spanish dollars in exchange for the immediate abolition of the slave trade.[82] The Spanish government, though in serious need of the money, declined the offer.[83] A month later, the Spaniards—perhaps still hoping for the money—made a counteroffer, suggesting that they would immediately ban the trade everywhere except in the zone from the equator to ten degrees north of the equator.[84] Anything short of total abolition, however, remained unacceptable to London.[85]

Negotiations with Portugal proved more promising. Before the war had begun, the Portuguese government had grudgingly agreed to a treaty in 1810 in exchange for British support against the French. That treaty committed Portugal to the gradual abolition of the slave trade and, in particular, limited the trade of slaves by Portuguese subjects to that carried on between Portuguese ports in Africa and Brazil.[86] During the war, Portugal had become indignant when Britain had invoked the treaty as an excuse to unilaterally seize and condemn Portuguese ships in its vice-admiralty courts, and the issue remained an irritant in Anglo-Portuguese relations at the end of the war. But Portugal was heavily dependent on England for military and financial support, and, in January 1815, Britain finally succeeded through a combination of bribery and threats in persuading Portugal to enter into new treaties restricting the slave trade. In the first of these treaties, the Convention of January 21, 1815, Britain agreed to pay Portugal £300,000, ostensibly as compensation for Portuguese ships illegally condemned by British vice-admiralty courts.[87] In a companion treaty, signed on January 22, 1815, Britain forgave the remainder of a £600,000 loan made earlier to Portugal, and Portugal agreed to ban the slave trade north of the equator and to adopt measures necessary to enforce the ban.[88] Although this was progress, it was not a great victory since the majority of Portugal's slave trade was destined for Brazil, which lies south of the equator.

While pursuing these various bilateral negotiations, Britain was simultaneously trying to obtain a multilateral agreement on the slave trade at the Congress of Vienna, where representatives of all the European powers had gathered to sort out a wide variety of issues related to the settlement of the war.[89] Beginning in December 1814 and throughout January and February 1815, the diplomatic representatives meeting in Vienna intermittently discussed the slave trade.[90] While Russia, Austria, and Prussia were quite supportive of Britain's proposals related to the slave trade, none of these countries had significant maritime empires. France, Portugal, and Spain were as recalcitrant in the multilateral negotiations as they had been separately.

It appears that the idea of an international body aimed at suppression of the slave trade first emerged during these negotiations at Vienna. And while no permanent international legal structures were created as a result of either the Congress of Vienna or the subsequent meetings between the great European powers, the idea of such structures was very much on the table. The Russian czar Alexander I had some grandiose ideas about a permanent international league of like-minded Christian monarchs that would preserve peace and order in Europe.[91] This line of thinking culminated in the Holy Alliance initially signed between Russia, Prussia, and Austria in the fall of 1815, and later joined by most of the "crowned heads" of Europe.[92]

Britain stayed out of the Holy Alliance—which Castlereagh privately pronounced "a piece of sublime mysticism and nonsense."[93] But Britain did spearhead the more limited and less metaphysical November 1815 treaty of Quadruple Alliance, which established a kind of mutual security and cooperation system for Europe and provided for regular meetings among the major powers.[94] Consistent with the overall discussion at Vienna of creating stable frameworks for cooperation, Britain firmly supported the creation of some kind of permanent international commission to deal specifically with the slave trade, although it was not yet clear what the powers and responsibilities of such a commission would be.[95]

The effort to address the slave trade issue at the Congress of Vienna ended on February 8, 1815, with the delegates adopting a nonbinding declaration that condemned the slave trade but placed no firm time limit on its abolition:

> Having taken into consideration that the commerce, known by the name of "the Slave Trade" has been considered, by just and enlightened men of all ages, as repugnant to the principles of humanity and universal morality;
>
> . . . [T]he Plenipotentiaries . . . proclaim, in the name of their Sovereigns, their wish of putting an end to a scourge, which has so long desolated Africa, degraded Europe, and afflicted humanity; . . . Too well acquainted, however, with the sentiments of their Sovereigns, not to perceive, that however honorable may be their views, they cannot be attained without due regard to the interests; the habits, and even the prejudices of their subjects; the said Plenipotentiaries at the same time acknowledge that this general Declaration cannot prejudge the period that each particular Power may consider as most advisable for the definitive Abolition of the Slave Trade.[96]

In modern international relations terms, this would be classified as soft law at best, and cheap talk at worst. Soon thereafter, the allies had more pressing problems to worry about. Napoleon returned with his army from exile, and the war restarted. Oddly enough, the renewal of the war proved to be a good thing for the abolitionist cause. In an apparent bid for English support, Napoleon did what the restored royal government had refused to do and issued a proclamation completely banning the slave trade on March 29, 1815.[97] Though clever, this was not enough to win British support. Napoleon met final defeat before Wellington's army at Waterloo in June 1815.

Napoleon's return broke the diplomatic impasse with France on the slave trade issue. On July 30, 1815, Talleyrand informed the British government that Louis XVIII had issued a complete and immediate ban on the slave trade.[98] The final peace treaty, signed in Paris on November 20, 1815, included the ban.[99]

While the French agreement served to assuage British public opinion somewhat, it was clear to the British government that a substantive ban on the slave trade was likely to be ineffective without some provision for mutual rights of search and seizure.[100] British colonial officials in Sierra Leone (the site of the most active vice-admiralty courts during the Napoleonic Wars) responded to an inquiry from Castlereagh about the state of the slave trade and the most effective means of suppressing it by noting that such treaty provisions were needed. They also noted that any scheme for enforcement of the ban was "less liable to objection" if the captured vessels were to be condemned "either by the Courts of his own Country, or by a Tribunal to be specially appointed for that purpose."[101]

The idea of mixed arbitral commissions to settle disputes between nations had already become an established part of international diplomacy. The 1794 Jay Treaty between Britain and the United States had ushered in the modern era of international arbitration by including provisions for the establishment of an arbitral commission consisting of representatives from each country to settle claims arising out of the American Revolutionary War.[102] More recently, the November 1815 peace treaty with France had included a provision for arbitration of public and private claims arising out of the Napoleonic Wars.[103] The previous arbitration commissions had all been created to settle past claims; none had prospective jurisdiction over future disputes. But the talk of forward-looking international cooperation mechanisms at Vienna combined with the concept of mixed commissions to adjudicate disputes to form the idea for the antislavery courts.

Continuing negotiations finally bore fruit in 1817 when Britain successfully concluded agreements with the Netherlands, Portugal, and

Spain that allowed for mutual rights of search and established mixed courts to try and condemn captured slave ships. The Anglo-Portuguese Treaty was signed on July 28, 1817, the Anglo-Spanish Treaty on September 23, 1817, and the Anglo-Dutch Treaty on May 4, 1817.[104] Unlike all of the previous, retrospective arbitration commissions, the courts set up by the new treaties would have prospective jurisdiction, that is, jurisdiction to adjudicate cases that might arise in the indefinite future.

It is not entirely clear what induced these three countries to agree to this novel scheme, or whether they fully understood just how novel it was at the time. The Netherlands, which had readily agreed to the treaty banning the trade in 1814, seemed easily persuaded to take additional steps to make the paper ban effective in practice. For their part, Spain and Portugal seemed motivated by financial incentives, though the amounts they were paid did not come close to compensating them for the economic losses that would accompany real abolition of the trade. Britain agreed in the 1817 treaty to pay Spain £400,000,[105] ostensibly to settle claims for vessels captured during the years of unilateral antislavery activity by Britain, as well as to compensate Spain "for the losses which are a necessary consequence of the abolition of the said Traffic."[106] Britain had already agreed in the 1815 treaties to pay Portugal £300,000 in cash and forgive £600,000 in loans. Apparently, though, Britain had never made good on these earlier promises. In the 1817 Anglo-Portuguese Treaty, Britain agreed to pay the £300,000 owed under the 1815 treaty in two installments along with interest.[107] As discussed more fully in chapter 3, the United States resisted joining the mixed court system until 1862. France never participated.

The scope of each treaty was slightly different. The Spanish treaty banned the trade throughout the Spanish empire as of May 30, 1820, with a five-month grace period for vessels that had "cleared out" lawfully prior to that date.[108] Slave trading from ports on the coast of Africa north of the equator was banned immediately as of the date of ratification, again with a grace period for the completion of voyages already underway.[109]

The Portuguese agreement reiterated the limits in the 1815 treaty, namely that the prohibition extended only to Portuguese ships trading north of the equator or to non-Portuguese possessions.[110] The Dutch had already agreed in 1814 to ban the trade completely, and the new treaty simply created an international enforcement mechanism.

Most significant, these treaties, unlike earlier declarations and treaties, were not merely cheap talk. They contained robust enforcement mechanisms to carry out the promised ban on the trade. Each of the new treaties provided for the mutual right of search and seizure of suspected slave vessels and the vessels' trial and condemnation before the courts of mixed commission:

> In order to bring to adjudication with the least delay and inconvenience, the Vessels which may be detained for having been engaged in an illicit Traffic of Slaves, there shall be established . . . 2 Mixed Commissions, formed of an equal number of Individuals of the 2 Nations, named for this purpose by their respective Sovereigns.[111]

These new courts were empowered to "judge without Appeal, according to the letter and spirit of the Treaty of this date."[112]

In addition, all three treaties were explicitly directed at the slave trade as an offense against humanity. The opening paragraph of the Anglo-Spanish treaty, for example, stated, "His Catholic Majesty concurs in the fullest Manner in the sentiments of His Britannic Majesty, with respect to the injustice and inhumanity of the Traffic in Slaves."[113] And so in 1817, the world's first international courts directed at the protection of human rights were created.

In sum, in the years following the Napoleonic Wars, Britain had effected a sea change in the status of the slave trade under international law. Just a few years earlier, the trade had been presumptively lawful under the law of nations. Now, the most powerful nations in the world had all agreed in principle to its suppression. Britain had moved beyond unilateral action based on vague conceptions of natural law toward concrete, positive treaty obligations and international enforcement mechanisms. Even when, in later years, Britain was sometimes forced to turn back to unilateral action, it was able to do so with greater legitimacy because it could point to the international commitments embodied in these treaties and argue that the treaties justified its actions. Time and again, British diplomats would remind other nations that they had agreed by treaty to suppress the slave trade. In one typical letter from 1836, British Foreign Secretary Lord Palmerston implored the Portuguese "to redeem the honour of Portugal" by fulfilling their promises to suppress the slave trade.[114] Once a nation had agreed that the slave trade was contrary to the laws of nature and nations, they could dodge and delay, but they could no longer defend the trade as lawful or legitimate. It might take decades for reality to line up with rhetoric, but once the course toward abolition was charted, it would prove impossible to go back.

CHAPTER 3

The United States and the Slave Trade

An Ambivalent Foe

From the beginning, slavery and the slave trade were delicate questions in American politics. Slave imports to North America had begun in the 1600s and had increased steadily through the mid-1700s. By the time the Declaration of Independence proclaimed in July 1776 that "all men are created equal," there were hundreds of thousands of African slaves in North America. The slave-owning revolutionaries may have been hypocritical, but they were not totally blind to the issue; the tension between slavery and the ideals of liberty on which the nation was founded was widely acknowledged.[1] The first early steps toward abolition were already being taken, though no one could have predicted then by what course slavery would eventually be eliminated or how long it would take. Northern states in which slavery had been practiced began abolishing it by the 1770s and 1780s. Antislavery societies in the upper South filed suit on behalf of slaves claiming freedom in the courts of Virginia and Maryland and lobbied their legislatures to pass manumission laws allowing individual owners to free their slaves.[2] The First Continental Congress had even temporarily banned the import of slaves, though this was primarily a measure aimed at British shipping interests, and imports resumed (albeit in relatively small numbers) following the end of the Revolutionary War.[3] Under the Articles of Confederation, Congress also passed the Northwest Ordinance of 1787 prohibiting slavery in the new territory it created out of the region north and west of the Ohio River, a measure foreshadowing later debates about whether slavery would be allowed in newly admitted states.

The U.S. Constitution, drafted in Philadelphia in the summer of 1787, is oddly evasive on the issue of slavery, a word that it studiously avoids. The first hint of the institution appears in Article 1, Section 2, which provides for the apportionment of representatives and taxes by a counting of "free persons, including those bound to Service for a term of years," excluding "Indians not taxed," and including "three-fifths of all other Persons"—that is, slaves were to count as three-fifths of a person.[4] The fugitive slave clause refers to "Person[s] held to Service or Labour in one State" and provides that their escape into another state should not result in their discharge from service but rather that they must be returned (which could preclude American courts from following the reasoning of the British court in *Somerset*, whereby a slave would be freed upon entering a free state).[5] Finally, on the issue of the slave trade, the constitutional convention compromised by limiting the power of Congress to prohibit the importation of "such Persons as any of the States now existing shall think proper to admit" until 1808 (and prohibiting amendment of this provision until the same year).[6] Reportedly, South Carolina, Georgia, and North Carolina persuaded the convention that this protection for the slave trade was vital for their support for ratification.[7]

During this time period, people managed to distinguish between slavery and the slave trade in moral and legal terms, and even supporters of slavery were often against the slave trade. Indeed, the constitution of the Confederate States of America included a provision banning the slave trade.[8] Nevertheless, it was apparent in the United States as in Britain that the treatment of the slave trade might have some impact on the institution of slavery. Early abolitionists certainly hoped that ending the slave trade would help end slavery itself. At the Pennsylvania ratifying convention on the Constitution, James Wilson suggested that the abolition of the slave trade would lay "the foundation for banishing slavery out of this country; and though the period is more distant than I could wish, yet it will produce the same kind, gradual change [for the whole nation] which was pursued in Pennsylvania."[9]

Though the federal government could not constitutionally ban the importation of slaves until 1808, the states had begun to prohibit the importation of slaves on their own even by the time of the Constitutional Convention. Indeed, "[b]etween 1776 and the Constitutional Convention in 1787, ten of the thirteen states banned the importation of slaves from abroad," while two others imposed prohibitively high duties or did not have significant slave imports to begin with.[10] In the late 1780s, the total annual slave imports to the United States were actually quite small, as shown in figure 3.1. By the early 1790s, abolition societies began asking Congress for some sort of national legislation against the slave trade in petitions that denounced the trade as "an

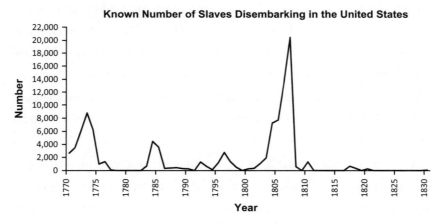

Figure 3.1. Number of Slaves Disembarking in the United States

outrageous violation of one of the most essential rights of human nature" and "degrading to the rights of man."[11] In 1794 Congress passed an act prohibiting the fitting out of slave ships in American ports to carry on the slave trade "to any foreign country."[12] The statute provided for the forfeiture of the ship and cargo and also for fines.

Abolitionist societies in New York, Philadelphia, and Providence, Rhode Island, began collecting information on illegal slave trading voyages and forwarding this information to authorities in hopes that cases would be brought under the new act.[13] One of the first ships condemned under the 1794 statute was the ironically named *Hope*.[14] The ship had been commissioned for its slave trading voyage in Rhode Island by John Brown, a prominent merchant and slave trader from Providence. From one of the leading families of Rhode Island, Brown was one of the founders of what would become Brown University. Though this John Brown was no relation to the famous abolitionist of the same name who led the raid at Harper's Ferry in 1859, he was related to Moses Brown, who was an active Quaker abolitionist and who had been one of the authors of the 1794 Slave Trade Act. The two brothers spent years debating the slave trade in person and in letters.

The *Hope* set sail from Providence, picked up a cargo of captives in Africa, delivered them into slavery in Cuba, and then returned to Rhode Island, making no attempt to hide the nature of its voyage or the profits it had earned. Members of the Providence Abolition Society petitioned the U.S. attorney for the city to bring an action against John Brown under the 1794 act, providing affidavits from crew members describing the voyage. The case came to trial in the U.S. district court in August 1797. The district judge easily found that the 1794 act had been violated and ordered the ship forfeited.[15] Following this favorable outcome, the abolition society urged a second lawsuit seeking fines under the act. Unlike the forfeiture action—which was an admiralty action triable by judge, not jury—the lawsuit seeking to impose a fine on Brown personally was subject to jury trial. In front of a Providence jury sympathetic to the slave trade and the profits it brought the seaport, Brown prevailed in this latter action, an outcome that dismayed the abolition society.[16]

The Supreme Court soon confirmed that there was no jury trial right, at least in forfeiture actions. In 1805, the Supreme Court held in the case of the *Schooner Sally* that forfeiture of a vessel under Congress's 1794 act against the slave trade fell within admiralty rather than common law jurisdiction and did not trigger a jury trial right.[17] In forfeiture cases, at least, prosecuting attorneys could avoid the prospect of a jury sympathetic to slave trading merchants, though of course the judges might prove biased as well.

The 1794 act was strengthened by Congress in an 1800 act that made it illegal for citizens to have any interest, even indirect, in slave voyages to foreign countries or to serve on slave ships engaged in the foreign slave trade in any capacity.[18] This statute provided not just for the forfeiture of ships but also for criminal sanctions including imprisonment. The same John Brown whose ship had been condemned under the 1794 act was now a member of Congress from Rhode Island and argued forcefully against any expansion of the laws against the slave trade.

> We want money, we want a navy; we ought therefore to use the means to obtain it. We ought to go farther than has yet been proposed, and repeal the bills in question altogether, for why should we see Great Britain getting all the slave trade to themselves; why may not our country be enriched by that lucrative traffic?[19]

Brown's views did not carry the day, and the measure passed the House by a vote of 67–5.[20]

In the following years, there were a number of actions in federal court involving civil forfeitures under these statutes, as well as a few criminal prosecutions.[21] In one criminal prosecution in Maryland in 1803, the jury convicted the defendant of violating the act by transporting slaves between two Caribbean ports, but the judge imposed imprisonment of only twenty-four hours upon a finding that the prisoner was ignorant of having violated any law.[22]

As the constitutional date on which Congress could prohibit slave imports into the United States approached, there was a dramatic uptick in the number of slave imports to North America, perhaps in anticipation that the trade would soon be prohibited. President Thomas Jefferson's message in December 1806 urged total abolition of the slave trade at the soonest possible date:

> I congratulate you, fellow-citizens, on the approach of the period at which you may interpose your authority constitutionally, to withdraw the citizens of the United States from all further participation in those violations of human rights which have been so long continued on the unoffending inhabitants of Africa, and which the morality, the reputation, and the best interests of our country, have long been eager to proscribe.[23]

Legislation to prohibit the slave trade was introduced the following day and was passed by Congress on March 2, 1807, to take effect in January 1808, the first constitutionally allowable date. As soon as the new law took effect, slave imports plummeted from more than 20,000 in 1807 to 593 recorded in 1808 and none the following year, as shown in figure 3.1.[24] The number of American ships engaged in the slave trade to other countries also declined substantially, as shown in figure 3.2.

Britain, of course, had just passed its own law against the slave trade, and, as early as 1808, the British abolitionist leader William Wilberforce was writing to Thomas Jefferson to see if it would be possible "to obtain some agreement between the two nations, for giving effect to Abolition, by allowing each country to take the other's ships."[25] But the mood in the United States was ill disposed toward allowing the British the right to board American ships. Already, British interference with American commercial trade to France and Britain's practice of impressing into British naval service sailors aboard U.S. merchant ships had led

Figure 3.2. U.S. Flagged Ships in Slave Trade

to tension between the two countries. This tension would eventually boil over as war broke out between the two countries in 1812. It was not until after the war that the countries would be able to really cooperate on the slave trade issue. Following peace negotiations, the United States agreed with Britain in the Treaty of Ghent in 1814 to use its best efforts to suppress the slave trade, though that treaty had no enforcement mechanism.[26] While Britain was negotiating treaties with other European powers on the slave trade in 1816 and 1817, it continued to press the United States for further action, suggesting provisions for mutual search and for mixed commissions—suggestions that the Americans chose to ignore.[27]

Multilateral negotiations among the European powers regarding the slave trade continued throughout 1818. At the Congress of Aix-la-Chapelle in 1818, the Russian government pushed for a permanent international institution "composed of elements drawn from all civilized States" including "a directing Council, and a judicial system" that would form "a Body Politic, neutral in its character, but exercising these High authorities over all States."[28] In its most ambitious iterations, such an organization would have criminal as well as civil jurisdiction over persons engaged in the illegal slave trade and would have at its disposal an international naval force with the right to visit and search ships flying all flags. By late 1818, however, the British government (perhaps because of its unsuccessful attempts to convince France to agree to courts of mixed commission) was skeptical of the "practicality of founding, or preserving in activity, so novel and so complicated a system" and began suggesting that it might be more feasible to treat slave traders as pirates, subject to trial in national legal systems. Castlereagh proposed to the parties at Aix-la-Chappelle that "it would be useful, and perhaps necessary, to consider the trade in slaves as a crime against the law of nations, and to this effect to assimilate it to piracy." If the slave trade were "universally prohibited" and "raised in the criminal code of all civilized nations to the standard of piracy," it would be "amenable to the ordinary tribunals of any or every particular state." The individuals charged with piracy could "plead no national character in bar of such jurisdiction," for pirates were "*Hostes humani generis*,"[29] or enemies of the human race, and fell "under the protection of no flag." The "verification of the fact of Piracy, by sufficient evidence, brings them at once within the reach of the first Criminal Tribunal of competent authority, before whom they may be brought."[30]

The British had by no means given up on the mixed courts idea, however, and they continued to try to persuade the United States to join the mixed courts regime, like Spain, Portugal, and the Netherlands. Certainly, the United States was no stranger to international courts. Although various forms of arbitration had been used to resolve disputes for many centuries,[31] the modern era of international adjudication is considered to begin with the Jay Treaty of 1794, through which Britain and the United States agreed to settle claims from the Revolutionary War by arbitration.[32] The commissions created under Article VII of the treaty yielded the most significant results;[33] they were charged with deciding property claims of American citizens "according to the merits of the several Cases, and to Justice, Equity and the Laws of Nations."[34] There were over 500 awards between 1798 and 1804.[35] The Jay Treaty arbitration panels were, in some sense, a model for the proposed slave trade tribunals, and the British referred to the precedent.

But other tension points in Anglo-American relations thwarted the negotiations. Britain had the world's most powerful navy. The Americans were concerned that the British would use this naval power to interfere with their commercial interests and trade, as they had in the past through the practice of boarding American ships and impressing sailors they deemed British citizens into service in their navy. This had been one of the causes of the War of 1812, and the issue lingered as a tension point even after that war ended. As then–Secretary of State John Quincy Adams noted in his diary, the Americans viewed the British proposals related to the slave trade as a "barefaced and impudent attempt of the British to obtain in time of peace that right of searching and seizing the ships of other nations which they so outrageously abused during war."[36] For decades, the concern that the right to search would be abused by the British kept the Americans from joining with the British in a stronger treaty.

One typical discussion of American concerns took place in October 1818, when the cabinet of President James Monroe met to decide what the American position should be in new negotiations with the British on impressment and the slave trade.[37] As the entry in Adams's diary shows, the members of the administration considered these to be politically sensitive issues. Monroe noted that impressment was a cause of the recently ended war and, according to Adams, noted, "There was a deep anxiety in [the public] minds, from an apprehension that it would again give rise to war."[38] Any missteps in the negotiations could be used by political rivals to gain the upper hand. Secretary of War John C. Calhoun joked, "what will the Kentucky and Western country newspapers say," which "occasioned a general laugh" as they "all knew that" political rival Henry Clay "would think well of anything which might excite dissatisfaction with the Administration."[39] Calhoun was concerned about any proposal that "would allow a British officer to muster and pass under inspection the crew of every American vessel boarded by him. It would give rise to altercations, and expose the American master to the insolence of the British officer, scarcely less galling than the injury of impressment itself." This would, Calhoun suggested, "give great dissatisfaction to the nation, and would be used as a weapon against the Administration."[40]

The main concern raised in respect to the British proposal for a slave trade treaty allowing a mutual right of search and trial in mixed commissions was that

> we have suffered so much from the practice of foreign officers to search our vessels in time of war, particularly by its connection with a British doctrine that after an officer has entered for one purpose he may proceed to search for another, that we ought to be especially cautious not to admit of the right of search in time of peace.[41]

Some of the Americans also had other concerns about the British proposal for mixed commissions. Attorney General William Wirt suggested that "there was no constitutional authority in the Government of the United States to establish a Court, partly consisting of foreigners, to sit without the bounds of the United States, and not amenable to impeachment for corruption," citing Article III, Section 1 of the Constitution, which vests the judicial power of the United States in the Supreme Court and such inferior courts as the Congress shall establish. Adams responded, "[I] thought there was sufficient authority by the Constitution, and likened it to the joint commissions which we have had by treaties with Great Britain and Spain, and to the Courts of Admiralty which it has been proposed to establish at Naples if we could have obtained the consent of that Government."[42] Wirt "pointed out distinctions between the two cases—between Courts constituted under the laws of nations and Courts to carry into effect our municipal and penal statutes."[43] Adams responded, "as the power of making treaties is without limitation in the Constitution, and treaties are declared to be the supreme law of the land, I still hold to the opinion that there is no constitutional difficulty in the way."[44] Notwithstanding his initial defense of the constitutionality of the proposed slave trade tribunals, Adams would eventually come around to Wirt's view and would argue, in negotiations with the British, that the courts presented constitutional problems for the United States, though it was never clear how sincere he was in offering these arguments.[45]

All of these men—President James Monroe, Secretary of State John Quincy Adams, and Attorney General Willliam Wirt—would continue to play a prominent role in debates over slavery and the slave trade in the following years. When Monroe was sworn in as president in March 1817, he became the fifth man to hold that office and the last to have played a prominent role in the American Revolution.[46] A Virginian, he had served as secretary of state under James Madison, and he came into power at the beginning of what many described, then and since, as an "era of good feelings" in American politics.[47] He was a slave owner, though his feelings on slavery seem to have been somewhat ambivalent.

John Quincy Adams would succeed Monroe as president following the 1824 election. The son of President John Adams and Abigail Adams, he had been born in Massachusetts. In his early career, he served as a senator and also spent a number of years abroad as the American ambassador to various European powers. He was one of the main negotiators of the Treaty of Ghent with the British in 1814, and was the American ambassador in London until 1817 when he returned and became Monroe's secretary of state. Adams was an opponent of slavery who famously defended the Africans onboard the slave ship *Amistad* in the Supreme Court in the 1840s as an old man, but in the 1820s he was an ambitious younger man who was sensitive to political circumstances. The British viewed Adams's political ambitions as an impediment to the conclusion of a slave trade treaty.[48] Throughout the negotiations over the treaty in the early 1820s, Adams undoubtedly had his political future in mind. As one historian puts it, "Being a New Englander and a former Federalist, Adams could not afford the slightest imputation of being pro-British."[49] Adams would run for president in the four-way election of 1824 against Senator Andrew Jackson, Treasury Secretary William H. Crawford, and Speaker of the House Henry Clay. The election was extraordinarily close and was ultimately decided in the House of Representatives, where Adams was selected as the next president.

Attorney General William Wirt is a less familiar name today, but at the time he was a very prominent and successful lawyer; today, he is viewed by legal historians as having increased the power and prestige of the office of attorney general.[50] Adams appeared to have no great fondness for him and complained in his diary that Wirt "appeared to think more about his salary, or what he called bread and meat for his children, than of any other subject."[51] He did seem to be perpetually in search of a way to pay his bills; in 1823 and 1824, Wirt argued almost as many cases for private parties in the U.S. Supreme Court as he argued for the United States government (something that ethics rules would never allow today).[52] Wirt was a slaveholder and more generally a defender of slavery, though he did support certain anti–slave trade measures.

Once Monroe's administration rejected the initial British overtures for a new treaty in late 1818, Congress chose to act against the slave trade through further domestic legislation. On March 3, 1819, Congress passed two important bills that would affect the slave trade. One bill, An Act in Addition to the Acts Prohibiting the Slave Trade, renewed authorization for the use of naval vessels to intercept illegal slavers; included within the prohibition ships that were equipped for the slave trade but that did not actually have slaves onboard at the time of capture; and authorized the federal government to make arrangements for the safekeeping of slaves from forfeited ships and for removing them to the coast of Africa, where the recently formed Colonization Society planned to set up a haven for freed slaves in what would eventually become Liberia.[53] On the same day, Congress also passed An Act to Protect the Commerce of the United States and Punish the Crime of

Piracy, which provided for punishment by death of any person who "on the high seas, commit[s] the crime of piracy, as defined by the law of nations" and who "shall afterwards be brought into or found in the United States."[54] The Supreme Court in *United States v. Smith* eventually upheld the piracy statute and rejected the argument that piracy was insufficiently definite under the law of nations to constitute a crime under American law.[55] "There is scarcely a writer on the law of nations, who does not allude to piracy as a crime of a settled and determinate nature," the Court noted, and the definition could easily be "ascertained by consulting the works of jurists, writing professedly on public law; or by the general usage and practice of nations; or by judicial decisions recognizing and enforcing that law."[56]

One thing that the law of nations did not yet include within the offense of piracy was the slave trade, for no country had yet taken up Britain's suggestion at Aix-la-Chapelle to assimilate the slave trade to piracy. Soon, Congress would change the definition of piracy in American law, but it would take more than the act of one nation to change the international definition. The following year, on May 15, 1820, Congress amended the 1819 piracy act to redefine piracy to include not only robbery on the high seas but also slave trading. Specifically, the statute made it piracy for "any citizen of the United States" or any person serving onboard a ship "owned in the whole or part, or navigated for, or in behalf of, any citizen or citizens of the United States" to "land, from any such ship or vessel, and, on any foreign shore, seize any negro or mulatto . . . with intent to make such negro or mulatto a slave."[57]

The new statute subjected offenders to the death penalty, making it perhaps the strongest measure against the slave trade in any nation, at least on paper. In the end, only one person was ever hung for slave trading by the United States, and that was not until 1862. Efforts to enforce these laws did increase, with some eleven slave ships captured by the navy between May 1818 and November 1821.[58] For a brief time in 1820, the United States had five naval vessels off the coast of Africa.

One of them, the USS *John Adams*, met up with the British HMS *Snapper*, and the captains of the two ships cooperated in an attempt to capture a slave ship in the River Pongas. But the American ships did not stay on the coast for long and were soon recalled to service in other waters.[59]

At the same time Congress was dealing with the slave trade, it was also confronting the issue of slavery itself. Beginning in 1819, the federal government was forced to address the issue of slavery in newly admitted states and territories as Missouri sought admission to the Union as a slave state. Northern states were concerned that this would tilt the balance in favor of slavery, while Southern states hoped to keep the balance from shifting in the other direction. After more than a year of acrimonious debate, the Missouri Compromise passed in 1820. The compromise preserved a balance between free and slave states by admitting Missouri as a slave state and Maine as a free state, and by prohibiting slavery in the Missouri Territory north of the 36°30′ parallel except within the proposed new state of Missouri itself.

Though the Missouri Compromise passed, it was obvious to Secretary of State John Quincy Adams that the "bargain between freedom and slavery contained in the Constitution of the United States" was a ticking time bomb: "If the Union must be dissolved, slavery is precisely the question upon which it ought to break," Adams mused in his diary.[60]

At the same time, both Congress and the British began pushing Monroe's administration to take even further action against the slave trade. In 1821, a proposed resolution in the House requested the president "to consult and negotiate with all the Governments, where Ministers of the United States are, or shall be accredited, on the means of effecting an entire and immediate abolition of the African slave trade."[61]

But the negotiations over a British treaty were stalled. Adams's diary suggests that the main and almost insurmountable objection of the U.S. government was to the right of search, though at times Adams would also raise the constitutional arguments he initially viewed as dubious.

In his diary in April 1819, for example, Adams records that Rush, the American minister in London, had been instructed to reject the British mixed courts proposal "for two reasons," the first being that "the United States, having no Colony or possession in Africa, had no territory where the joint Court could hold their sessions" and the other "that the Constitution of the United States admitted no appointment of Judges who would not be amenable to impeachment."[62] But Adams went on to say, "There was a third reason which had been mentioned to Mr. Rush, but which he had not been desired to urge, if the others would appear to be entirely satisfactory to the British government."[63] In an informal conversation with the British minister in Washington, Charles Bagot, Adams "thought it well to come directly to the point of . . . difficulty by stating" this third objection, namely that "the United States ought on no consideration whatever to listen to any proposal for admitting a right of search in their merchant vessels by the commanders of foreign armed vessels so long as the question remains open between them and Great Britain concerning impressment for men."[64] Tellingly, Adams explained to Bagot, "[W]e had no wish to stir this question unnecessarily, or to awaken the feelings connected with it, when it can be avoided, we had scarcely mentioned it in regular communications to the British Government," and that he thought it best to mention it only in an "informal manner."[65] In other words, the Americans were hoping that the British would accept the constitutional objection so that they would not have to discuss the troublesome issue of search and impressment.

Soon, the British sent a new negotiator, Stratford Canning, to Washington with full instructions to engage the Americans in a new slave trade treaty.[66] But the change of personnel had little impact on the negotiations. In a meeting with Canning in October 1820, Adams rebuffed Canning with objections to the right of search in peacetime and also argued that there was a "want of Constitutional authority to establish such a Court."[67] Adams continued by noting "there were other [reasons]" that "it was best in candor to mention" in this private meeting.[68]

The first was "the general extra-European policy of the United States."[69] The second was that the United States "had had one war with Great Britain for exercising what she alone claims of all the nations of the earth as a right—search of neutral vessels in time of war to take out men."[70] The nations had tried without success to work out a satisfactory agreement on this point, and "[i]t was a point upon which, more than any other, not only the people but the Government of the United States were sensitive, and which would fix [them] in the determination in no case to yield the right of search in time of peace."[71] Canning's response that the mutual right of search in the slave trade was unlikely to be abused gained little traction.[72]

Later meetings covered much of the same ground.[73] In one meeting, when Adams raised concerns about impressment, Canning "hint[ed] some regret that [Adams] should even harbor the sentiment that there was any analogy between" the right of search in the slave trade treaties and the issue of impressment.[74] Canning returned on October 26 to lobby Adams again for "two hours or more upon the subject of the slave-trade," bringing with him a "long written paper" summarizing and responding to the various American objections.[75] The conversation frustrated both participants. "We went over the whole ground of impressment, as usual, to no purpose," Adams recounted in his diary.[76] "I told him it was not my wish to debate the point," for "w[e] had more than once exhausted the argument with his Government."[77]

Little changed in the next two years of negotiations. In June 1822, Adams recounted another meeting with Canning where they debated search and impressment: "We went over this ground again, as we had often done before, repeating on both sides the same arguments as before."[78] But when it came time for public statements, Canning as well as Adams seemed loath to focus too much on impressment. Indeed, Adams recounts in his diary that when he told Canning that his latest response to the British proposal was before the president for review, Canning "appeared to be uneasy at the idea that in my reply the subject of impressment would be discussed, and said he hoped, in the disposition between the two Governments so strongly tending towards conciliation, whatever was of an irritating character might be avoided."[79]

Other statements by the administration echoed the roadblock in the negotiations around the topic of impressment. President Monroe, for example, noted in a letter in 1821, "We should be guarded, in the pursuit of this object [of suppressing the slave trade], to give no countenance by any act of ours to the right of search, which may be applied to other purposes" and cautioned against any policy that "might give some countenance to the practice of impressment."[80]

Meanwhile, two important court cases concerning the slave trade were working their way through the federal court system. The first concerned a ship called *La Jeune Eugenie*. The USS *Alligator*, commanded by Captain Robert Stockton, was cruising off the coast of Africa in 1821, when it fell in with the schooner *La Jeune Eugenie* and captured it on suspicion of slave trading.[81] Though no slaves were onboard at the time, the ship was equipped with movable decks and irons and far too much food and water for its small crew. The Americans placed a prize crew onboard and sailed the captured ship to Boston, where they sought condemnation of the ship in federal court under various statutes including the 1807, 1819, and 1820 acts. The captors claimed that the ship was American, though it flew the French flag and carried French papers. In support of their claim, they asserted that the ship had been built in the United States, that there were no legal papers showing its transfer to French citizens, and that it was well known that the French flag and papers were used to shield slave traders. In the alternative, they alleged that the slave trade was prohibited by French laws and that the court would be justified on that ground from returning the ship, as the alleged owners had no legal claim to it under their own nation's law. Finally, they argued that "the slave trade was contrary to the law of nations, as at present understood and received" because it was "a violation of the law of nature, which constituted a component part of the law of nations."[82] Noting that "[m]ost or all of the civilized nations of the globe, had declared their sense of the illegality of this trade, by enacting laws to suppress it, and by various other public acts, treaties, and declarations," they contended that "it might now therefore be considered as contrary to the conventional law of nations."[83]

On the other side of the case, the French consul entered a claim on behalf of the alleged owners of the *Eugenie*, and "a protest against the seizure and judicial proceedings, on behalf of the French government."[84] In addition to arguing that the ship was French and that there was inadequate proof that it was engaged in the slave trade, the French claimants also argued that there was no belligerent right under the law of nations that authorized the initial search and seizure of the ship. They asserted that the customary law of nations did not prohibit the slave trade and that there were no grounds upon which the courts of the United States could rightly exercise jurisdiction.

The case almost immediately incited diplomatic controversy, and, upon the advice of Secretary of State Adams, President Monroe soon issued orders to the navy against intercepting foreign-flagged vessels.[85] When Monroe and Adams were inclined to ask that the ship be turned over to the French government, Attorney General Wirt was actually more skeptical. Wirt noted, "You have certainly taken the safe side as it affects our questions of search with Great Britain." But he questioned whether the administration's position was "too far within the line," noting that "vessels are in the constant habit of using the flags of all nations to cover their illicit operation" and that the laws against the slave trade would be unenforceable if there was no right to question their nationality.[86] Adams responded that there was no peacetime right to board and search foreign vessels and that "[b]y the law of nature, no vessel has a right to board another at sea without its consent."[87] Adams's views prevailed within the administration, and the district attorney was instructed to inform the court that the president desired that the ship be turned over to the French government.

It was the practice in those days for Supreme Court justices to "ride circuit" and decide cases in the regions to which they were assigned, and Justice Joseph Story of the U.S. Supreme Court decided the case as circuit justice. Story was one of the most prominent members of the early Supreme Court, and in 1833 and 1834 published his influential *Commentaries on the Conflict of Laws* and *Commentaries on the Constitution of the United States*. Later, he would write the majority opinion in the Supreme Court in the *Amistad* case.

In his opinion in the case of *La Jeune Eugenie*, Story wrote that he was "fully aware of the importance and difficulty of this case," including the diplomatic trouble it had caused between the United States and France. He determined that the ship was American built and American owned, though carrying French papers, and that it was equipped for the slave trade. Story noted that the statute making the slave trade piracy and punishable by death meant that American citizens involved in the slave trade would have a strong incentive to disguise their nationality, and that false papers were easy to obtain. "Sitting as I do in a court of the law of nations, accustomed to witness, in many shapes, the artifices of fraud . . . I think, that I should manifest a false delicacy . . . if I did not borrow somewhat that experience of the world, to enable me to disentangle the network, which covers up unlawful enterprises."[88] Given the circumstances, he thought that more proof was necessary to show that the ship was actually French rather than American.

But even assuming the ship was French, he went on to explain, the French claimants were still not entitled to its return. In an action *in rem*, he stated, anyone seeking title to the property must establish good title; even if the prize crew's claim should fail, that did not mean the ship should be returned to the French claimants if they could not themselves establish good title. While acknowledging that there was no peacetime right of search under the law of nations, he distinguished the right of seizure, noting that "vessels and property in the possession of pirates might be lawfully seized on the high seas," though in such cases the captors acted at their own peril if they turned out to be mistaken about the captives' piratical character.

Turning then to the question whether the law of nations prohibited the slave trade, Story acknowledged that slavery "existed in all ages of the world" and "forms the foundation of large masses of property in a portion of our own country." He could not deny that "under some circumstances [slavery] may have a lawful existence" and "may form a part of the domestic policy of a nation."[89] Nevertheless, he concluded that the lawfulness of the African slave trade was a separate and distinct issue. In great detail drawn from abolitionist writings of the period,[90] he described the particular ways in which the African slave trade involved "a breach of all the moral duties, of all the maxims of justice, mercy and humanity." The law of nations, he explained,

> may be deduced, first, from the general principles of right and justice, applied to the concerns of individuals, and thence to the relations and duties of nations; or, secondly, in things indifferent or questionable, from the customary observances and recognitions of civilized nations; or lastly, from the conventional or positive law, that regulates the intercourse between states.[91]

Universal agreement since time immemorial was not necessary, in his view, to make something part of the law of nations, for certain aspects of that law could change over time. The major European powers had recently acknowledged the injustice and inhumanity of the slave trade and pledged to promote its abolition, as had the United States. Story therefore described himself as "bound to consider the trade an offence against the universal law of society and in all cases, where it is not protected by a foreign government, to deal with it as an offence carrying with it the penalty of confiscation."[92]

Story went on to distinguish the recent British decision invalidating the seizure of the French slave ship *Le Louis*. That seizure had been made "when no public ordinance of France prohibited the slave trade, and before the recent [international] discussions at Aix-la-Chappelle [condemning the trade]." While "cognizance of penalties and forfeitures for breaches of municipal regulations exclusively belongs to the tribunals of the nation, by whom they are enacted," Story noted that the courts of another nation were able to take judicial notice of foreign laws "which come incidentally before it in the exercise of its general jurisdiction over persons or property."[93] Thus, in determining who had a valid claim to ownership of the vessel, the court was entitled to take notice that French municipal law also prohibited the slave trade.

In the end, Story stopped short of declaring the ship forfeit. He noted that the district attorney had submitted, by direction of the president, a suggestion that the ship be turned over to the French government for final adjudication. Though he concluded that the private French owners were not entitled to return of the ship, he decreed that the ship should be turned over to the French government. That ended the case.

At the same time, a similar case was working its way through the courts, with the additional element of slaves having been found onboard at the time of capture. That case, *The Antelope*, would eventually reach the U.S. Supreme Court, where Chief Justice Marshall would reach a conclusion quite different from Story's on the status of the slave trade under the law of nations.[94] The case began when the United States revenue cutter USS *Dallas* captured the *Antelope* in June 1820 with some 281 slaves on board. The ship was brought to Savannah for trial on suspicion of being illegally engaged in the slave trade.[95] The local U.S. attorney was not entirely certain how to proceed and sought instructions from Washington, DC. When the issue reached President Monroe's desk, the president instructed Adams on how to respond:

> Instruct the D. Attorney to pursue the affair in its several relations with the utmost attention; first, to contend for the complete liberation of every African against every claimant . . .; and secondly, for the punishment of all concerned in taking them who are exposed to it under our laws.[96]

Further, Monroe noted his belief, "I do not think that any foreigner can sustain a claim against an African brought directly from Africa as a slave, in our Courts, but that when brought within our jurisdiction he must be free."[97]

The captain of the ship, John Smith, was indicted and tried for piracy, based on the allegation that he had stolen the *Antelope* from its true Spanish and Portuguese owners; the American statute declaring the slave trade to be piracy was not used because it had been enacted too recently, on May 15, 1820. Smith's defense was that he was operating not as an unlawful pirate but as a lawful privateer under commission from a revolutionary South American government, the predecessor of modern-day Uruguay. After the trial, he was acquitted by the jury.[98] Smith then entered the parallel civil proceeding in admiralty as a claimant, seeking return of the *Antelope* and its cargo as against the competing claims of the captain of the *Dallas* and Portuguese and Spanish claimants on behalf of the ship's original owners.[99] The district judge ruled that the ship should be returned to the Spanish, dividing most of the slaves between the Spanish and Portuguese claimants and awarding bounty and salvage to the captain of the *Dallas*.[100] The case was appealed to the Sixth Circuit, which described the suit as having been brought "on behalf of the United States and officers and crew of the cutter *Dallas* who claim the vessel and cargo as forfeited under the act of the 20th April, 1808, or under the modern law of nations on the subject of the slave trade."[101] The appeals court held that the U.S. statutes prohibiting the slave trade were not applicable to foreign-flagged ships; the court believed the general law of nations still allowed the slave trade, and it thus concluded that the ship and its cargo had to be returned to its original owners, a view that would ultimately be upheld by the Supreme Court.[102]

Although the case was docketed in the Supreme Court in early 1822, it was not argued immediately. The Monroe administration was apparently not eager to have the case decided and so, without public explanation, the case was held over for three full years without argument, a rather unusual delay. Indeed, the case was not argued in the Supreme Court until 1825—after a slave trade treaty with the British had finally been agreed to by the Monroe administration and then failed upon amendment in the Senate, and after Adams had won the closely contested 1824 presidential election.

A number of important developments occurred between 1822 and 1825. In 1822, at the Congress of Verona, Britain attempted to get other European powers to agree to stronger measures against the slave trade, again pressing for an agreement that each country should denounce the slave trade as piracy.[103] In 1823, the American Congress began pushing harder for the conclusion of a treaty with the British, with the House passing a resolution calling upon the president "to enter upon . . . negotiations with the several maritime Powers of Europe and America, as he may deem expedient for the effectual abolition of the African slave trade, and its ultimate denunciation, as piracy, under the law of nations, by the consent of the civilized world."[104] In support of the resolution, Congressman Mercer argued that "[t]he consent of nations may make piracy of any offence upon the high seas" and that declaring the slave trade piracy would provide a "definite and competent remedy" that would be "understood, and punished by all nations." Moreover, the slave trade was analogous to piracy, for, he asked, "is it not robbery to seize, not the property of the man, but the man himself?" As for the mixed courts, he opined that "Great Britain cannot but perceive the inefficacy of those mixed courts on which she has relied to give effect to her laws and treaties for the abolition of the slave trade, and, above all, that her present system, complicated and difficult of execution in peace, must be exposed to great derangement, if not abandoned, in war." Declaring the slave trade to be piracy, by contrast, would be "simple" and "effective."[105] This approach—the "piracy" strategy—would dominate American-British negotiations for the next two years.

Broader developments in U.S. foreign policy were also afoot. Many of the Latin American countries had declared their independence from

Spain, and the United States felt the need to weigh in on their independence. At the same time there were rumors that the Russian government had designs on areas in the Pacific Northwest. The United States wanted to discourage other countries from trying to gain control of the former Spanish colonies or from attempting to colonize the as-yet-unsettled regions of the Western Hemisphere. Later that year, President Monroe laid out what would become known as the Monroe Doctrine in his State of the Union message in December 1823. The doctrine, actually drafted by Secretary of State Adams, became a cornerstone of American foreign policy into the twentieth century. The doctrine asserted that North and South America should not be colonized further by any European powers; that any European intervention in the hemisphere would be treated as "dangerous to our peace and safety"; and that the United States would not become involved in European wars or "internal concerns."[106]

It was against this backdrop of asserted independence from European affairs that the United States continued to negotiate a treaty on the slave trade with the British in 1823 and 1824. In March 1823, Adams wrote to Canning proposing a treaty whereby the two countries would mutually stipulate "to annex the penalties of *Piracy* to the offence of participating in the Slave Trade, by the Citizens or Subjects of the respective Parties."[107] Adams noted "[t]he distinction between piracy by the law of nations and piracy by statute," and the fact that "while the former subjects the transgressor guilty of it to the jurisdiction of any and every country into which he may be brought, or wherein he may be taken, the latter forms a part of the municipal criminal code of the country where it is enacted, and can be tried only by its own courts."[108] Though the United States "expressed their desire that the change [in the definition of piracy to include the slave trade] should become general by the consent of every other power," Adams acknowledged that Britain and the United States alone could not redefine piracy under the general law of nations. Until the general agreement of nations on the matter was achieved, Adams asserted that the United States was bound to punish its own citizens in its own courts, and the treaty had to provide that captured slave ships be brought back to their own nation for trial.[109] At the same time, Adams also sent letters to American diplomats in a variety of countries including Spain, France, and the Netherlands seeking similar agreements to redefine the slave trade as piracy.[110]

It may seem odd that the 1824 treaty submitted to the Senate allowed a right of search, since the United States' main objections to British proposals over the past several years had concerned the right of search. But, in fact, policy concerns about the scope of the right to search and impressment drove this decision to put jurisdiction in national courts, and the members of the administration believed the treaty adequately cabined Britain's ability to abuse the right of search. As Secretary of the Navy Thompson explained in one cabinet meeting, if arrangement "could be made so that vessels under our flag should be brought for trial into our own jurisdiction and tried by our own Courts," there was little chance it "would give any countenance to the British practice of impressing men from our merchant vessels in time of war."[111] Adams likewise explained, "The objections to the right of search, as incident to the right of detention and capture, are also in a very considerable degree removed by the introduction of the principle" that the home courts of the captured ship would be able to review the legality of the search and impose damages on the captor if the search was unwarranted. "This guard against the abuses of a power so liable to abuse would be indispensable," Adams believed.[112]

As Monroe explained in his 1824 message to the Senate, the problem with the original British proposal was that "[t]he right of search is the right of war of the belligerent toward the neutral" and "[t]o extend it in time of peace to any object whatever, might establish a precedent which might lead to others with some powers, and which, even if confined to the instance specified, might be subject to great abuse."[113] On the other hand, assimilating the slave trade to piracy would not set a precedent for expanding peacetime search but would merely fit the slave trade into a preexisting category where search was allowed. "By making the crime piracy, the right of search attaches to the crime, and . . . when adopted by all nations, will be common to all."[114]

The British readily agreed to the proposal, and Parliament enacted a statute declaring the slave trade to be piracy. The treaty foundered, however, when in ratifying the final treaty the Senate tried to make changes to which the British would not agree.[115] Although the British were willing to accept some modifications, including a provision allowing either party to withdraw from the treaty, they were unwilling to accept the Senate's insistence that the waters off the coast of America be excluded from the treaty.[116] The two countries found themselves at an impasse.

It was against this background of diplomatic failure that the Supreme Court finally decided the case of the *Antelope* the following year. By then, the case had been lingering for years on appeal, the unfortunate Africans from onboard the ship still waiting to learn their fate. The results were not good. Writing for the Court, Chief Justice Marshall concluded that the ship and the enslaved passengers must be returned to their owners. With the recent failure of the treaty no doubt in mind, Marshall began by observing "[t]hat the course of opinion on the slave trade should be unsettled, ought to excite no surprise."[117] While "abhorrent," he explained, "it has been sanctioned in modern times by the laws of all nations who possess distant colonies" and "has claimed all the sanction which could be derived from long usage, and general acquiescence." Thus, he went on, "That trade could not be considered as contrary to the law of nations which was authorized and protected by the laws of all commercial nations."[118] Marshall, relying in part on the British decision in *Le Louis*, concluded that "the legality of the capture of a vessel engaged in the slave trade depends on the law of the country to which the vessel belongs."[119] Marshall specifically noted the holding in

Le Louis that there is no peacetime right of search except against pirates, who are the "enemies of the human race."[120] But the slave trade was not yet piracy under the law of nations.[121]

As for slavery itself, "That it is contrary to the law of nature will scarcely be denied," for "every man has a natural right to the fruits of his own labor."[122] But slavery had been allowed since ancient times and thus "could not be pronounced repugnant to the law of nations" for "[t]hat which has received the assent of all must be the law of all."[123] Marshall—whose decision in *Marbury v. Madison* had helped launch the practice of judicial review—explained the role of a judge in circumspect terms:

> Whatever might be the answer of a moralist to this question, a jurist must search for its legal solution in those principles of action which are sanctioned by the usages, the national acts, and the general assent of that portion of the world of which he considers himself a part, and to whose law the appeal is made. If we resort to this standard as the test of international law, the question as has already been observed, is decided in favor of the legality of the trade.[124]

The opinion went on to explain, "Each [nation] legislates for itself, but its legislation can operate on itself alone. . . . As no nation can prescribe a rule for others, none can make a law of nations."[125] Marshall further explained the relation of the slave trade to piracy: "If it is consistent with the law of nations, it cannot in itself be piracy. It can be made so only by statute; and the obligation of the statute cannot transcend the legislative power of the state which may enact it."[126] Thus, the court concluded, "the right of bringing in for adjudication in time of peace, even where the vessel belongs to [a] nation which has prohibited the trade, cannot exist"; for "[t]he Courts of no country execute the penal laws of another."[127] Like the British decision in *Le Louis*, Marshall's decision in the *Antelope* closed American courts as an option for condemning foreign ships engaged in the slave trade, at least in the absence of further treaties. Natural-law arguments about the evil of slavery would not be enough.

Shortly thereafter, James Kent's influential treatise *Commentaries on American Law* in 1826 reflected this same understanding of the status of the slave trade under the law of nations. Kent described the turn of sentiment against the transatlantic slave trade, as it was "repugnant to the principles of Christian duty, and the maxims of justice and humanity."[128] But Kent agreed it was "not piratical or illegal by the common law of nations."[129] He explained that "a pirate, who is one by the law of nations, may be tried and punished in any country where he may be found."[130] But acts that were not piracy under the law of nations, but solely under the municipal laws of a particular country, were "punishable exclusively by the nation which passes the statute." Although the slave trade was declared to be piracy by statutes in England and the United States, those two nations could not speak for the whole world, and the slave trade was still not piracy under the law of nations. The American statute of 1820 making the slave trade piracy, he explained,

> operates only where our municipal jurisdiction might be applied consistently with the general theory of public law, to the persons of our citizens, or to foreigners on board of American vessels. Declaring the crime piracy does not make it so, within the purview of the laws of nations, if it were not so without the statute.[131]

In order to "make it piracy" under the law of nations, "it must have been so considered and treated in practice by all civilized states, or made so by virtue of a general convention."[132]

Thus, in the 1820s the law of nations was in an ambiguous and transitional state with respect to the slave trade. International law could no longer be said to expressly authorize slave trading, as it had in the time of Grotius. But neither did the law of nations prohibit the practice. Instead, it was up to each country to decide, either through its own legislation or through ratification of treaties. This was where things stood as the new Anglo-Spanish, Anglo-Portuguese, and Anglo-Dutch courts of mixed commission got down to work thousands of miles away. Their work would help turn international law away from its troubled past in supporting and justifying the slave trade and toward the future of abolition.

CHAPTER 4

The Courts of Mixed Commission for the Abolition of the Slave Trade

THE SLAVE TRADE TRIBUNALS IN OPERATION

On the coast of Africa, the slave traders were acutely aware of the state of the law, for their livelihood depended on it. News of the signing of treaties between Britain and the Netherlands, Spain, and Portugal quickly reached the slave coast, as did news when the treaty between Britain and the United States had failed.

In 1820, soon after the first mixed commission treaties went into effect, the British commander of the African squadron, Commodore George Collier, explained that "the knowledge the slaving masters have of the treaties" meant that it had become difficult to catch ships of the covered nations with slaves on board. At this point, the treaties allowed only for the condemnation of ships that actually had slaves onboard at the time of capture. In some instances, while British boats were approaching slave vessels near the coast, the slavers quickly relanded all their slaves on shore and then paraded them on the beach, compelling them to "dance, and make every sign of contempt for the boats crews."[1] But challenges in capturing the slave ships, Collier explained, were not the "only difficulties His Majesty's naval officers have to surmount, as every sort of objection has been urged even by the foreign Commissary Judges against the condemnation of slave vessels."[2]

In their first few months of operation, the new mixed courts frustrated the British captains to no end. At first, the courts were even uncertain about what procedures they should use. For the first few cases, they would not allow anyone to be present for most of the proceedings—even the captain of the capturing ship. Moreover, they refused to allow the parties to be represented by professional advocates in the proceedings, insisting that each British captain present his case personally and then wait around in port for the court to decide. This was a major departure from the procedures used in normal admiralty courts and provoked much outrage among the naval officers, particularly since they could be held personally liable for damages in case of wrongful capture.[3] The procedures were not, in the view of the captains, in conformity with the "law of nature and of nations."[4] Indeed, Commodore Collier argued, these were "the most extraordinary of all courts of justice I have ever heard or read of" in operating secretly and not allowing the parties to appear with representation.[5] After a deluge of strenuous objections from the naval officers suggesting that the whole scheme would be a failure unless more reasonable procedures were adopted, the British judges persuaded their foreign colleagues to allow the parties to be represented by advocates and to open their proceedings so that both sides could participate.[6]

As challenging as it was to figure out the procedural rules, the substantive law proved just as troublesome. One of the earliest cases before the mixed commission was that of the Dutch ship *Eliza*. In that case, the slave captain had unloaded all the slaves but one by the time the British gained control of the ship. The Dutch judge insisted that the ship was no longer covered by the treaties, since they referred to ships with "slaves" onboard, and therefore were inapplicable when there was only one slave onboard at the time of capture;[7] the British judge thought this was ridiculous. The judges drew straws to pick a third judge (the "arbitrator") to break the tie. A Dutch arbitrator was selected, but in this case he sided with the British judge and found that the *Eliza*, even with only one slave onboard at the time of capture, was subject to condemnation under the treaties.[8] This, unfortunately, was indicative of some of the troubles that the courts would face throughout their many years of operation.

Under each of the treaties creating mixed commissions, one court was to be set up in a British possession, and another in a Spanish, Portuguese, or Dutch possession, respectively. Thus, courts were set up in Freetown, Sierra Leone; Havana, Cuba; Rio de Janeiro, Brazil; and Suriname.[9] Annexes to the treaties provided detailed regulations for the courts, including the basic procedural rules under which the courts operated, but as with modern international courts, their procedures evolved over time in light of practical circumstances and as the treaties were amended to close loopholes. Pursuant to the treaties, each nation appointed a commissioner, sometimes referred to as the "commissary judge." Each nation also appointed a "commissioner of arbitration" or "arbitrator." These two officers were often collectively referred to as the "commissioners." Finally, the government of the territory in which the court sat appointed a registrar, who acted as the court's chief administrator and assisted in the taking of evidence.[10]

In the event that the two judges could not agree on the outcome of the case, one of the two arbitrators would be selected by lottery to cast the deciding vote.[11] As it happened, on many occasions one or more of the judges or arbitrators was absent. Due to the prevalence of tropical diseases in the locations where the courts sat, it was not uncommon for the European officials to fall ill, and many died in the course of duty.[12] While Britain promptly replaced its fallen representatives, many other nations did not, leaving very long stretches in each of the courts when at least one and sometimes both of the non-British slots remained vacant. For example, of the 109 cases heard by the Anglo-Brazilian court at Sierra Leone, only twenty-eight were decided with the participation of Brazilian judges, while the remaining eighty-one were decided by British judges alone. Of the cases in which a Brazilian judge was present, in eighteen the British and Brazilian judges agreed on the outcome, while in the other ten, the judges did not agree and the case was decided by the arbitrator. In each of these cases, the selected arbitrator voted with the judge from his own nation.[13] After some initial confusion and controversy, the governments generally agreed that in the absence of one or more officials, the courts should proceed with whomever was present.[14]

The judges and arbitrators were not always lawyers.[15] Sometimes they held other public offices contemporaneously. For example, the governor of Sierra Leone and other colonial officials were occasionally called upon to serve as the British judge or arbitrator on the mixed courts after the incumbent died and until a replacement could arrive from London.[16]

Pursuant to the treaties, ships of each nation's navy were to be provided with "special Instructions" entitling them to "visit such merchant Vessels of the two Nations as may be suspected, upon reasonable Grounds, of having Slaves on board."[17] The instructions were quite detailed, specifying that the searches should be conducted "in the most mild manner, and with every attention which is due between allied and friendly nations." To avoid insult, the search was to be conducted by officers of suitable rank.[18] If the ship was in violation of the treaty, the captor had authority to "detain and bring away such Vessels, in order that they may be brought to trial before the Tribunals established for this purpose."[19]

British naval vessels captured the vast majority of ships.[20] In addition to the overall commitment of the Royal Navy to the antislavery patrol, individual officers had a financial incentive to capture slave ships since they were entitled to a share of the prize money.[21] In addition, many captains of ships in the antislavery patrol were horrified by what they found aboard slave vessels and pursued their duty with moral zeal. As one British naval officer testified before Parliament of his experience on boarding a slave ship:

[A] great many of the slaves had confluent small-pox; the sick had been thrown down in the hold in one particular spot, and they appeared on looking down to be one living mass; you could hardly tell arms from legs, or one person from another, or what they were; there were men, women and children; it was the most horrible and disgusting heap that could be conceived.[22]

Similarly, Captain Joseph Denman—an officer who spent many years trying to influence the British government's slave trade policies— explained that he had become interested in suppression of the trade fifteen years earlier, when as a young lieutenant he was placed in charge of a captured slave ship that had to be sailed first to Rio and then to Sierra Leone for trial: "I was . . . altogether four months on board of her, where I witnessed the most dreadful sufferings that human beings can endure. . . . Those sufferings have given me the deepest interest in the subject."[23]

Commodore George Collier similarly described his feelings upon the capture of a Spanish ship, the *Anna Maria*, in 1821. "I feel I should ill fulfill the duties falling upon me . . . if I did not describe the horrible state which this vessel was in when visited by British officers," he wrote. Although the *Anna Maria* was a relatively small ship of under 200 tons, she had "on board nearly 500 living souls!" Collier described "[t]he intense heat and filthy state of the slave rooms (being only 2 feet 11 inches high)" in which the captives were

[c]linging to the gratings to inhale a mouthful of fresh or pure air, and fighting with each other for a taste of water, showing their parched tongues, and pointing to their reduced stomachs as if overcome by famine. . . . [T]he crowded state of the vessel, the dirt and filth inseparable from such a state, the sickening and desponding appearance of most of the wretched victims, confined more loathsomely and more closely than hogs brought to a morning market for sale, was so appalling and distressing to our feelings.

The British officers had witnessed some of the enslaved passengers throw themselves overboard and be eaten by sharks. This "maddening act of self-destruction," Collier explained, was not surprising given the horror of the conditions on the ship.[24]

In each case, after determining that the ship under search was indeed engaged in the illegal slave trade and fell within one of the treaties, the commander of the capturing ship would typically place a junior officer and a small prize crew onboard the captured ship to sail it into the nearest port where a commission sat.[25] Sometimes the captor would send its ship's surgeon aboard the captured ship to try to provide medical treatment, or sick slaves might be taken aboard the captor ship to be treated and to relieve overcrowding.[26] In the case of the overcrowded *Anna Maria*, for example, Commodore Collier "was obliged to order twelve immediately to this ship to be placed under the care of the surgeon, and the day following, one hundred more, to afford the rest the chance of surviving the passage to Sierra Leone."[27] One British captain described in horrifying terms his capture of a ship with 560 slaves: "I had to remove the children on board of my own vessel; 200 of them," who ranged in age "[f]rom a few days old and upwards; some of them had been born on board" and most were "suffering from dysentery."[28] If many of the slaves were too sick to make the voyage at all, the sickest would be landed at the nearest available port.[29]

Almost invariably, some of the slaves died between the time of capture and the time of adjudication.[30] Once they arrived at the site of the court, the slaves would often be kept onboard the ship while the court decided the case, with often devastating consequences for the health of the slaves if the adjudication were prolonged for any reason. This provoked frequent concern on the part of the naval captains and the commissioners alike. For example, Commander Keith Stewart of HMS *Ringdove* sent one prize to Havana with a note imploring the court to remove the Africans from the ship immediately; most of the slaves were emaciated children between the ages of ten and fifteen, and

Commander Stewart pronounced the ship "the most miserable craft I ever saw in the shape of a slaver."[31] Although the treaties were not clear on what should happen to the captives while the case was pending, the British commissioners argued, "In such circumstances, the duties of humanity have pre-eminence over every other object."[32] At Sierra Leone, the judges would often successfully petition the colonial governor to allow the slaves to disembark.[33] Local governments in Havana and Rio, however, generally did not allow the slaves to go ashore, viewing their presence as a security risk.[34] Eventually, the British stationed special ships in the harbors of Havana and Rio to provide more humane housing for the slaves during the pendency of cases before the courts.[35]

The treaties specified that cases should ordinarily be resolved in twenty days.[36] In reality, adjudication of cases took anywhere from a few days to several months, with the court at Sierra Leone typically working most efficiently.[37] After the initial confusion about procedures, cases typically proceeded in an orderly fashion using procedures very similar to those employed in the national admiralty courts of Britain. The proceedings began with the capturing officer turning over the captured ship's papers along with an affidavit describing the circumstances of the capture.[38] The registrar would then administer a standard set of interrogatories to witnesses from both ships, recording a summary of their responses.[39] The ship's captain and senior crew were usually questioned. The slave crews lied under oath without compunction. In one case, for example, they testified that "the men slaves had been received as hired men to navigate the vessel, and the slave boys as servants."[40] The court had little trouble rejecting this testimony. The lengthy list of questions ranged from the identity of the witness and how he came to serve on the captured ship to questions about the ship's owners, its course during the current voyage, the circumstances of capture, and whether any of the ship's papers were missing or destroyed.[41] Only occasionally were the captive Africans called upon to give testimony.[42] The registrar would then turn over the file of evidence to the two commissary judges, who were not generally present at the initial examination of the witnesses.[43] The "proctors" (who were not always attorneys) representing the two parties would then argue the case. On occasion, the judges might ask to hear further evidence from one of the witnesses, or from an additional witness.

Many of the trials were quite summary in nature. For example, if a Brazilian ship was caught on the high seas with slaves onboard, the British and Brazilian judges would have little difficulty agreeing that it should be condemned.[44] Other cases presented more complex factual and legal issues. For example, in many cases the courts had to determine the true nationality of a ship. Quite often—and in violation of the law of nations—slave ships carried more than one flag and set of papers, with the hope of deploying whichever seemed most expedient to avoid seizure and condemnation. Thus, a slave ship might carry both French and Portuguese flags, hoisting the Portuguese flag when a French man-of-war appeared on the horizon (since no treaty authorized the French to search Portuguese ships) and the French flag when a British or Portuguese cruiser was spotted. Captain Henry John Leeke reported a typical incident of this sort. After a chase, he boarded a schooner with 140 slaves onboard, but "being under French colours I could not detain her, though I am satisfied that she was carrying on this disgusting traffic for the Spaniards, having seen a paper to that effect on board her."[45] Leeke apparently did not think the case was strong enough to take to court. But in many cases where the ship's papers might seem irregular or forged, the court would determine that the ship was for that reason not entitled to the protection of the flag it claimed. In so doing, the judges often drew upon the broader law of nations of the time period, invoking doctrines from admiralty courts that based a ship's entitlement to a particular nationality on its ownership and course of trade and not merely the papers it carried.[46] The courts' opinions were brief but often included citations to precedents from the mixed courts or to the decisions of British vice-admiralty courts. They were not published in separate law reports, though they did appear in annual printed reports to Parliament.

The determination of the ship's nationality was often dispositive of the case, particularly during the years when the coverage of the various treaties varied (e.g., during the years when the Anglo-Spanish treaties were broader than the Anglo-Portuguese treaties).[47] For example, from 1820 until 1842, the Portuguese treaty prohibited slave trading only in the region north of the equator, while the Spanish treaty prohibited slave trading both north and south of the equator.[48] Similarly, the Spanish government agreed in 1835 to an amendment covering ships that were equipped for the slave trade but that had not yet taken any slaves onboard, while the Portuguese treaty was not amended to include an "equipment clause" until 1842.[49] Given the discrepancies between the Portuguese and Spanish treaties, many trials turned on where precisely the ship had been sailing before it was caught and whether it was really Portuguese or Spanish.[50]

The trials also became factually more complicated after the treaties were modified—first, to cover cases where there was evidence that slaves had been onboard earlier in the voyage,[51] and second, to cover ships that were equipped for the slave trade but that had not yet boarded their human cargo.[52] In the first set of cases, the judges would base their decision on the ship's papers, testimony of witnesses, the circumstances of capture, items found aboard the ship, and even the well-known stench of a ship that had recently carried hundreds of slaves.[53] In the "equipment clause" cases, the court would examine evidence such as the presence of manacles and chains or wood planks for a slave deck, or the fact that a ship was carrying much more food and water than necessary for its crew.[54] In some cases, the evidence of a ship's illegal mission was quite obvious, but in others it was less so, particularly as slave traders became more sophisticated.

In simple cases, the judges usually were unanimous.[55] When the judges disagreed and an arbitrator was drawn, the arbitrator would often agree with the judge from his own country,[56] though occasionally, the arbitrator would side with the judge of the other nationality.[57] Many, though not all, of the non-British judges appear to have carried out their duties honestly, if not always with great zeal.[58] When the British government complained to Brazil that its judge at Sierra Leone was associating with slave traders, for example, the Brazilian government responded promptly by removing him from office.[59] British officials praised one long-serving Spanish judge at Havana, though some later judges in Havana were men who owned large slave plantations.[60] The courts' decisions were final, and there was no system for appeals.

The great majority of cases resulted in condemnation of the ships, with the rates of condemnation highest in the courts at Sierra Leone and lowest in the Anglo-Portuguese courts at Rio and Loanda, Angola. At Sierra Leone, 485 ships were condemned, while twenty-nine were released. In Havana, forty-eight were condemned and seven were released, while at Rio twenty-five were condemned and fourteen were released and at Loanda five were condemned and six were released. All five cases at Cape Town resulted in condemnation.[61] The greatest disagreement among the judges seems to have occurred in the Anglo-Brazilian courts at Sierra Leone and Rio, where the British judges adopted a creative reinterpretation of the existing treaties to cover ships equipped for the slave trade but not yet loaded with slaves. Given that Brazil had refused to ratify a treaty amendment to that effect,[62] the Brazilian judges probably had the better legal argument.

If the court held that a ship should be condemned, the ship would be auctioned off and the proceeds would be split between the two governments.[63] In later years, some ships were broken up and sold in pieces to avoid being redeployed in the slave trade by the persons who purchased them at auction.[64] Some of the money was allocated to the expenses of the courts, and a substantial portion of the rest was generally awarded as prize money to the captor.[65]

The crews of slave ships were generally made up of "suspicious and dangerous characters," some of whom were also engaged in piracy.[66] The mixed courts themselves had no criminal jurisdiction over them, but the crews would occasionally be sent to the courts of their own country for criminal trial.[67] In other cases, they fled, were let go in port, or on a few occasions were reportedly left stranded somewhere on the coast of Africa.[68] The emancipated slaves would be given certificates of freedom, and their personal details (name, age, language, identifying marks) would be recorded in a logbook.[69] If, on the other hand, the judges agreed that the ship had been wrongfully seized, they would allow it to continue on its voyage with its human cargo. The judges had the power to order the captor to pay compensation to the owner in such cases, though depending on the circumstances, they did not always do so.[70]

While they were instructed to be mindful of their judicial character and apply the law neutrally and fairly,[71] the judges and arbitrators were not independent in the modern sense. The Foreign Office in London provided a great deal of guidance to the British judges in the field on how they should carry out their business. The Foreign Office provided regulations for the operation of the courts, including elaborate instructions on everything from the form of the captor's affidavit to the oaths for swearing in witnesses and the form for decisions.[72] Officials in London would provide detailed praise or criticism of particular aspects of the commissions' operations, from the speed of their operations down to the color of the ink used in their correspondence.[73] On occasion, the Foreign Office would suggest that a particular decision involved an incorrect interpretation of the law and urge the judges not to repeat the mistake.[74] For their part, the judges would from time to time request the opinion of legal officials in London on a point of law.[75] In a similar manner, the non-British judges also took instructions from their own governments.[76]

The courts were but one aspect of the highly coordinated British effort to suppress the slave trade. The British judges in Cuba might send the Foreign Office information about ships that had recently set sail for the African coast equipped for the slave trade, which that office would in turn forward to the commissioners in Sierra Leone.[77] Similarly, useful information received by the Foreign Office from the navy would be forwarded to the judges, and vice versa.[78] Reports from the courts would be sent to British diplomats in various European capitals, and they would be instructed to bring difficulties with the courts to the attention of the partner governments.[79] On some occasions, the commissioners communicated more or less directly with naval captains, providing information about the rules for captures or sharing information about slave vessels or notorious traders.[80]

Based on the volume of their correspondence on the topic, it appears that the slave trade consumed an enormous amount of the time and attention of the men who served as foreign secretary during the years of the suppression effort, notably Viscount Palmerston and the Earl of Aberdeen (both future prime ministers). The suppression of the slave trade was an issue in British relations with almost every country and often proved a source of diplomatic tension.[81]

THE COURTS IN OPERATION: IMPACT AND LIMITATIONS

The original courts created by the Anglo-Spanish, Anglo-Portuguese, and Anglo-Dutch treaties began operations in 1819. These courts sat in Sierra Leone, Havana, Rio de Janeiro, and Suriname. Over the years, new treaties added new courts. Brazil agreed to sign onto the treaty regime in 1826 in exchange for recognition of its independence by Britain.[82] Thus, an Anglo-Brazilian court was added to the three courts already in Sierra Leone, and the court in Rio was transformed into an Anglo-Brazilian court.[83] In the late 1830s and early 1840s, Chile, the Argentine Confederation, Uruguay, Bolivia, and Ecuador also agreed to participate in the mixed commission in Sierra Leone.[84] In 1842, a new Anglo-Portuguese treaty was signed and mixed courts were added in Luanda, Boa Vista,

Spanish Town, and Cape Town.[85] Finally, in 1862 the United States—which had long resisted participation in the regime—agreed to the establishment of mixed courts in New York, Sierra Leone, and Cape Town.[86]

Of all the courts created by the treaties, the courts at Sierra Leone were by far the most active, hearing more than 500 cases in total. Two factors explain the Sierra Leone courts' preeminence. First, the British Royal Navy's antislavery patrol was most active in the areas off the west coast of Africa, where most of the slaves originated. Second, the commissions in Sierra Leone were strongly supported by the British colonial government there, while the courts in foreign ports often received only marginal support from the local government and faced outright hostility from the public.[87] The courts at Havana and Rio heard fifty and forty-four cases respectively, and the remaining courts received only a handful of cases.[88] The belated Anglo-American courts never heard any cases at all, though, as discussed below, that was more a measure of the effectiveness of the Anglo-American treaty than its weakness, since the slave trade was squelched in the immediate aftermath of the 1862 treaty.

The Sierra Leone courts led in terms of the number of slaves freed as well. British logbooks show that the Sierra Leone courts emancipated approximately 65,000 slaves between 1819 and 1846.[89] The Havana courts freed some 10,000, and the Rio courts freed 3,000.[90] Because the courts eventually gained jurisdiction over ships equipped for the slave trade even if no slaves were actually onboard at the time of capture, an unknown number of other individuals were saved from slavery by the seizure off the African coast of ships that had not yet been loaded with their unfortunate human cargo. During the life of the commissions, at least 225 ships were seized and condemned without slaves onboard. Given that between 1830 and 1850, the average cargo is estimated to have been approximately 400 slaves per ship, that would represent another 90,000 individuals, though it is impossible without more sophisticated econometric analysis to estimate how many of those would actually have been onboard the captured ships or how many ended up embarking on other vessels instead.

The courts were most active between 1819 and the mid-1840s.[91] During their peak years of operation in the late 1830s and early 1840s, an average of one out of every five or six vessels known to have been engaged in the transatlantic trade was brought for trial in the courts of mixed commission, with the highest annual percentage occurring in 1835 when some 39 percent of known slave ship voyages that departed that year ended up in the mixed courts.[92] Both before and after the mixed courts' peak years of operations, the British also tried a significant number of captured slave vessels in domestic vice-admiralty courts.

Figures 4.1 and 4.2 give a rough indication of the number of slave ship voyages that led to adjudications in the courts of mixed commission and vice-admiralty courts. These figures are based on information from the annual reports of the British commissioners combined with data from the new online revised version of the Trans-Atlantic Slave Trade Database.[93] The database contains information on close to 35,000 known slave-trading voyages, or more than 80 percent of all the estimated transatlantic slave-trading voyages that took place during the four centuries of the traffic. The data are even more complete for later years for which better records exist.

Two cautions must be given with respect to these data. First, voyages that ended up in adjudication—in either national or the mixed courts— are likely overrepresented in the data, since court records were one of the sources used to compile the database. Second, certain nationalities of slave ships are likely overrepresented in the data because of differences in the quality and accessibility of historical records in different countries. Nevertheless, for the purposes of this book, the quantitative information amply demonstrates possible trends and rough estimates of magnitude. More precise statistical analysis would involve complex methodological issues and is well beyond the scope of this book.[94]

A few observations emerge from the available quantitative data. First, during the mixed courts' peak years of operation in the 1830s and 1840s, it appears that they heard cases involving a significant

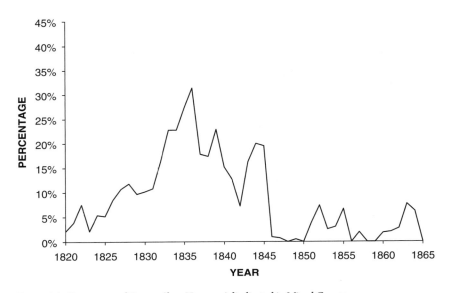

Figure 4.1. Percentage of Known Slave Voyages Adjudicated in Mixed Courts

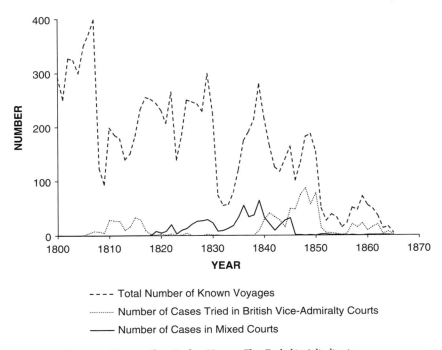

- - - - Total Number of Known Voyages

.... Number of Cases Tried in British Vice-Admiralty Courts

———— Number of Cases in Mixed Courts

Figure 4.2. Number of Known Slave Trading Voyages That Ended in Adjudication

percentage of the total transatlantic slave trade. Because voyages that ended in adjudication are overrepresented in the Slave Trade Database, the percentages in figures 4.1 and 4.2 are likely to be overestimates. Nevertheless, the raw numbers and estimated percentage of cases suggest that the courts made a substantial impact. Another general trend that is apparent from the data is that, beginning in 1839, the British shifted from use of the mixed courts back to the use of the domestic vice-admiralty courts. The reluctance of Portugal and then Brazil to continue to participate in the treaty system led to this shift, as discussed further below.

In addition to the quantitative data, firsthand accounts from those who actually participated in the treaties and court system provide evidence about their impact on the slave trade. For example, in the late 1840s and early 1850s, the British Parliament engaged in a contentious reexamination of the amount of energy and resources being devoted to suppression of the slave trade. Special committees were convened in both the House of Commons and the House of Lords; dozens of witnesses appeared, giving thousands of pages of testimony.[95]

Not surprisingly, the witnesses gave conflicting opinions. Some testified that suppression efforts had increased the cruelty of the traffic by inducing slavers to pack the slaves in more tightly and that it would be better to relegalize and regulate the trade, while others argued that the trade had always been cruel and the only humane course was to stamp it out.[96] Some witnesses and members of Parliament doubted whether the decades of suppression efforts had made any difference at all.[97] William Smith, who had served for several years between 1825 and 1834 as a judge on the mixed court in Sierra Leone, testified gloomily of the suppression effort, "I should say that it is a failure," and he predicted that no system was ever likely to succeed "because the demand for slaves will always create a supply."[98] Commodore Charles Hotham— who had commanded the African squadron from 1846 to 1849 but was criticized for his ineffectiveness—testified that the slave trade could not be suppressed by any means he knew and suggested that it would be more realistic to sign a new treaty with Brazil authorizing the trade for a fixed period of time.[99]

On the other hand, many witnesses testified that the antislavery treaties and Britain's attempts to enforce them had made a difference. Their views ultimately carried the day, when in March 1850 the House of Commons voted 232 to 154 to reject a motion that would have called for Britain to be "released from all the treaty engagements with foreign states and from maintaining armed vessels on the coast of Africa to suppress the traffic in slaves."[100]

In the months leading up to that critical vote, Foreign Secretary Palmerston, a devoted abolitionist during his many years in office, testified before Parliament that but for the suppression efforts, the slave trade would have "increased in a vast proportion," and cheap slaves would have been used to bring huge tracts of Brazilian land into cultivation.[101] Palmerston estimated that over a ten-year period, the number of slaves that might have been carried on ships captured without slaves onboard was around 190,000.[102]

In addition to the ships that were actually captured and condemned, the threat of capture made the trade more difficult and expensive, and sometimes more inhumane, as slave traders were forced to take precautions to evade capture. A wide array of sources indicates that the price of slaves increased significantly during the years of the suppression effort.[103] At times, increased suppression activity also reportedly increased insurance costs and sometimes made insurance unavailable.[104] In addition, some underwriters began including clauses in their insurance policies exempting from insurance ships seized under the treaties.[105]

Individual participants in the suppression effort also testified to its effects and its limitations. One witness, David Turnbull, was an ardent abolitionist who served controversially as British consul at Havana from 1840 to 1842 and then as a judge on the mixed court in Jamaica.[106] He testified that, although he believed the treaties should be revised to expand the power of the mixed courts, he felt that the existing system, even with its weaknesses, had reduced the trade.[107]

Another witness, Captain Edward Butterfield, had served on the coast of Africa in command of the *Fantome*, the *Waterwitch*, and the *Brisk*—three of the fastest boats in the squadron—and had captured an astonishing forty vessels between 1840 and 1842. He testified that he was told by Portuguese merchants that he had captured at least three-fifths of the slave vessels attempting to sail from that portion of the coast, and he felt that the slave trade was much diminished by his frequent captures.[108] He noted that the slaves onboard the last ship he captured had been kept in the barracoons for fourteen months because no slave ships were able to sail from that port during his blockade. In one case he boarded a legal merchant ship carrying slave traders back with their families to Rio because they had given up the trade as unprofitable.[109]

Captain Christopher Wyvill, who had been stationed on the east coast of Africa, testified that the trade had dramatically fallen off there between 1844 and 1846 because of a treaty with local chiefs, the new treaty with Portugal, and the presence of British cruisers.[110] Likewise, Captain Henry James Matson argued that the trade on the west coast had decreased a great deal following the adoption of the equipment clause with Spain in 1835. In response to skeptical questioning from members of Parliament about the basis for his assertion, Matson responded that he was relying on firsthand knowledge: "I think there are facts to prove the opinion. I was on the coast during the whole of that time, or very nearly so."[111]

In response to questioning about whether the possible additional suffering of slaves on the Middle Passage made the suppression effort a net negative from a humanitarian perspective, several witnesses asserted that any such negative had to be weighed against the enormous benefit in terms of individual lives saved from slavery.[112] Such a view is reinforced by paging through the courts' logbooks of tens of thousands of freed slaves, with names, ages, and descriptions. These were real people, and their lives were made at least a little bit better because of the efforts to enforce the international treaties against the slave trade. In sheer human impact, no other international court has directly affected so many individuals. Indeed, regardless of whether or not the mixed courts were "successful" in terms of their impact on the overall transatlantic slave trade, they were successful in their impact on the nearly 80,000 individuals who were granted their legal freedom by the courts.

Still, even the witnesses who supported continuation of the effort recognized that the slave trade had not been suppressed despite forty years of struggle and a vast expenditure of resources. These witnesses, along with more hostile witnesses, identified a number of weaknesses and limitations in the system.

The first major weakness in the treaty regime was the lack of participation by two of the most significant naval powers of the time, France and the United States. France never agreed to the mixed courts at all. Although it signed a treaty with Britain agreeing to mutual search rights in 1831, the treaty provided that ships were to be tried in the courts of their own nation.[113] The United States eventually joined the international mixed court system, but not until 1862.[114]

Though the absence of both France and the United States from the mixed courts regime for most of the courts' existence hindered their effectiveness, it did not prevent a substantial portion of the trade from being suppressed. By the 1830s, the importation of slaves into the United States and into French possessions in the Caribbean had been effectively squelched by domestic authorities, and the major remaining trade was to Cuba and Brazil.[115]

Trade to Cuba and Brazil by slave traffickers using the French or American flag was intermittently a serious problem, though agreements with the United States and France that stopped short of participation in the mixed courts helped ameliorate the situation. In 1831, France and Britain concluded a treaty granting mutual rights of search, though it provided for captured ships to be turned over to their own governments for trial. With the adoption of this treaty and the prospect of capture by both British and French warships, the French flag was no longer particularly attractive to slave traders. After 1831, the number of ships sailing under the French flag was relatively insignificant. It remained so even after the right of mutual search was rescinded in 1845 due to domestic political pressure in France and replaced with a new treaty committing France to maintain a certain number of its own warships off the coast of Africa.[116]

As noted previously, negotiations between Britain and the United States fell apart following the Senate's unsuccessful attempt to modify the 1824 treaty.[117] Diplomatic efforts continued without success in the 1830s, when the United States was repeatedly invited to join the treaty with France and Britain but declined to do so.[118] Notwithstanding these facts, in the late 1830s and early 1840s, the Anglo-Spanish mixed court at Sierra Leone actually condemned a number of American-flagged ships on the grounds that they could be treated as Spanish under the law of nations, a move that elicited surprisingly little reaction.[119] Moreover, by the late 1830s, the Americans had sent several patrol ships to Africa. The commander of the American naval squadron on the west coast of Africa and the British commander in the region were able to work together in a way their governments could not. An informal agreement between the two commanders on the scene led to a period of joint patrol. Under the agreement, American ships that came upon a slave ship covered by one of the British treaties would hand it over to the nearest British ship, while a British vessel that found a slaver flying the American flag would deliver it to the closest American warship.[120] During a brief period of confusion, British naval captains even brought captured American-flagged slave ships into American ports, where they were sometimes condemned by U.S. courts.[121] In two notable cases in 1839—those of the *Eagle* and the *Clara*—the U.S. government refused to exercise jurisdiction over two American-flagged ships captured by the British and brought to New York, based on the conclusion of the

American attorney general that the ships were actually Spanish. The cases were then submitted to the mixed court at Sierra Leone, which issued orders of condemnation.[122]

This period of informal cooperation was short lived. A combination of disease and lack of support on the home front hampered the American squadron in its patrols of the African coast.[123] The U.S. government eventually disavowed the informal agreement between the navies in 1841,[124] and U.S. courts began refusing to condemn ships captured by the British. Diplomatic protests by the United States about the boarding of American ships led to a crisis in U.S.-British relations, with the Americans claiming the policy was "alarming to national sovereignty and sensibility, and the friendly relations of the two countries."[125] After several months of tense correspondence,[126] the government in London ordered British naval officers to be more deferential to American-flagged ships.[127] In 1842, the Webster-Ashburton Treaty between the two countries committed the United States to maintaining an antislavery squadron on the African coast but did not include a right of search or any provision for trial in mixed courts.[128]

The U.S. government did engage in reasonably vigorous efforts to suppress the slave trade at various times, notwithstanding the delicate status of slavery in American politics and the nation's reluctance to enter into slavery-related treaties that it viewed as an infringement of its sovereignty or the freedom of the seas. Some 103 slave ships were captured by the U.S. Navy and brought for trial in U.S. courts between 1837 and 1862, most of them in the years after 1842. The fact that U.S. law classified the slave trade as piracy subject to the death penalty also deterred use of the U.S. flag. Criminal proceedings were brought against more than 100 individuals in U.S. courts, though relatively few of these cases resulted in convictions, and the death penalty was actually imposed in only one case.[129]

At the same time, however, one notable weakness in American law was the fact that for many years it was not interpreted to cover ships equipped for the slave trade but without slaves on board. Because of this loophole, it was reportedly a common practice for ships to sail into the African coast under the American flag (thereby evading capture by the British). They would then change their colors to those of another nation once slaves were actually taken onboard, to avoid possible capture and prosecution by the Americans.[130]

British officials involved in the slave trade suppression effort generally agreed that full participation in the treaty and mixed court system by the United States and France would have been advantageous, but many contemporaries did not view those countries' participation as indispensable. When a member of the House of Commons asked Lord Palmerston whether the consent of France and America to mutual rights of search was essential to successful suppression of the trade, Palmerston answered, "My opinion is, that if the Spanish government, and if the government of Brazil, would honestly and effectually fulfill their treaty engagements . . . the slave trade would be practically extinct."[131] France, Palmerston argued, was effectively enforcing the slave trade ban against French-flagged ships.[132] Treaties had been concluded with native chiefs in Africa that gave England and France the right to enforce the slave trade ban in the chiefs' territories.[133] As for the United States, he contended, "I do not conceive that the mere refusal of the United States to concur in mutual right of search would, of itself, be sufficient to defeat the naval police if all other nations had united in the common league."[134] Even without the cooperation of the United States, the slave trade to Brazil and Cuba could be brought "to a very narrow limit indeed."[135]

Palmerston was certainly correct as to Brazil. As it happened, the traffic to Brazil was effectively suppressed by the Brazilian government itself (under pressure from the British) beginning in 1850, notwithstanding the absence of the United States from the mixed court regime until 1862. The available data on the usage of particular flags in the slave trade also suggest that claims about the heavy use of the French and

American flags in the later years of the slave trade were somewhat exaggerated. Figure 4.3 reflects the available data on the national registration of ships involved in the slave trade from 1815 to 1865. Of course, data about the flag used are unavailable for many voyages, but the overall trends shown in the figure are likely to be accurate.[136]

Despite the changes to the international legal regime that made these other flags less attractive, the French flag does not appear to have been a substantial part of the trade after 1830. Nor does the American flag appear to have accounted for a dominant portion of the traffic between 1830 and 1850, though it is difficult to say how commonly ships used the flag on the inbound portion of the voyage to Africa.[137] During these years, the dominant preference of the slave traders under increasing pressure seems to have been to shift to no flag at all. Although a ship flying no flag could be boarded, from the slave traders' perspective, the advantage of this approach may have been to avoid susceptibility to criminal punishment under the law of their "home" country.[138]

As discussed more fully below, the participation of the United States in the mixed courts regime was more critical to the suppression of the slave trade to Cuba, which lies a mere ninety miles from Florida. After a

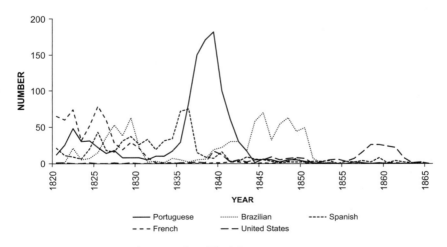

Figure 4.3. Known Voyages by Nationality of Ship's Registration

sharp decline in the late 1840s, the trade to Cuba began to increase again in the 1850s. Unflagged and American-flagged ships dominated this final period of the trade.

It is possible that even without the American treaty, the trade to Cuba could eventually have been suppressed by Cuban authorities acting against slave markets on shore in much the same way it was finally suppressed in Brazil. But in 1862, the United States finally ratified the treaty with Britain granting the right of mutual search and establishing mixed courts at New York, Sierra Leone, and Cape Town.[139] This ratification appears to have been part of the catalyst for the final suppression of the trade to Cuba. Ratification of the treaty eliminated the final "safe" flag under which slavers could sail and triggered more active enforcement by Cuban authorities who began to see the end of the trade as inevitable. To put it somewhat differently, the Brazilian case shows that the participation of the United States may not have been a necessary part of the suppression of the slave trade. But the Cuban case shows that the participation of the United States in the treaty regime was likely sufficient to end the trade.

Other loopholes in the treaties also created serious impediments to the courts' effectiveness. For example, one significant loophole was the exclusion from the courts' jurisdiction of certain types of ships, such as ships that were traveling in some parts of the ocean or that did not actually have slaves onboard at the time of capture.

The case of the *Maria da Gloria* provides one good example of such loopholes in action. A British ship captured the *Maria da Gloria* with more than 400 slaves onboard, but the mixed court at Rio de Janeiro rejected the case on the grounds that the ship was Portuguese, not Brazilian. Transported back across the Atlantic by a prize crew, the mixed court at Sierra Leone reluctantly concluded that the ship was immune from condemnation because it was seized south of the equator, where the slave trade was arguably still permitted by the Portuguese treaty. The case had a profound impact on the captain of the British prize crew, Joseph Denman, who, as mentioned previously, became an ardent abolitionist because of his experiences onboard the *Maria da Gloria*.[140] The case also left a strong impression on the judges at the Sierra Leone court. With some dismay, the British judges wrote to Viscount Palmerston:

> Although it has been our duty as Judges to restore the "*Maria da Gloria*," we cannot forbear expressing to your Lordship our deep regret on witnessing the sailing of that vessel with her cargo of unhappy beings, destined to another miserable voyage across the Atlantic. As men, our feelings have been greatly distressed.[141]

The judges expressed their hope that the case would enable the British government to conclude a new, more effective treaty with Portugal that covered traffic sailing in all latitudes.[142] Viscount Palmerston himself was also upset by the case, writing to the British diplomats in Lisbon in regard to the *Maria da Gloria*'s claim for damages against its captor that "[t]he Claimant was engaged in a proceeding that was in violation of the laws of God and man; it was undertaken in fraud, and defended by perjury; and he escaped the punishment due to his crime, not because he did not deserve to suffer it, but because he was found in a place, where, under the strict letter of the Treaty, he was not liable to be detained."[143]

In addition to the exclusion of Portuguese ships sailing south of the equator, the other significant initial loophole in the treaties was the lack of authority to condemn ships that were equipped for the slave trade but that had not yet taken slaves onboard. The Netherlands had readily agreed to such a clause, but since the Dutch flag was not used much in the trade after 1817, this was not a significant development. The British judges at Sierra Leone repeatedly urged their government to negotiate for an equipment clause with Spain and Portugal and viewed such a clause as vital to the courts' success.[144] Although Spain resisted for several years, it finally agreed in principle to a revision of the treaty in September

1834, and the treaty was signed on June 28, 1835, although news of it still had not reached the Spanish officials in Havana by January 10, 1836.[145] As figure 4.3 suggests, after the equipment clause was adopted, traffic under the Spanish flag decreased noticeably.

Despite strong encouragement from the British, Portugal would not agree to a new treaty including an equipment clause, and this reluctance proved a serious barrier to suppression efforts.[146] As figure 4.3 indicates, the adoption of the Spanish equipment clause in 1835 coincided with a remarkable uptick in the trade under the Portuguese flag. Although the trade as a whole was increasing during these years and other factors may have played a role in the increasing use of the Portuguese flag, the trend is noticeably correlated with, if not verifiably caused by, the change in the Spanish treaty. Trade under the Portuguese flag only decreased when, in 1839, Britain attempted to close the loopholes by unilaterally seizing Portuguese ships under a creative reinterpretation of the 1817 treaty. In response, in 1842, Portugal finally agreed to a new, comprehensive treaty.

The equipment clause loophole in the Brazilian treaty was closed not by treaty amendment but by judicial initiative. Although the Brazilian legislature had failed to ratify the equipment clause amendment, in 1839, the Anglo-Portuguese courts in both Rio de Janeiro and Sierra Leone independently began condemning ships equipped for the slave trade under a creative reinterpretation of the existing treaties. Although the Brazilian judges objected to this reinterpretation, the practice soon became settled and a large number of Brazilian ships were condemned simply for being equipped for the slave trade, occasionally with the concurrence of a Brazilian judge but more often with the toss of the coin choosing the British arbitrator to break the tie if the British and Brazilian judges disagreed.[147]

Some participants in the system believed that the courts would have been more effective if, in addition to closing the loopholes in the substantive coverage of the treaties, the courts were granted additional powers, including the ability to punish criminally slave ship crews and owners and the ability to declare slaves found on plantations in Cuba and Brazil free unless it could be proven that they had not been imported illegally.[148] While perhaps desirable, these additional powers were not within the realm of diplomatic plausibility. In the later years of the courts' operation, however, the governments agreed that the courts at least had the power to detain captured slave crew members until they could be turned over to their own nation for criminal prosecution.[149] Rather than leading to more prosecutions, however, this practice may simply have increased the incentives for slavers to claim no nationality at all.

But the most serious impediment to the success of the mixed court system was the reluctance of Spain, Portugal, and Brazil to enforce strictly the ban on the slave trade. This lack of cooperation was not principally manifested in the behavior of the mixed court judges from those countries, although these judges did sometimes vote to acquit, especially in the commission at Rio de Janeiro.[150] To the contrary, the British judges often spoke quite favorably of their colleagues. Upon the death of a Brazilian judge who had served for six uninterrupted years in Sierra Leone (during which time admittedly few cases were heard), the British commissioners wrote to London that "his public conduct was marked by a spirit of courtesy and conciliation towards his colleagues in office, with whom he at the same time lived privately on terms of intimacy and friendship."[151]

The British judges at Havana spoke of some of their Spanish colleagues in similarly favorable terms, in one early case noting that "the most perfect unanimity prevailed during the whole of the proceedings; and that my Spanish colleagues continued to manifest the same zeal to uphold the dignity and authority of the Court, which I before stated they had displayed at the commencement."[152]

Nor was the main problem outside pressure on the courts, though the mixed courts at Rio de Janeiro and Havana did sometimes face threats stemming from popular opposition to their work. For example, in Rio, one individual who had acted as a proctor for British captors in a number of cases was threatened that should he be involved in any more cases, he would be "waylaid and murdered." As a result, the captors were left without "professional assistance" in prosecuting their cases because he had abandoned his work out of fear.[153] Although these threats sometimes slowed the courts' proceedings, local authorities took sufficient measures—albeit sometimes reluctantly—to protect the physical safety of the courts and the threats do not appear to have seriously hampered their functioning.

In terms of lack of cooperation, the far more serious problem was the unwillingness of the Spanish, Portuguese, or Brazilian governments to engage in any meaningful enforcement of domestic laws against the slave trade by preventing the landing of slave ships, blocking the sale of imported slaves, or criminally prosecuting those involved. Though laws against the slave trade were on the books in all these countries, there was no intent to enforce them. Indeed, even today Brazilians describe laws that will never be enforced as "laws for the British."

Viscount Palmerston, British naval officers, and British officials in the field all believed that the governments of Cuba and Brazil could end slave importations if they wanted to by taking these measures.[154] It turned out that they were correct, for once each of these countries finally began enforcing its domestic laws, the slave trade was finally and successfully extinguished. Changes in attitudes that led to the enforcement of laws against the slave trade in Brazil and then later Cuba were essential to the final suppression of the trade.

When the treaties were first signed, it was not initially obvious how essential the cooperation of local officials in Cuba and Brazil would be to the successful suppression of the slave trade. By giving the British the power to search, seize, and condemn slave ships in international courts, the treaties seemed to embody strong international enforcement mechanisms. These powers were unprecedented at the time and have been unmatched in human rights treaties and international courts created since then. But as robust as these powers were, and as much energy and expense as the British devoted to the effort, the oceans were vast, and the most vulnerable part of the slave trade system turned out to be the point of sale in the Americas. Just as modern efforts to interdict drugs on the high seas are unsuccessful when uncoupled from effective enforcement on land, naval enforcement alone was unlikely to end the slave trade.

The correspondence from British officials in Brazil and Cuba is filled with complaints about the supineness and outright corruption of local authorities, who turned the other way when slave ships landed and auctioned off their cargos. When the new captain-general of Cuba assured the British diplomats in Havana that he was determined to enforce the antislavery treaties, Viscount Palmerston was skeptical:

> No doubt can be entertained that he has a power of putting a stop to it if he will: if the Cuba Slave Trade has ceased, General Valdes will have proved himself sincere: if that trade still continues, he will have demonstrated that his professions are all as hollow and valueless as those of all his predecessors.[155]

For many years, port officials in Havana would clear for departure ships obviously equipped for the slave trade.[156] The tolerance of local governments for the slave trade was so great that until very late in the game, slave traders who safely escaped British patrols on the high seas and reached the territorial waters of Cuba and Brazil engaged in only token efforts to conceal their illegal activities. In 1836—more than fifteen years after the Spanish treaty took effect—British officials were outraged but not surprised by the appearance in one Havana newspaper of an advertisement for the open sale of newly imported Africans.[157]

In response to continual complaints from British diplomats, the other governments would engage in denials and token responses. For example, when the British commissioners at Havana reported that the

Portuguese consul there was granting papers to slave vessels, the British complained to the Portuguese government in Lisbon, which revoked the consul's authority and declared invalid documents furnished by him.[158] Yet such minimal, occasional efforts to sanction participants in the slave trade were little more than meaningless gestures. For many years, the other governments did not deploy significant numbers of their ships in suppression efforts even in their own territorial waters.[159] Their national courts often did not condemn ships obviously engaged in the slave trade,[160] and slave traders brought in for criminal trial were routinely acquitted.[161]

The occasional faltering in domestic support within Britain for the slave trade suppression effort also limited the courts' effectiveness. More than sixty years elapsed from the moment Britain banned the slave trade under its flag in 1807 until the trade as a whole was finally extinguished. Understandably, domestic political interest and support for the effort waxed and waned over the decades, and with it the resources and attention devoted to crafting the most effective policies for suppression. As noted previously, this simmering debate reached a crisis point when, from 1848 to 1850, Parliament engaged in almost continuous hearings and discussions about whether to stay the course in suppressing the slave trade or to abandon the system of treaties and courts backed with naval power. One political faction, which included some abolitionists who opposed all use of military force because of their Quaker beliefs, wanted to withdraw the African squadron from its antislavery patrol and even withdraw from the antislavery treaties.[162] Another faction wanted the government to redouble its efforts at suppression of the trade.

In addition, hard-learned lessons about which tactics were effective were sometimes lost due to changes in personnel in the British Foreign Office and the admiralty, changes made both for simple administrative reasons and because not all officials were equally committed personally to the cause of abolition. When officials committed to abolition were replaced by officials who were less enthusiastic, treaty enforcement often became less effective.

The Gallinas expedition in 1840 is one prime example. The provocation for the expedition was the kidnapping of a free African woman and her infant, both of whom were British subjects at Sierra Leone. With the support of the British governor there, Captain Denman of the HMS *Wanderer* went ashore at Gallinas to rescue the woman. Having done so, he induced the local chief to sign a treaty banning the slave trade and enlisted the chief and his men in burning the Spanish slave traders' storehouses.[163]

When news of Captain Denman's endeavor spread, two other British captains then undertook similar actions elsewhere on the African coast. Initially, London reacted positively: the admiralty granted Denman a promotion, and Parliament gave him a reward of £4,000. Foreign Secretary Palmerston wrote that "[t]he course pursued by Captain Denman seems to be best adapted for the attainment of the object in view" and encouraged other captains to follow his example.[164] The initial reaction by the slave traders was dramatic as well. The slave trade in that region of the African coast dropped precipitously,[165] and word of the incident quickly reached as far as Cuba, where slave traders viewed the new tactics as a serious threat to their livelihood.[166]

But a few months later, the Earl of Aberdeen replaced Viscount Palmerston as foreign secretary. Aberdeen was more conciliatory toward foreign powers and more legalistic, and he circulated a letter stating that the queen's legal advisers believed such raids to be illegal under international law.[167] News of Aberdeen's letter and the change in policy also reached the slavers quickly, and the trade resumed.[168] New and inexperienced officers on the African coast began engaging in safer, but less effective, distant offshore patrols.[169] One of the Spanish slave traders whose slaves Denman had liberated and whose warehouse he had burned sued Denman in a British court for an astonishing £180,000. The court eventually ruled in Denman's favor, but not until 1848.[170] The queen's advocate then issued another opinion stating that such raids of onshore barracoons were lawful when authorized by a treaty with the local chief, which Denman's raid had been. British captains in the African squadron then began entering into new treaties with local chiefs and pursuing such raids again, but several years had been wasted in the interim.[171]

CHAPTER 5

Am I Not a Man and a Brother?

T he mixed commissions had a dramatic human impact in terms of the number of people directly implicated by their work. As noted earlier, more than 80,000 men, women, and children were legally granted their freedom by the courts in some 600 cases—an astonishing number in comparison to contemporary international courts. (The International Court of Justice, for example, has only heard some 120 contentious cases in its more than sixty years of existence.) But the voices of these individuals are curiously absent from the courts' proceedings. Only occasionally did they give testimony as witnesses. They were not directly represented in the trials. And while the slave trade is sometimes described as violating "human rights" in documents from the nineteenth century, the slaves themselves rarely appear in any legal proceedings as claimants of rights. Instead, they are silent bystanders—beneficiaries of the system, to be sure, but hardly active participants in it.

Given these limitations, what can we glean about the impact of the slave trade tribunals on their intended beneficiaries? In the British colony at Sierra Leone, the slaves emancipated by the mixed courts seem to have fared no worse (though also no better) than the rest of the large population of free Africans. A few of the emancipated Africans were employed as messengers and clerks by the court,[1] while the rest took their place as ordinary laborers in the colony. Thus, as long as they remained in British-controlled territory near Sierra Leone and were not recaptured by slave traders, the 65,000 Africans freed by the mixed courts at Sierra Leone actually received some of the benefit of their freedom.

The several thousand *emancipados* in Cuba and Brazil, however, were "virtually slaves" kept in repeated apprenticeships.[2] No money was available to pay to return those freed by the courts to their homes in Africa, and, in these slaveholding societies, free Africans were often in a precarious position. In Brazil, the emancipated slaves were hired out as apprentices, many employed by the government itself.[3] At first, it was reported that they were "well treated, and not overworked."[4] Eventually, it became clear that this was not the case, and the Brazilian government established a commission of inquiry in Rio to investigate allegations of mistreatment of *emancipados*.[5]

In Havana, a number of *emancipados* who had been effectively reenslaved in the hands of private individuals were forced to seek the help of the British government in obtaining their freedom.[6] In one particularly poignant case, the British consul in Havana helped rescue from slavery a woman who had been granted her freedom by the mixed commission, along with her ten-year-old daughter. The British consul in Havana at that time, David Turnbull was, as noted in the preceding chapter, a controversial figure.[7] Turnbull had apparently become interested in the slave trade while working as a reporter for London's *Times* newspaper in Madrid in 1835 during the negotiations over the revised Anglo-Spanish slave trade treaty.[8] In 1837 and 1838, he traveled throughout the West Indies, a journey he chronicled in his book *Travels in the West*, which described the cruelty of slavery in the plantations of Cuba and elsewhere and argued for stronger measures against the slave trade.[9] Among other things, Turnbull suggested that the courts of mixed commission should be given the power to order the freedom of any slave in Cuba or Brazil based on a determination that he or she had been illegally imported.[10] This, he argued, would be simple factually since it was easy based on language and other characteristics to distinguish slaves who had been born in Africa from those who had been born in the Americas. The British and Foreign Anti-Slavery Society became interested in Turnbull's proposal, particularly since it emphasized legal rather than forceful means for suppressing the trade.[11] Turnbull presented his proposal at the world Anti-Slavery Convention of 1840, which brought together abolitionists from both sides of the Atlantic. Though some at the convention were initially skeptical of Turnbull's proposal, believing that it did not go far enough toward immediate and total abolition of slavery itself, eventually the convention voted its support for his proposal for expanding the jurisdiction of the mixed courts.[12] The suggestion was taken seriously by the British government, and Lord Palmerston ordered the preparation of a draft treaty that would encompass such powers, although he acknowledged, "It is not very likely that we shall persuade the Spanish Government to accede."[13] Palmerston was, of course, correct—in the end, the Spanish would flatly reject the proposal.

In the meantime, with the support of the Anti-Slavery Society, Turnbull began a campaign to get himself appointed as British consul to Havana. Palmerston agreed to appoint him to the post, but Turnbull's stay in Havana proved short lived and extraordinarily contentious. His zeal annoyed even his British colleagues in Havana. Turnbull, along with the Anti-Slavery Society, had successfully lobbied Palmerston to adopt a policy prohibiting British officials from having any interest in slave property.[14] As a result of this policy, Turnbull almost immediately became involved in a squabble with Kennedy, the British commissioner on the slave trade tribunal in Havana, because Kennedy was in the habit of hiring slave labor.[15] Worse still from his colleagues' perspective, Turnbull sought the removal of the mixed commission's British clerk, a man named Jackson, whom Turnbull accused of having owned slaves and having punished *emancipado* servants "'after the manner of the Country.'"[16] More substantively, Turnbull and the British civil servants working on the mixed commission ended up fighting over the scope of their respective duties, with the commissioners feeling that Turnbull was encroaching on areas under their jurisdiction.[17]

But the reaction of his fellow countrymen was nothing compared to the reaction of the Spanish. The Spanish government described Turnbull as a "fanatical abolitionist" and asked for his removal almost as soon as he was installed in office,[18] a demand they repeated with increasing stridency throughout his stay there.[19] They finally succeeded in driving him from the country in 1842, but by then he had stirred up quite a lot of drama in Havana.[20]

During his short stay in Cuba, Turnbull played a central role in several incidents concerning *empancipados* who had been deprived of their freedom.[21] One such incident involved a man named Gavino, who was emancipated by the slave trade tribunal in Havana in 1821. According to Turnbull, Gavino had been assigned to a master for renewed five-year periods, during which he had been treated as a slave, and he had never received wages.[22] The captain-general of Cuba was hostile to Turnbull's efforts to intercede on behalf of Gavino and other *empancipados*, and he threatened to expel Turnbull from the island.[23] The British government defended Turnbull's actions—apparently not having yet realized how much of a liability to them he would become—and the British ambassador in Madrid demanded from the Spanish government the "immediate freedom of all the negroes, who have been emancipated in Cuba by sentence of the Mixed Commission since the Treaty of 1817, but who appear hitherto to have been retained in practical slavery by the authorities of Cuba."[24] Since the colonial government officials in Cuba seemed unable to protect the freedom of the *emancipados*, the British suggested that everyone on the lists of the mixed commissions be brought before the court again and given the opportunity to be put under the protection of the British Superintendent of Liberated Africans and sent to British colonies "where they would by law as well as by treaty be free."[25] The Spanish viewed this proposal as a reflection of Britain's insincerity in opposing the slave trade on humanitarian grounds and its secret desire to bolster the labor forces in its own colonies.

Turnbull's encounter with the *emancipada* named Matilda and her daughter Isabel Marina was even more dramatic. Matilda had arrived in Cuba onboard the Spanish schooner *Xerxes* in 1827 and had been granted her freedom by the mixed commission. Little about Matilda's life story remains, but she was born in West Africa among the Caravali people;[26] the term Caravali was apparently applied by European traders to several different ethnic groups from areas near the ports of Elem Kalabari and Old Calabar in what is now Nigeria, and who likely spoke the Igbo language.[27] It is likely that she was captured in or near her home village and sold to a local slave dealer before reaching one of the barracoons, or slave forts, on the River Bonny in the Niger delta. The Spanish schooner *Xerxes* picked up its cargo of slaves somewhere on the River Bonny in May 1828, and Matilda was one of the unfortunate captives loaded onto the ship.

The British commissioners in Havana first mentioned the schooner *Xerxes* in their reports to the Foreign Office in February 1828, when they included that ship on a list of ships engaged in the slave trade that left Cuba bound for Africa, lists that were then sent to the admiralty and on to ship's captains so they could be on the lookout for the illicit voyages.[28] But the *Xerxes* had eluded British patrols on the African coast and was returning to Havana when the British caught it almost by accident. Admiral Fleeming of the Royal Navy had ordered the *HMS Grasshopper*, under Commander Abraham Crawford, to patrol in *Los Colorados*, the barrier reefs on Cuba's northwest coast that were said to be a haven for pirates. It was there that the *HMS Grasshopper* came across the *Xerxes* on its approach to Cuba. The *Xerxes* was heavily armed, with an eighteen-pound cannon, four other guns, sixty-six small firearms, and sixty swords.[29] The *Grasshopper* began a twenty-six-hour chase that finally ended in the middle of the Gulf of Mexico, where the British crew succeeded in capturing the Spanish ship with its crew of forty-four and some 406 slaves onboard.[30] According to the ship's captain, some twenty slaves had already died on the voyage from Africa,[31] and the rest were in such poor health that some five more would die before the ship arrived in Havana. Of the captive passengers, 217 were men, thirty-seven were women, and the balance were children; a large percentage of the last group were determined by the British to be sick at the time of capture, including many who suffered from the "putrid dysentery" that had also killed some of the crew.[32]

The *Grasshopper* sailed into port in Havana with its prize on Saturday, July 5, 1828. The *Xerxes* crew was handed over to the Spanish captain-general in Havana, who had them held in the public prison for the duration of the trial; the Africans were also taken onshore and held in custody in a warehouse.[33] The British and Spanish judges on the mixed commission at Havana began considering the ship's fate the next Monday and continued with hearings for the next five days.[34] The crew had been careful to keep the nature of the ship's cargo absent from the *Xerxes* logbooks, though in this case no proof of the illegality of the voyage was needed since slaves were found onboard.[35] The ship's captain and owner was Don Felipe Rebel, an unmarried twenty-eight-year-old Spanish citizen. Rebel claimed that he had set out to trade for palm oil and ivory and had been deceived by a local king in Africa who had insisted on giving him slaves instead after he had already paid him with merchandise and silver.[36] This story was implausible, to say the least, but that also did not really matter—the slaves onboard were irrefutable evidence of a violation of the treaty, and Rebel's argument that he was an accidental slave trader may have made him feel better but was entirely beside the point. The "only difficulty" in the proceedings concerned a young African boy, Manuel Perez, whom Rebel claimed was his own personal servant.[37] The boy's name was not recorded in the ship's crew roster, but because the boy could speak Spanish, the commissioners concluded that the master was telling the truth and found that they had no legal basis on which to emancipate him.[38]

On July 14, the commission declared that the *Xerxes* should be condemned and that the Africans found onboard were "free from all slavery and captivity."[39] The British commissioner reported to London that the case had gone well overall, and that he felt that his Spanish colleagues demonstrated "the utmost good faith, as well as . . . their desire to carry into execution the stipulations of the Treaty in the most friendly manner."[40] The Africans onboard this ship, however, were "in a very unhealthy state" and another fifteen or so had died since the ship had been brought into port, leaving only 385 alive.[41] Even so, that was a large number of people. The *ayuntamiento*, or city council, in Havana reportedly expressed concern about the emancipation of so many Africans at one time and asked that the passengers of the *Xerxes* be transported to Europe, with the expense of transport to be defrayed by increasing duties in imports. But nothing came of that suggestion and the captain-general informed the British commissioner that he would apprentice the freed Africans out "as usual."[42]

At this point, Matilda was placed as an apprentice with a Spanish woman in Havana named Maria del Carmen Carrillo. On May 8, 1830, Matilda was baptized as a Catholic in the church of Santo Cristo del Buen Viage of the Havana; the church's book of the "Baptisms of coloured people" described her as "an adult emancipated woman of the Carabali nation, one of those introduced in the Spanish schooner 'Xerxes,' a prize to Her Britannic Majesty's corvette 'Grasshopper'" and noted that she had been placed "under the tutelage" of Carrillo, a member of the parish.[43] But this good Christian woman Carrillo proceeded to treat Matilda as a slave for the next fourteen years.[44] In the summer of 1831, Matilda gave birth to a daughter, whom she named Isabel Marina. The infant was baptized in the same church under the name Marina; her baptismal record included her mother's name and repeated the circumstances of her emancipation by the mixed commission. The infant's godmother was a woman named Susanna Carrillo,[45] who would at some point end up in service to the man who was the British consul in Havana before Turnbull, David Tolmé.[46] Tolmé, who was an active merchant as well as British consul, had been criticized for being too entwined with slave trading interests and was replaced by Turnbull as part of a conscious policy on the part of the British to ensure that their representatives in Cuba were fully devoted to the suppression of the slave trade.[47] It was a lucky break for Matilda and her daughter that the godmother should have ties to the British, for it was through this avenue that both mother and child would eventually gain their freedom.

Some ten years later, upset that her daughter was being treated as a slave and fearing that she might even be sold, Matilda delivered the child over to "two white men, the one a creole of this island, named Joaquin Saguez, the other a native of the Canaries, named Francisco Abreu."[48] Abreu was, in fact, Matilda's husband "in all but the ceremony of the church,"[49] though it is not clear if he was also Isabel Marina's father. The two men kept the child concealed in their houses for several months to protect her from the Carrillo family. During this time, Matilda was subject to "all sorts of cruelty and torture, for the purpose of compelling her to disclose the place where she had concealed her daughter,"[50] but she would not talk. Matilda was sent to the sugar plantation of Don Jose Maria Carrillo, a cruel situation where hard labor would threaten her life.

By that point, the police had begun a search in Havana for the child. Saguez and Abreu became afraid and approached then–British Consul David Turnbull for help. Susanna was reportedly willing to hide her godchild, but the men were uncertain whether this would be safe.[51] Turnbull asked to speak with Susanna. Upon meeting her, he found her (somewhat condescendingly) to be "a person of considerable intelligence, having been with her mistress for some time in England."[52] Having apprised the situation, Turnbull decided the best solution was to take matters into his own hands and "to receive the child under [his] own roof," where she would be safest.[53] He immediately wrote to the captain-general to try to resolve the situation with respect to both Matilda and her mother.[54] The child was delivered to his house and thus was safely sheltered under the diplomatic immunity of a foreign consulate. Soon afterward, Turnbull learned that Susanna, Saquez, and Abreu had all been arrested and were being held incommunicado in the Havana prison. Turnbull fired off another angry letter to the captain-general and soon found that Matilda herself had finally been retrieved from the sugar plantation and had also been thrown in prison.

The captain-general then appointed an "assessor" to investigate the situation and asked Turnbull to visit the assessor at his home the following day. Suspicious, Turnbull refused and sent a letter back demanding that Matilda be liberated from her situation, which was "in violation of the Treaties between Spain and Great Britain, in defiance of the laws of the country, and in contempt of the decree of the Court of Mixed Commission, by which she was declared to be free."[55] The captain-general sent back the report of his assessor, who apparently had rejected Matilda's claim to freedom and insisted, "somewhat suspiciously, on confining his attention to the pretended concealment of her daughter; as to which he declare[d] that a proceeding ha[d] been instituted, in order to discover by whom it had been effected."[56] In other words, despite evidence that a free woman and her child had been held in slavery for more than ten years, the only people the government was interested in investigating were the people who had hidden the child to prevent her from being sold or abused. The assessor's excuse was that the child's baptismal certificate gave her name as Marina, while most people called her Isabel, and so it was not clear that she was, in fact, free. Turnbull replied that there was no serious dispute over who she was, that her name was Isabel Marina Carrillo, and that she was undoubtedly Matilda's daughter and Matilda was undoubtedly free by judgment of the mixed commission. Having refused to show up at the assessor's house with the girl, Turnbull invited the assessor to come to his house, the consulate, and to bring Matilda with him. The captain-general then demanded that Turnbull turn over the child, with a vague promise that if the assessor determined that she was Matilda's daughter they would both be given their freedom. But Turnbull had no confidence in the proposed proceeding and refused to let the child leave his house.

Finally, the captain-general invited Turnbull to come with the child to meet with him at the Government House to resolve the matter. Turnbull decided it was his best chance of reuniting mother and child. Soon after they arrived, Matilda was brought in and, he said, "the poor girl was called forward, when a scene ensued which I shall not trust myself to describe," but which he compared to the biblical scene where Solomon's judgment reveals indisputably who is the true mother of the disputed child.[57] Mother and child wept tears of joy and relief at their reunion. Both were given certificates of freedom in Turnbull's presence, and minutes of the meeting were taken down by a notary and signed by both Turnbull and the captain-general. Susanna's owner, Mr. Tolmé, was able to buy her release from prison, and Saguez had enough funds to buy his own release. But Matilda's husband Abreu remained stranded in jail for lack of money to pay the bribe or bail. Turnbull suggested to the Foreign Office that he should arrange "to send the whole family to some British colony, there to enjoy that security for person and property of which they have no hope in this country."[58]

It is unclear whether Turnbull ever carried out this plan and what happened after that to Matilda and her family. Letters between Turnbull and the British commissioners some months later suggest that the commissioners disapproved of Turnbull's conduct, for when he asked for their assistance in trying to get Abreu out of jail, they replied, "as the man, according to your statement, has got into serious difficulty by acting in concert with you in the matter, it appears to us a question solely for your consideration."[59] The case of Matilda and her daughter was far from the only hornet's nest Turnbull had stirred up. And so it was perhaps not too surprising when, in February 1842, Palmerston's successor in the office of Foreign Secretary, Lord Aberdeen, decided to take a more conciliatory approach toward Spain by stripping Turnbull of his consulship, though leaving him in office for another few months as superintendent of liberated Africans in Havana.[60] Throughout the spring of 1842 in his new capacity as superintendent, Turnbull continued to receive visits from *emancipados* seeking his help. In May, for example, he wrote to the British commissioners in Havana reporting, "Another female *empancipado* . . . one of the cargo of the 'Midas' of 1831, has come to my house to complain that her pretended mistress [has been mistreating her]," and availing himself "of this opportunity to recall your attention to the condition of the *emancipados* as a class" and to ask what the commissioners would do about it.[61] During those months, Turnbull sent additional letters to both the captain-general and the British commissioners, referring to still other *emancipados* who were in dire straits and who had sought his help.

His efforts did not engender great sympathy, and by the summer of 1842, Turnbull feared for his life and fled to a British hulk in the harbor, the HMS *Romney*.[62] From there he eventually left the island, though he would return briefly in a private capacity before being permanently expelled by the Spanish government.[63] Even after he had left Cuba, he was accused by the Spanish government of having played a role in fomenting the alleged *Escalera* slave conspiracy in 1844.[64] Although Aberdeen was at best lukewarm on Turnbull, Aberdeen appointed him as a judge on the Anglo-Portuguese court of mixed commission in Jamaica, where Turnbull served for another several years after leaving Cuba and continued to advocate forcefully in the cause of abolition.[65]

After Turnbull's departure, the remaining British officials in Havana continued to press local officials to ensure the protection of *emancipados*,[66] both in general and in particularly egregious cases.[67] The captain-general put in place a system for issuing renewed certificates of freedom to *emancipados*, which was apparently successful in hundreds of cases.[68] The British eventually succeeded in making arrangements for many

emancipados to be transported to British colonies,[69] though this continued to give rise to sinister allegations that the British were hoping to benefit their colonies by taking African laborers away from Cuba and Brazil.

Aside from the issue of treatment of those emancipated by the mixed
commissions, another issue concerned the impact of the treaties on the
mistreatment of captives on slave ships as part of efforts to evade detec-
tion and capture, as well as the problem of delays in adjudication. Even
strong supporters of the effort to suppress the slave trade acknowledged
that the faster, smaller ships used in attempts to evade capture increased
to some degree the suffering onboard.[70]

The case of the *Maria da Gloria*, also mentioned in the preceding
chapter as an example of loopholes in the treaties, provides an illustra-
tion of the problems caused by delays in adjudication and the unfortunate fate of captives onboard ships that were ultimately acquitted by the
mixed courts and sent on their way again. The *Maria da Gloria*, a barque
of 238 tons, left Rio bound for Angola in May 1833. On October 26, the
ship was cleared by the customs officer in Angola for a return to Rio,
with a manifest showing cargo to consist of "18 barrels of gum copal,
105 hides, and 1,500 mats," an implausibly worthless cargo for a trans-
atlantic voyage.[71] A letter from the owner of the ship (no doubt intended
for prying eyes in the event of capture) directed the master to take "the
greatest care and vigilance" against carrying "contraband goods, particularly new slaves," and that "it should be ascertained, when outside the
bar of the port, that none are hidden onboard."[72] Not much of a search
would have been required to find the more than 400 slaves that the master took onboard once outside the bar of the port. The ship was sailing
under the Portuguese flag, but also carried onboard English, Brazilian,
and American flags.[73] One month later, the *Maria da Gloria* fell in with
the HMS *Snake*, a sloop under the command of Commander William
Robertson off the mouth of the harbor of Rio de Janeiro.[74] The *Snake*
detained the *Maria da Gloria* and turned the ship over to the mixed
commission for trial. But the mixed court at Rio de Janeiro rejected the

case on the grounds that the ship was Portuguese, not Brazilian, and therefore was in the wrong jurisdiction.[75]

The admiralty ordered the ship to be transported back across the Atlantic by a prize crew led by Lieutenant Joseph Denman, and the ship arrived at Freetown, Sierra Leone, in February 1834. The ship's crew asked that the slaves be landed "on account of their crowded and sickly state, and their long confinement on board the detained vessel."[76] The commissioners were reluctant to let the slaves be landed as they feared that "in the event of the '*Maria da Gloria*' and her cargo being restored, a serious commotion in the colony might result from an attempt to re-ship them."[77] It was decided that it would be safer to keep them all off-shore during the trial, but that the sickest should be removed to a different ship to prevent the further spread of disease. The governor provided another ship, the *Adelaide*, for receiving the sick slaves. The assistant surgeon of the *Snake*, who had been sent as part of the prize crew, continued to tend to the sick.

The fate of the ship was decided by the Anglo-Portuguese mixed court at Sierra Leone. The judges there "reluctantly" concluded that the ship was immune from condemnation because it was seized south of the equator, where the slave trade was arguably still permitted by the Portuguese treaty.[78] The ship was not carrying a valid royal passport authorizing the transportation of slaves, as required by the 1817 treaty between Britain and Portugal.[79] Nevertheless, that was apparently a matter to be dealt with by the Portuguese government, and not a basis for the mixed commission to act given that the ship had been sailing south of the equator. The master of the ship gave testimony so inconsistent that the mixed commission judges noted that never had "perjury been more un-blushingly practised" before them.[80] At one point, he tried to claim that the "black people" onboard the ship were passengers and had paid him 250 dollars each for passage to Monte Video.[81] It took four weeks for the court in Sierra Leone to adjudicate the case, a pace which it said was a "much shorter period of time than ever yet was occupied by any Case of a similar description."[82] In the end, however, the commissioners felt obliged to order the acquittal of the ship because it had been captured south of the equator, though they denied any costs or damages to the *Maria da Gloria*'s crew on the grounds that they were engaged in an illegal traffic and should not profit, even if they had been wrongly detained.

The case had a profound impact on Denman, who, as mentioned previously, became an ardent abolitionist because of his experiences onboard the *Maria da Gloria*.[83] Dispirited, Denman and the rest of the prize crew took passage to London onboard a "very fast-sailing vessel" a day or two after the case was resolved. The case also left a strong impression on the judges at the Sierra Leone court, as previously noted. With some dismay, the British judges wrote to Viscount Palmerston:

> Although it has been our duty as Judges to restore the *"Maria da Gloria,"* we cannot forbear expressing to your Lordship our deep regret on witnessing the sailing of that vessel with her cargo of unhappy beings, destined to another miserable voyage across the Atlantic.
>
> As men, our feelings have been greatly distressed.[84]

The commissioners noted that sixty-four of the sickest slaves onboard had been freed from slavery through the "humane interposition" of the lieutenant governor at Freetown:

> This is indeed an incalculable advantage, and may serve, in some degree, to console humanity under the horrid prospect, which now lies before the survivors of the unhappy slaves, of having a third time to cross the Atlantic ocean, after the sufferings which they have already endured during a period of more than 5 months.[85]

The judges expressed their hope that the horrifying outcome of the case would prompt the British government to conclude a new, more effective treaty with Portugal that covered traffic sailing in all latitudes.[86] Out of the original 400 slaves loaded on the *Maria da Gloria*, some 150 slaves landed and were sold in Brazil after a third miserable passage across the Atlantic. More than 200 Africans had died onboard the ship of disease during the long months as it bounced from court to court.[87] In testifying before Parliament more than a decade later, Denman still seemed marked by this experience:

> In my own case I was four months on board a particularly large and roomy slaver, and I can speak from my own experience of the sufferings which were there incurred.
>
> . . . Under the best of circumstances, it is abhorrent to humanity in every step of its progress.[88]

In sum, like many legal regimes, the international regime for the suppression of the slave trade had certain unintended consequences. The purpose of the regime was to benefit the victims of the slave trade—to preserve the freedom of the millions of Africans who might otherwise be torn from their homes and carried to slavery on the other side of the globe. Ultimately, this goal was achieved. But along the way, many individual Africans were harmed. Some were crowded onto ships in worse conditions than they might otherwise have endured, as slavers tried to maximize the value of each voyage while evading capture. Some were thrown overboard to drown when a British cruiser was spotted, a most vicious way of destroying the evidence of wrongdoing. Some died of disease as the courts took too long to decide cases. Some were formally freed but fared no better than slaves because the courts lacked adequate mechanisms for following up on enforcement. To the extent that the mixed commissions delivered justice, it was imperfect justice at best.

CHAPTER 6

Hostis Humani Generis

Enemies of Mankind

In addition to the suprising role of international slave trade tribunals in the suppression of the slave trade, the history of the abolition of the transatlantic slave trade sheds light on other issues in international human rights law, including the role of domestic courts in the enforcement of international norms. One of the more intriguing aspects of the law governing the slave trade in the nineteenth century relates to two important concepts in contemporary international human rights law: the concept of universal jurisdiction over human rights abusers, and the concept of crimes against humanity. By the middle of the nineteenth century, a number of countries had agreed to declare the slave trade a form of piracy in the hopes of making slave traders, like pirates, *hostis humani generis*, or enemies of mankind, subject to capture and trial in the courts of any nation. Moreover, some commentators—notably the prominent American jurist Henry Wheaton—had begun to refer to the slave trade as a "crime against humanity," putting that term into legal use more than a century before its more famous debut at Nuremberg. The two developments were not unrelated. That is, describing the slave trader as *hostis humani generis* helped solidify the idea that these crimes were offenses against humanity generally.

The link between slave trading and piracy, and between slave trading and universal jurisdiction, has not been entirely forgotten in international law, but unfortunately it has often been misunderstood. This chapter seeks to clarify that link.

While the description of slave traders as *hostis humani generis* is not likely to surprise most international lawyers, the fact that the term "crimes against humanity" was used in conjunction with the slave trade is likely to surprise them. The conventional wisdom is that the term originated in the early twentieth century. For example, one leading and careful scholar of international law asserts in his treatise *International Criminal Law* that "[t]he notion of crimes against humanity was propounded for the first time in 1915, on the occasion of mass killings of Armenians in the Ottoman Empire."[1] Another prominent and thorough scholar agrees that "[t]he specific origin of the term 'crimes against humanity' as the label for a category of international crimes goes back to 1915" in connection with the slaughter of Armenians as "crimes against civilization and humanity."[2] He further argues that the term "crimes against humanity" emerged in connection with war crimes, drawing on the Martens Clause of the 1899 and 1907 Hague Conventions on the laws of war,[3] though he does acknowledge that the concepts of *hostis humanis generis* and offenses *jure gentium* are older.[4]

But the actual term "crime against humanity" was used long before 1915, and in connection with the slave trade, not war crimes. In his 1842 treatise *Right of Visitation and Search*, the prominent American international law scholar Henry Wheaton describes the slave trade as a "crime against humanity," which is so far as I know the first use of that term in international law.[5] Wheaton uses the term again in his 1845 *History of the Law of Nations*, where he states that "[p]ublic opinion, stigmatizing the traffic [in slaves] as a *crime against humanity*" had led to action against the slave trade.[6] Wheaton's phrasing is the most directly similar to the modern usage, but he is not the only one to speak of the slave trade as an offense against humanity or a violation of the laws of humanity. Indeed, such language appears frequently throughout discussions of the slave trade. In his 1810 message to Congress, for example, President James Madison said that "it appears that American citizens are instrumental in carrying on a traffic in enslaved Africans, equally in violation of the *laws of humanity*, and in defiance of those of their own country."[7]

But does violating the laws of humanity make one an enemy of all mankind? How did slave traders get their reputation as enemies of mankind? And did this label reflect a judgment about the heinousness of their actions, or was it merely a clever legal technicality to gain jurisdiction over them? These issues are relevant to several contemporary debates related to international human rights law. In 1980, a federal appeals court in New York famously opened the door for the prosecution of civil lawsuits against human rights abusers from other countries in United States courts under the Alien Tort Statute. These cases, along with criminal cases brought against figures like Chilean dictator Augusto Pinochet and Israeli leader Ariel Sharon in countries such as Spain and Belgium, launched a modern debate about the use of so-called universal jurisdiction against human rights abusers. In the 1980 case, *Filartiga v. Pena-Irala*, the appeals courts said that "for purposes of civil liability, the torturer has become—like the pirate and slave trader before him—*hostis humani generis*, an enemy of all mankind."[8] This idea has been frequently repeated by courts and commentators since then, with the treatment of pirates and slave traders under international law cited as the main precedents for the contemporary doctrine of universal jurisdiction.

In fact, jurisdiction over both pirates and slave traders was more complex and more contested than these modern references suggest, though ultimately it does support at least the beginnings of a concept of universal jurisdiction based on actions that are crimes against humanity.

As is often the case with international law, the road does eventually lead back to the laws of war, which formed a major part of the early law of nations. Historically, pirates were individuals who engaged in armed violence on the high seas without the sanction of a sponsor state. Writers on the law of nations from the Middle Ages forward typically include pirates as proper objects of just war. The idea that human rights violators and pirates are analogous in their assault on the social order of the world community is quite an old one. This link makes an early appearance in the writings of Alberico Gentili (1552–1608), an Italian Protestant who left his home for lands more tolerant of his religious beliefs and ended up as the Regius Professor of Civil Law at Oxford University in 1587. Gentili espoused a theory of just war that encompassed the common interests of mankind (*communi ratione et pro aliis*). He believed that just war could be "undertaken for no private reason of our own, but for the common interest and in behalf of others," explaining that if "men clearly sin against the laws of nature and of mankind, I believe that any one whatsoever may check such men by force of arms."[9]

Gentili thus set out a case for something like the modern doctrine of violations of international law *erga omnes* (against all) that may be raised not only by the injured, but by anyone—a concept that is distinct from (but related to) the idea of universal jurisdiction over certain offenses. Just as "in a state any one whatsoever is allowed to accuse an offender against the community, even one who is not a member of the state," when the matter concerns something "which is not peculiar to the state but of interest to all men," anyone may take action.[10] For example, Gentili explained that "a foreigner may not conduct a case relating to a road and highway of the state, but he may do so in a question affecting a man's liberty or the like."[11] Gentili further argued, in a chapter "On defending the Subjects of another Sovereign," that war might be waged to protect subjects of a foreign sovereign "treated cruelly and unjustly."[12]

[T]he subjects of others do not seem to me to be outside of that kinship of nature and the society formed by the whole world. . . . And unless we wish to make sovereigns exempt from the law and bound by no statutes and no precedents, there must also of necessity be some one to remind them of their duty and hold them in restraint.[13]

Practices like human sacrifice that were contrary to "a right of humanity" thus justified waging war on their practitioners, "for the innocent must be protected."[14] Indeed, speaking of rape, Gentili suggested that "to violate the honour of women will always be held to be unjust" even in war, and the party that allows it will be accountable "to the rest of the world, if there is no magistrate here to check and punish the injustice of the victor. He will render an account to those sovereigns who wish to observe honourable causes for war and to maintain the common law of nations and of nature."[15]

Gentili not only described piracy as being of universal concern but also analogized war waged for humanitarian interests to wars waged on pirates:

And if a war against pirates justly calls all men to arms because of love for our neighbour and the desire to live in peace, so also do the general violation of the common law of humanity and a wrong done to mankind. Piracy is contrary to the law of nations and the league of human society. Therefore war should be made against pirates by all men, because in the violation of that law we are all injured, and individuals in turn can find their personal rights violated. . . . Therefore, since we may also be injured as individuals by those violators of nature, war will be made against them by individuals.[16]

Gentili was not by any means the only writer to suggest that humanitarian intervention could be a justification for war—the Spanish scholastic Francisco de Vitoria (ca. 1480s–1546) espoused similar notions before Gentili, and Hugo Grotius did so after. (Unfortunately, these sorts of ideas were used in justifying the European conquest and colonization of other lands, tainting the idea of humanitarian intervention with a reputation as a tool of imperialism.) But Gentili was especially explicit in linking the idea of wars waged against pirates to wars on offenders against the common law of humanity.

Many modern writers have characterized the treatment of piracy as an offense against all as a tool for reinforcing state sovereignty, by solidifying the monopoly on the use of force by nation-states to the exclusion of nonstate actors (e.g., pirates). But in Gentili's writings, nation-states are not inviolate but instead are subject to the "common law of nations and of nature." Those who violate these common laws of humanity are of concern to all members of the human community, whether the violators bear the mantel of sovereignty or not.

To add greater complexity to the matter, jurisdiction over pirates was not as clear under the law of nations as many assume. Certainly, there are many statements supporting the idea that pirates were subject to some sort of universal jurisdiction. Reflecting the *ius gentium* rationale for jurisdiction over piracy, for example, British admiralty courts in the seventeenth century described pirates as "*hostis humani generis*" and therefore "out of the Protection of all Princes and of all Laws."[17] In the eighteenth century, Blackstone similarly wrote:

> the crime of piracy . . . is an offence against the universal law of society;
> a pirate being . . . *hostis humani generis*. As therefore he has renounced all
> the benefits of society and government, and has reduced himself afresh
> to the savage state of nature, by declaring war against all mankind, all
> mankind must declare war against him: So that every community hath a
> right, by the rule of self-defence, to inflict that punishment upon him,
> which every individual would in a state of nature have been otherwise
> entitled to do.[18]

Nevertheless, actual instances of the exercise of jurisdiction over pirates by nations with no connection to their crimes appear relatively uncommon—that is, nations were mostly in the habit of punishing pirates who were their citizens, who sailed under their flag, or who attacked ships under their national flag.[19] The boundaries of jurisdiction over piracy were litigated in several early Supreme Court cases in the United States. The first U.S. statute against piracy was enacted in 1790 and provided that:

> if any person or persons shall commit upon the high seas, or in any river, haven, basin or bay, out of the jurisdiction of any particular state, murder or robbery, or any other offence which if committed within the body of a county, would by the laws of the United States be punishable by death . . . every such offender shall be deemed . . . to be a pirate and a felon, and being thereof convicted, shall suffer death.[20]

In *United States v. Palmer*, the Supreme Court found that, although Congress had the power "to enact laws punishing pirates, although they may be foreigners, and may have committed no particular offence against the United States," the 1790 act was not intended to encompass such broad jurisdiction.[21] With respect to the provision of the act applying to "any captain or mariner of any ship or other vessel, [who] shall piratically run away with such ship or vessel," the Court noted that:

> These are offences against the nation under whose flag the vessel sails, and within whose particular jurisdiction all on board the vessel are. Every nation provides for such offences the punishment its own policy may dictate; and no general words of a statute ought to be construed to embrace them when committed by foreigners against a foreign government.[22]

In other words, the Court saw a jurisdictional distinction between piracy in the form of one ship robbing another and piracy in the form of mutiny onboard one ship. The former was the classic type of piracy recognized under the law of nations as of general concern, while the Court viewed the latter as primarily up to the particular state whose ship was involved to define and punish.[23]

Apparently displeased with the Supreme Court's decision, the U.S. Congress enacted a new, broader law against piracy in March 1819. This law, An Act to Protect the Commerce of the United States and Punish the Crime of Piracy, provided that "if any person or persons whatsoever shall, on the high seas, commit the crime of piracy, as defined by the law of nations, and such offender or offenders, shall afterwards be brought into or found in the United States, every such offender or offenders shall, upon conviction thereof . . . be punished by death."[24] By defining piracy in terms of the law of nations, Congress also suggested that it intended for U.S. courts to exercise jurisdiction in cases where international law would allow it.

Two significant cases on piracy reached the Supreme Court in 1820. In the first, the charges had been brought under the older 1790 act. This case was against Ralph Klintock, a U.S. citizen who had been sailing onboard a foreign ship under ostensible commission as privateer sponsored by "Aury, styling himself Brigadier of the Mexican Republic and Generalissimo of the Floridas"—a commission that was not recognized as valid by the United States. The ship on which Klintock served as first lieutenant had captured a Danish vessel by way of a fraud involving forged papers planted on the ship. The jury convicted Klintock of piracy. On appeal in the Supreme Court, Attorney General William Wirt argued in support of the conviction that:

> [a] pirate, being *hostis humani generis*, is of no nation or State. He and his confederates, and the vessel on board of which they sail, are outcasts from the society of nations. All the States of the world are engaged in a tacit alliance against them. An offence committed by them against any individual nation, is an offence against all. It is punishable in the Courts of all.[25]

Writing for the Court, Chief Justice Marshall upheld the conviction, distinguishing cases of ships "sailing under the flag of a foreign State, whose authority is acknowledged" from those of ships "in possession of a crew acting in defiance of all law, and acknowledging obedience to no government whatever.... Persons of this description are proper objects for the penal code of all nations."[26] The statute, the Court concluded, "applied to offences committed against all nations, including the United States, by persons who by common consent are equally amenable to the laws of all nations."[27]

The next day, the Court decided *United States v. Smith*, its first case under the 1819 statute, which, as noted previously, expressly defined piracy in terms of the "law of nations." The defendant, Thomas Smith, was serving on a vessel with a commission from the government of Buenos Aires, which had declared its independence from Spain. The crew mutinied, then seized another ship, and then set about plundering and robbing a Spanish ship from onboard the new vessel, which lacked papers and commission altogether. The Court upheld Smith's conviction, holding in an opinion by Justice Story that Congress had acted constitutionally in defining piracy in terms of the "law of nations" and that the law of nations as to piracy was sufficiently definite to support criminal punishment.[28] Shortly thereafter in *U.S. v. Furlong, alias Hobson*, the Court further explained that "when embarked on a piratical cruize, every individual becomes equally punishable . . . whatever may be his national character, or whatever may have been that of the vessel in which he sailed, or of the vessel attacked."[29] Nevertheless, the Court distinguished between piracy and murder, holding that:

> Robbery on the seas is considered as an offence within the criminal jurisdiction of all nations. It is against all, and punished by all. . . . Not so with the crime of murder. It is an offence too abhorrent to the feelings of man, to have made it necessary that it also should have been brought

within this universal jurisdiction. And hence, punishing it when committed within the jurisdiction, or, (what is the same thing,) in the vessel of another nation, has not been acknowledged as a right, much less an obligation. It is punishable under the laws of each State.[30]

Thus, the court held that the murder of one British citizen by another onboard a British ship would not be punished by an American court, notwithstanding the fact that the 1790 act had defined piracy to include murder. The Court described the limits of Congress's power to redefine piracy under the law of nations:

> If by calling murder *piracy*, it might assert a jurisdiction over that offence committed by a foreigner in a foreign vessel, what offence might not be brought within their power by the same device? The most offensive interference with the governments of other nations might be defended on the precedent. Upon the whole, I am satisfied that Congress neither intended to punish murder in cases with which they had no right to interfere, nor leave unpunished the crime of piracy in any cases in which they might punish it.[31]

Under the rationale of these cases, when the United States in 1820 passed a criminal statute making slave trading punishable as piracy, it was changing municipal law only, and not the law of nations. Both the United States and Britain hoped that slave trading would eventually become piracy under the general law of nations but recognized that changes to the general law of nations required the agreement of more than just two nations. Making the slave trade piracy under the law of nations would have several advantages. First, suspected pirate ships were susceptible to search under the law of nations even in peacetime, when there was generally no right to board and inspect the ships of another country. Second, all countries had jurisdiction to punish individuals who committed piracy as defined in the law of nations. Finally, the traditional characterization of the pirate as an enemy of humanity lent itself naturally to the extension to the slave trade, which was by then being characterized as an offense against humanity.

As noted previously, Britain proposed at the Congress of Aix-la-Chapelle in 1818 that the European powers act in concert to declare the slave trade to be piracy under the law of nations, but was initially unsuccessful in winning broader agreement on this point.[32] In 1823, the United States—having already declared the trade to be piracy under municipal law in 1820—also took up the project of making it such under the law of nations. The U.S. House of Representatives passed a resolution calling upon the president "to enter upon . . . negotiations with the several maritime Powers of Europe and America, as he may deem expedient for the effectual abolition of the African slave trade, and its ultimate denunciation, as piracy, under the law of nations, by the consent of the civilized world."[33] Congressman Mercer, in support of the resolution, explained that "[t]he consent of nations may make piracy of any offence upon the high seas" and that declaring the slave trade piracy would provide a "definite and competent remedy" that would be "understood, and punished by all nations." Moreover, he contended, the slave trade was analogous to piracy, for "is it not robbery to seize, not the property of the man, but the man himself?"

Pursuant to these instructions, Secretary of State John Quincy Adams proposed that Britain and the United States enter into a treaty agreeing to declare the slave trade piracy in their municipal laws and to endeavor to get other countries to make it so under the law of nations. At the same time, Adams also sent letters to American diplomats in a variety of countries including Spain, France, and the Netherlands seeking similar agreements to redefine the slave trade as piracy.[34]

The British were receptive to the proposal, as Canning put it, to "join with other powers in declaring slave trade piracy, under the law of nations, and treating the perpetrators of this crime as *enemies of the human race*."[35] As President Monroe explained in his message to Congress in

1824, the United States had objected to British proposals for conceding the right of search on the grounds that as "the right of search was a right of war of a belligerent towards a neutral power, it might have an ill effect to extend it, by treaty . . . to a time of peace."[36] On the other hand, by "making it piratical," that objection would be eliminated since there was already a right of search for piracy. "In that mode, *the enormity of the crime* would place the offenders out of the protection of their Government, and involve no question of search, or other question, between the parties, touching their respective rights."[37]

At the same time, the negotiators recognized that, under the prevailing understanding of the law of nations, they could not alone change the customary international legal definition of piracy. Adams, for example, noted "[t]he distinction between piracy by the law of nations, and piracy by statute," and the fact that "while the former subjects the transgressor guilty of it, to the jurisdiction of any and every country, into which he may be brought, or wherein he may be taken, the latter forms a part of the municipal criminal code of the country where it is enacted, and can be tried only by its own courts."[38] This was reflected in the recent U.S. Supreme Court decisions on the topic, with which Adams was no doubt familiar. Although the United States "expressed their desire that the change [in the definition of piracy to include the slave trade] should become general by the consent of every other power," Adams acknowledged that Britain and the United States alone could not redefine piracy under the general law of nations. Until the general agreement of nations on the matter was achieved, Adams asserted that the United States was constitutionally bound to punish its own citizens in its own courts for what was a municipal law offense, and the treaty had to provide that captured slave ships be brought back to their own nation for trial.[39]

Adams noted: "Piracy being an *offence against the human race*, has its well known incidents of capture and punishment by death, by the people and tribunals of every country."[40] However, he also asserted that in some cases "by the prevailing *customary* law, they are tried only by the tribunals of the nation to which the vessel belongs in which the piracy was committed" and that "[t]he crime itself has been . . . in modern times, of so rare occurrence, that there is no uniformity in the laws of the European nations with regard to this point."[41] In this regard, he distinguished "a piracy committed on board of a vessel by its own crew"— that is, a mutiny—from "[e]xternal piracies, or piracies committed by, and from one vessel against another," which "may be tried by the courts of any country, but are more usually tried by those of the country whose vessels have been the sufferers of the piracy."[42]

As noted, the British eagerly agreed to the American proposal, and Parliament enacted a statute declaring the slave trade to be piracy.[43] Thus, an 1824 draft treaty between Britain and the United States noted that each country "separately, by its own laws" had subjected "their subjects and citizens" engaged in slave trading to the penalties of piracy, and agreed "to use their influence, respectively, with the other maritime and civilized nations of the world, to the end that the said African slave trade may be recognized, and declared to be, piracy under the law of nations."[44]

As detailed in chapter 3, the treaty foundered when the Senate tried to make changes before final ratification to which the British would not agree.[45] The British, however, were inspired by the American proposal to treat the slave trade as piracy, and many of the British treaties on the slave trade in succeeding years included a clause declaring the trade to be piracy. Britain's 1826 convention with Brazil, for example, provided that after three years, "it shall not be lawful for the subjects of the Empire of Brazil to be concerned in the carrying on of the African Slave Trade . . . and the carrying on of such Trade after that period, by any person Subject of His Imperial Majesty, shall be deemed and treated as piracy."[46] British treaties with Chile, Venezuela, Argentina, and Uruguay in 1839 described the slave trade as piracy, as did British treaties with Bolivia and Texas in 1840, with Mexico, Ecuador, Austria, Prussia, and Russia in 1841, Borneo in 1847, Belgium in 1848, New Granada in 1851, and Italy in 1889. These treaties included various formulations, with some countries promising to enact or enforce domestic legislation declaring the slave trade to be piracy, as with the Chilean treaty that promised "to promulgate a law imposing the punishment attached to piracy on all Chilean citizens who shall . . . take any part whatever in the traffic in slaves.[47] Others, such as the Texas treaty, simply promised "to declare such trade Piracy."[48] An 1839 treaty with Haiti referred to a recently passed Haitian law which asserted "La Traite est assimilée à la Piraterie,"[49] while the 1841 convention with Austria, Prussia, and Russia, to which Belgium acceded in 1848, provided that each country would "prohibit all trade in slaves, either by their respective subjects, or under their respective flags, or by means of capital belonging to their respective subjects" and "to declare such traffic piracy."[50]

The implications of a bilateral declaration that the slave trade was piracy became the subject of dispute between Britain and Brazil in the mid-1840s, when the portion of the Anglo-Brazilian treaty providing for mixed commissions expired and Brazil refused to renew it. Britain responded by reverting to the use of its own admiralty courts to try Brazilian ships. The political consequences of those actions are discussed more fully in chapter 7, but it is worth recounting here the legal arguments on both sides.

In 1845, in response to the crisis, the British Law Officers gave an opinion to the Foreign Office on the matter. They advised that under the 1826 treaty with Brazil, Britain had "acquired the right to order the Seizure of all Brazilian subjects found upon the High Seas engaged in the Slave Trade, or punishing them as Pirates, and of disposing of their vessels in which they may be captured, together with the Goods on board of them as *bona piratorum*." But they also concluded "that further Legislative Enactments are necessary in order to, and previous to carrying into full effect on the part of Her Majesty the above mentioned Rights."[51] Parliament obliged by passing a statute that became known as Aberdeen's Act, which provided that, since the 1826 Anglo-Brazilian convention had stated that the slave trade "should be deemed and treated as piracy," the British courts of admiralty and vice-admiralty were authorized "to take cognizance of and adjudicate any vessel carrying on the Slave Trade" in contravention of the 1826 treaty.[52]

Aberdeen wrote to the Brazilian minister arguing, "There is nothing here to show that the penalties of piracy are to be inflicted on the offenders by Brazil alone; or that a municipal regulation of Brazil, attaching the penalties of piracy to the offence, is to be considered as a fulfillment of the engagement." He went on to argue that "[t]he very term of piracy would imply, unless it were otherwise stated" that violators were subject to the jurisdiction of the other country. However, he "admitted that no act of Great Britain and Brazil alone" could make the slave trade "piracy as to other nations," but that between themselves "it should be so treated."[53] Aberdeen similarly explained before the House of Lords that "[t]hat declaration [in the 1826 treaty] could not, of course, render the Slave Trade piracy by the law of nations; but as between Great Britain and Brazil it became illegal by that compact."[54]

Brazil did not accept these legal arguments. "It is a principle of the law of nations, that no State can exercise any act of jurisdiction over the property or the individuals in the territory of another," the Brazilian government wrote to the British.[55] Britain's assertion of jurisdiction was an "unjustifiable abuse of power which threatens the rights and prerogatives of every free and independent nation."[56]

[The] trade is ranked with piracy only by a fiction of law; and it is known, that fictions of law are effectual only for the express purpose for which they were created. In truth, the traffic is not so easily carried on as robbery on the high seas. The same difficulty does not exist in detecting and convicting its agents, as with reference to pirates. In a word, the traffic does not menace the maritime commerce of all people, as piracy does. It follows then, that the penalties imposed on slave-traders cannot, without being deemed tyrannical, be rendered so severe as those which all nations award to piracy."[57]

The Brazilians suggested that the 1826 treaty did not expressly delegate the power to enforce the prohibition to Britain, and that such a delegation should not be inferred lightly. Moreover, the Brazilians noted, if the 1826 treaty were really meant to authorize the British to seize and try Brazilian slavers in their own courts as pirates, then why did it also provide for the mixed commissions, which would appear redundant? "Nor is it conceivable how the traffic can at this time be deemed piracy according to the law of nations" when "it is not many years since England herself did not conceive herself disgraced by trading in African slaves; and when other civilized nations only very recently proscribed that traffic."[58] Aberdeen's Act was, in the eyes of Brazil, "opposed to the most clear and positive principle of international law" and "in contempt of the sovereignty and independence of Brazil."[59]

As recounted in chapter 7, Brazil eventually responded to the British pressure by taking decisive action against slave traders by enforcing its own laws against the sale and importation of slaves, thus putting an end to the traffic to Brazil and mooting the controversy about the status of slave trading as piracy.

By then, the arguments about the slave trade and piracy had become well known even to naval officers. Testifying before the House of Commons in 1848, Captain Joseph Denman of the Royal Navy stated that "if the states of the civilized world were to declare slave trading an act of piracy," then "the slave trade would become perfectly extinct; that no one would incur the penalties and perils which the commission of acts of piracy would involve."[60] Denman explained, "We do practically exercise the right of search already with regard to America." (The Americans would have been displeased to hear that.) Britain claimed the right of visit to verify the flag, which he acknowledged was a new distinction from the right of search. The effect of this was that:

> if you go on board an American vessel, and see that she is a slaver (no search is required to see that), she becomes at once subject to seizure; because America having made the slave trade piracy by her law, it is a well-known fact that no such thing exists as an American slaver; and therefore the very fact of seeing her to be a slaver would make the inference so strong that she was not American, that you would be entitled to act upon the supposition that she was Spanish, Portuguese, or Brazilian.[61]

As for the crews onboard slave vessels, Denman said, "They are the greatest scoundrels on the face of the earth. They are accustomed, in their daily course of life, to commit murder, and to regard human life as of no more consequence than the lives of pigs or dogs." Were they, a member of Parliament asked, "that class of men who might become pirates or might be guilty of any atrocity?" Denman replied, "[I]t answers itself. When men are in the habit of treating human beings in the way that they do treat them, and when they are already violating the laws of their own country . . . then piracy, in its general sense, is an easy step."[62]

Although by this time a number of countries declared the slave trade piracy by treaty, it was apparently not enough to persuade some commentators in the mid-nineteenth century that slave trading was piracy by the law of nations. Writing in the early 1840s against British claims of the right to visit American ships suspected of slave trading to determine their true nationality, the American jurist Henry Wheaton argued that "the piracy . . . created by municipal statute must not be confounded with piracy under the law of nations."[63] He noted that even if the slave trade were "now forbidden by the municipal laws of all civilized and Christian countries, and is declared to be piracy," that "it does not therefore follow that the offence of trading in slaves is deemed piracy under the law of nations," noting that the proposal to make it such failed at the Congress of Verona, and that the 1824 Anglo-American treaty had failed.[64]

> It is, therefore, a looseness of language, fatal to all accurate reasoning, to call slave-traders "piratical outlaws," and to assert that, for the sake of discovering and punishing these persons as offenders against the law of nations, a general right of search is to be assumed in time of peace, as if cruising against slave-traders were to be put on the same footing with public war between sovereign communities.[65]

Wheaton suggested that unanimity in the international community was required before such a transformation in law could occur: "It is quite clear that such a right can never be established but by the voluntary consent of all civilized States."[66]

It is not clear to what degree Wheaton's views were colored by his focus on denying the British the right to visit and search American ships. In the 1866 edition of his treatise on international law— published after the United States had joined the mixed courts regime—Wheaton still insisted that the slave trade was not piracy under the law of nations, and therefore that no right of search attached to it. But he agreed that it was "now denounced as an odious crime, by the almost universal consent of nations."[67] Other commentators writing around this time agreed with Wheaton's assessment. British barrister and admiralty judge Robert Phillimore's 1854 treatise on international law reports:

> International Law has, on this subject, advanced towards, if it have not yet reached the elevation of Natural and Revealed Law. . . . By general practice, by treaties, by the laws and ordinances of civilized States, as well as by the immutable laws of eternal justice, [the slave trade] is now indelibly branded as a *legal* as well as a natural crime.[68]

He further noted, "Many countries have stamped the character of piracy upon this horrible traffic, so far as the authority of their own Municipal Laws may extend,"[69] though it was not yet piracy "*jure gentium.*"[70]

During the American Civil War, the Union military orders that are today famous as the Lieber Code somewhat radically suggested that international law did not recognize slavery at all, and that the law of nations shielded fugitives from slavery. The Lieber Code, which is now regarded as one of the foundational texts of the modern laws of war and which served as the basis for later law of war treaties, was drafted by Columbia University law professor Francis Lieber and issued by President Lincoln in 1863 as General Orders No. 100 to govern the conduct of the Union army.[71] The Code asserted

> Art. 42 Slavery, complicating and confounding the ideas of property, (that is of a thing,) and of personality, (that is of humanity,) exists according to municipal or local law only. *The law of nature and nations has never acknowledged it.* The digest of the Roman law enacts the early dictum of the pagan jurist, that "so far as the law of nature is concerned, all men are equal." Fugitives escaping from a country in which they were slaves, villains, or serfs, into another country, have, for centuries past, been held free and acknowledged free by judicial decisions of European countries, even though the municipal law of the country in which the slave had taken refuge acknowledged slavery within its own dominions.
>
> Art. 43. Therefore, in a war between the United States and a belligerent which admits of slavery, if a person held in bondage by that belligerent be captured by or come as a fugitive under the protection of the military forces of the United States, such person is immediately entitled to the rights and privileges of a freeman. To return such person into slavery would amount to enslaving a free person, and neither the United States nor any officer under their authority can enslave any human being. Moreover, *a person so made free by the law of war is under the shield*

of the law of nations, and the former owner or State can have, by the law of postliminy, no belligerent lien or claim of service.[72]

The Lieber Code was revisionist—clearly, the law of nations had very recently tolerated slavery and the slave trade—but it reflected the changing attitudes. By the 1870s, many writers were comfortable saying that the slave trade was an offense against the law of nations. An 1878 edition of James Kent's *Commentary* (edited for a British audience by J. T. Abdy, a judge and professor of international law at Cambridge University), in the chapter "Of Offences Against the Law of Nations," adds to Blackstone's list of classic offenses (violations of safe conduct, infringements of the rights of ambassadors, and piracy) the slave trade "as a trade condemned by the general principles of justice and humanity, openly professed and declared by the powers of Europe."[73] Others, particularly American writers, continued to maintain that the slave trade was not piracy under the law of nations, although they also suggested that conceding the right of search for slave traders might not be so bad after all. In the 1878 edition of his treatise on international law, for example, Yale professor Theodore D. Woolsey said:

> as the slave-trade has not hitherto become piracy by the law of nations, but only by the municipal and conventional law of certain nations, no state can authorize its cruisers to detain and visit vessels of other states on suspicion of their being concerned in this traffic, because the right of detention and visit is a right of self-defense. Every state may to carry out *its laws* and the *laws of humanity*, detain and search its own vessels in peace also, but if, in so doing, mistakes are committed, the commander of the searching vessel is responsible, and damages may be demanded.[74]

Moreover, he noted that the right "of reciprocal detention and visitation upon suspicion of being engaged in the slave-trade has been conceded by a considerable number of treaties."[75]

There is substantial language about human rights (or the "rights of man" or "natural rights") in the arguments presented against the slave trade. Woolsey's 1860 edition of *Introduction to the Study of International Law* explained that under the "correct views of human rights" slavery was a status unprotected by the law of nations and that "new views of men's rights" had led to the prohibition of the slave trade in international law.[76] Abolitionist writings in the 1840s referred to "the cause of human rights."[77] In 1806, petitions asking the U.S. Congress to prohibit the slave trade described the trade as "an outrageous violation of one of the most essential rights of human nature" and "degrading to the rights of man."[78] And, as recounted in chapter 2, abolitionism was rooted in part in Enlightenment ideas about natural rights.

Nevertheless, it is true that we also see quite a bit of language about the interests or laws of humanity and the language of humanitarianism. The Congress of Vienna, for example, declared the slave trade "repugnant to the principles of humanity and universal morality."[79] What is the significance of these differences in terminology? At first glance, the language of *humanity* might seem to detract from my attempt to describe the international actions against the slave trade as an example of early international human rights law by taking the focus away from individuals as rights bearers and suggesting instead a kind of benevolent concern grounded not in the idea of rights but in some kind of *noblesse oblige* toward the less fortunate. But in fact, it is precisely this language of humanity that captures the contemporary idea that violations of human rights are of international, and not just local, concern. That is, it is this language of humanity (drawn in part from much earlier writings about the *ius gentium*) that helps propel natural rights from their eighteenth-century link to social contract theory (with its focus on nation-states) to the twentieth-century idea of human rights as matters of international legal concern. A central aspect of international human rights law is that it considers harm to individual persons to be the proper subject of international concern. That is, it posits that the treatment of Mexican citizens in

Mexico is the proper subject of concern of France, and Japan, and South Africa. In this regard, human rights law does not focus exclusively on the relationship between the rights bearer and the rights violator (as might a purely domestic regime of protection for individual rights under a constitution). Instead, international human rights law brings in outsiders—the rest of humanity—and suggests that the rights violations are of concern to them as well. This is little appreciated but is significant for understanding the ways in which international human rights differ from purely domestic conceptions of individual rights.

The word *humanity* is today defined as "people in general" or sometimes as "understanding and kindness towards other people."[80] The 1828 edition of *Webster's Dictionary* defined it as "[t]he peculiar nature of man by which he is distinguished from other beings," as well as "[m]ankind collectively; the human race," and "kindness; benevolence; especially, a disposition to relieve persons in distress, and to treat with tenderness those who are helpless and defenseless; opposed to cruelty."[81] These multiple meanings are each represented in the discussions of the slave trade, and in ways that reflect the presence of these ideas in contemporary discourse about international human rights law.

The idea of humanity as a status—that humans have a particular nature that distinguishes them from other beings and objects—flows through writings from the scholastics through the Enlightment and undergirds the ideas of natural rights that not only helped give rise to the antislavery movement but also provide the foundation for contemporary international human rights law.

At the same time, the concept of humanity defined as "mankind collectively" appears in arguments that the slave trade violates the laws of humanity—that is, that it violates the *ius gentium*. The multiple meanings of the word *humanity* are also reflected in the impulse to define slave traders as *hostis humani generis*. Declaring slave traders to be *hostis humani generis* suggests that because their actions deny the humanity of those they abuse, they are an affront to humankind generally, and their punishment is thus the proper concern of humankind generally, regardless of national borders. As others have noted, the phrase "crimes against humanity" is particularly felicitous because it captures the duality of particular kinds of crimes—those that "offend against the human status and that all humankind shares an interest in repressing."[82] It was in connection with the slave trade that lawyers first began to deploy that duality in seeking to make certain egregious violations of human rights offenses cognizable under international law.

Moreover, the concept of crimes against humanity also stems from another linguistic ambiguity present in debates over slavery and international law, the ambiguity of the phrase *ius gentium*, which gradually grew from meaning the law of people generally to mean the law governing relations between nations. *Ius gentium* was originally a technical term used to describe the body of Roman law that applied to foreigners and governed mostly private civil matters. In this sense, it was quite distant from modern international law, as it was not really a body of law that governed the relations between nation-states.[83] Later Roman writers came to use the phrase *ius gentium* to describe a law that transcended individual nations, though even in this usage it primarily concerned private relations (such as contracts) rather than sovereigns' relations to one another. During this phase of its history, the *ius gentium* was considered related to, and in large part based upon, the *ius naturale*, or natural law.[84] As one Roman jurist in the second century A.D. described it:

> That law which a people establishes for itself is peculiar to it, and is called *ius civile* [civil law] as being the special law of that *civitas* [state], while the law that natural reason establishes among all mankind is followed by all peoples alike, and is called *ius gentium* [law of nations, or law of the world] as being the law observed by all mankind.[85]

It was only gradually that the term *ius gentium* came to mean "law which all the various peoples and nations ought to observe in their *relations with each other*,"[86] eventually to be translated as the law of nations. Describing the slave trade as a violation of the laws of humanity profitably exploits the multiple historical meanings of *ius gentium*.

And what of the word *humanitarian*? It is actually not in the 1828 *Webster's Dictionary*, and when it appears in the 1913 *Webster's Dictionary* the first two meanings are quite different from how it is used today: "One who denies the divinity of Christ, and believes him to have been merely human" or "[o]ne who limits the sphere of duties to human relations and affections, to the exclusion or disparagement of the religious or spiritual." Only the third definition, "benevolent; philanthropic," matches the modern usage, and this is described in 1913 as "recent."[87] The word *humanitarian* is today defined as "involved in or connected with improving people's lives and reducing suffering."[88] It denotes a kind of benevolence not necessarily connected with the idea of legal rights—as when people say, for example, that a prisoner has been released for "humanitarian reasons."[89]

As a technical term, the phrase "international humanitarian law" refers to the body of law applicable in armed conflict, which is considered distinct from international human rights law in both origin and content. The origins of contemporary international humanitarian law are usually traced to mid-nineteenth-century developments including the promulgation of the Lieber Code during the American Civil War and the founding of the International Red Cross.[90] The 1899 Hague Conventions on the Laws and Customs of War include the famous Martens Clause, which provides:

> Until a more complete code of the laws of war is issued, the High Contracting Parties think it right to declare that in cases not included in the Regulations adopted by them, populations and belligerents remain under the protection and empire of the principles of international law, as they result from the usages established between civilized nations, from the *laws of humanity* and the requirements of the public conscience.[91]

The Martens Clause is often described as the source of the concept of "crimes against humanity."[92] But the idea that the laws of humanity were a proper topic of international legal concern had been embedded in the nineteenth-century legal mind primarily in connection with the slave trade. The dominant interpretation of the relationship between international humanitarian law and international human rights law has international humanitarian law coming first historically. In fact, they both share common roots in the struggle against the slave trade, and in earlier conceptions of the *ius gentium*.

This is not to say that the laws against the slave trade resembled contemporary international human rights law in all respects. The Nuremberg trials of the Nazi war criminals were an important, and transformative, event. But the effort against the slave trade helped lay the legal groundwork that made Nuremberg jurisprudentially possible. One of the most important conceptual developments that made possible the contemporary international human rights regime was the idea that violations of human rights are properly of global and not just local concern. This idea was expressed in the writings of early just war theorists, but the ideas of humanitarian intervention threaded through the just war theories of Vittoria or Gentili or Grotius did not result in an elaborate body of treaty law or international courts. Rather, the idea first came to legal fruition with a global consensus in favor of concerted international legal action against the slave trade. The idea that nations should use international lawmaking to protect the rights of individuals outside their own territory was first put into practice with the effort to abolish the slave trade. A second central principle of the contemporary human rights regime is that national sovereignty is not an impenetrable barrier to international legal action in the case of human rights violations. Attempts to subject the slave trade to universal jurisdiction by declaring it piracy foreshadowed this development but were not entirely successful. The seed of the idea was planted in the nineteenth-century actions against the slave trade, but it was not until Nuremberg that the barrier would be shattered.

Given the heavy focus by international human rights scholars on the novelty and innovations of post–World War II developments in human rights law, it is startling to find some of the very same debates about the legitimacy of international human rights–based interventions occurring almost a century earlier. During the debate over whether to abandon efforts to suppress the slave trade, for example, one member of the British Parliament skeptically asked Palmerston whether suppression was in England's interest "apart from the interest of humanity." Palmerston argued that humanity was the main consideration, though there were others.[93]

"Assuming that it is simply from motives of humanity," the questioner continued, "do you think it a legitimate mode of disposing of the resources of this country?" Palmerston answered in the affirmative, calling it a "moral duty."[94] The prescient questioner then took Palmerston's argument to the extreme: "Supposing one nation abolished the punishment of death, would it not be a legitimate effort of that government to interfere with other nations, which had not done so, to induce them to follow the example?" Palmerston stated that it would be legitimate for a nation to pursue that goal, "or any other measure tending to the interests of humanity," in the same way England had pursued the abolition of the slave trade.[95] The antislavery effort was thus not only a precursor to modern international human rights law but foresaw and justified that body of law. States could legitimately be concerned with the welfare of individual persons in other states and could covenant with one another to protect the rights of those individuals. Crimes against humanity and violations of individual rights were a proper subject of international lawmaking.

CHAPTER 7

From Crisis to Success

The Final Abolition of the Slave Trade

Even as the mixed court system reached its peak of effectiveness in terms of volume of cases in the late 1830s and early 1840s, the weaknesses in the system discussed in the preceding chapters led the British government to augment, and then replace, the mixed court system with a combination of military force and domestic courts. The pressure brought to bear by this shift in strategy—along with other economic, political, and social changes—eventually led to changes in the domestic policies of Portugal and Brazil that culminated in the ultimate suppression of the slave trade under the domestic laws of those countries. But the final surviving branch of the transatlantic slave trade, the traffic to Cuba, was only extinguished once the British turned back to cooperative international legal action by concluding a treaty with the Americans.

PORTUGAL

In the late 1830s, negotiations between Britain and Portugal failed to produce a broader, more comprehensive treaty.[1] The Portuguese raised a number of objections to the proposed treaty, including its unlimited duration.[2] In response, the British resorted to a creative reinterpretation of the 1817 Portuguese treaty. That treaty allowed the slave trade to continue only between Portuguese possessions south of the equator. After the independence of Brazil in 1826, Britain argued that Portugal had no colonies in the Americas, and thus all trade under the Portuguese flag was illegal. Moreover, Portugal was in breach of its treaty obligations, and Britain was entitled to enforce those obligations by any means necessary.[3]

Viscount Palmerston recognized that this was a debatable legal argument and that the Portuguese were likely to view Britain's action as an affront to Portuguese sovereignty. In a private letter to the British diplomat in Lisbon, Palmerston wrote that if Portugal responded by declaring war, "so much the better. . . . There are several of her colonies which would suit us remarkably well."[4] In another letter, he stated, "We consider Portugal as morally at war with us and if she does not take good care and look well ahead she will be physically at war with us also."[5]

Thus, in 1839, the Parliament passed a statute popularly known as Palmerston's Act that authorized the capture and condemnation of Portuguese slaving vessels in British vice-admiralty courts rather than the mixed commissions.[6] The bill was initially rejected in the House of Lords, where the Duke of Wellington and others argued that it would encroach on the executive's powers by bringing the nation to the brink of war, not only with Portugal but with other maritime nations who were offended by Britain's aggressive efforts to police the oceans.[7] Their constitutional objections were answered by having the Crown first issue orders to British officers to seize Portuguese ships (thereby preserving the executive's prerogative to make decisions that might lead to war) and then by having the Parliament pass legislation to protect those officers from possible indemnity lawsuits.[8]

Portugal viewed Palmerston's Act as "a gross usurpation of power" and "a flagrant violation of international law" but did not go to war over it.[9] For the next three years, Portuguese-flagged slave vessels were captured by British cruisers and condemned either in the mixed courts on the grounds that they were actually Spanish or Brazilian under the law of nations, or in the British vice-admiralty courts under Palmerston's Act.[10]

Portugal finally signed a new treaty in 1842 that both closed the loopholes in the earlier treaties and expanded the number of mixed commissions.[11] Under the new treaty, the mixed commissions finally had the power to keep slave crews in custody until they could be turned over to their own government for prosecution,[12] and the Portuguese government began in earnest to prosecute at least some of these cases.[13] Portuguese warships began seizing slavers off the coast of Africa in greater numbers, and prize courts in the Portuguese colonies began condemning those captured in coastal waters, over which the mixed commissions lacked jurisdiction.[14] By 1848, witnesses testified before Parliament that Portugal had been seriously engaged in suppression efforts for the past few years, though they disagreed on how universal or effective those efforts were.[15] Portugal's decision to crack down on the trade meant that slavers were less willing to fly the Portuguese flag, and the business of the Anglo-Portuguese mixed courts never reached significant levels again.[16] In effect, the Anglo-Portuguese courts were killed by their own success.

BRAZIL

A similar breakdown in relations between Britain and Brazil over the slave trade occurred in 1845 and proved fatal to the Anglo-Brazilian mixed courts. The treaty authorizing the Anglo-Brazilian courts arguably expired on March 13 of that year.[17] Brazilian officials, though not willing to defend the slave trade publicly, refused to renew the treaty and its provisions for the right of search and trials in mixed courts, insisting that Brazil would suppress the trade with its domestic laws.[18]

Britain once again resorted to creative treaty interpretation. There was no saving the mixed courts, since the Brazilians appeared to be correct about the expiration of the treaty authorizing them. But, as noted in chapter 6, the British construed a separate provision of the Brazilian treaty, which had declared the slave trade to be piracy, to trigger the broader jurisdiction over piracy allowed by the law of nations and to authorize the condemnation of Brazilian-flagged slaving ships in British courts.[19] In August 1845, Parliament passed Aberdeen's Act, which, like Palmerston's Act, authorized the capture and condemnation of Brazilian and unflagged vessels. In the next few years, the volume of cases heard in the British courts increased dramatically.[20] For example, of the thirty-three cases heard by the vice-admiralty court at St. Helena in the first six months of 1848, nineteen were Brazilian, while the remainder had no papers.[21]

Aberdeen's Act was not well received in Brazil. In addition to the legal argument recounted in chapter 6, a number of other arguments against the British actions were raised. In 1848, a Brazilian citizen who was a former slave ship medical officer told the British Parliament that Brazilians viewed the British suppression effort as either "wild and impracticable" or an effort to "check the rising prosperity of Brazil."[22] But like Portugal, Brazil was neither willing nor able to go to war with Britain over the issue.[23]

Despite Britain's aggressive use of vice-admiralty courts against the Brazilian trade, the volume of the trade increased in the late 1840s. Ironically, the demand for slaves had been fueled by British free trade legislation that had removed tariffs on Brazilian sugar.[24] The tension between the two countries reached a climax in 1850–51, when a handful of British ships began attacking slave vessels in Brazil's territorial waters and even its harbors.[25] One of the British ships and a Brazilian fort even exchanged shots. It was a small display of force, but it was effective. Brazil could not afford to go to war with Britain (though it was also apparent that Britain, with its commercial ties to Brazil, was not eager for war either).

Moreover, in recent years, popular sentiment against the slave trade had grown in Brazil.[26] The only face-saving option seemed to be for

Brazil to put an end to the traffic itself. Thus, in September 1850, Brazil enacted new anti–slave trade legislation and began to enforce it. Once the Brazilian government began policing the landing and sale of slaves, the number of slaves imported into Brazil dropped precipitously, from more than 30,000 in 1850 to 5,000 in 1851 and none in 1853.[27] One of the last known slave ships to arrive in Brazil, the schooner *Mary E. Smith*, which had been illegally outfitted in Boston, sailed in 1855. The crew could not find any place to land its cargo of 400 slaves and began to run out of food and water. A Brazilian warship finally captured the unfortunate vessel. One American involved in the venture died in prison, and the Brazilian government punished the other crew members.[28] In this manner, the slave trade into Brazil was finally extinguished, though slavery itself was not abolished in Brazil until 1888.[29]

SPAIN, CUBA, AND THE UNITED STATES

Though relations between Spain and Britain were sometimes tense, they never broke down in the same way relations with Portugal and Brazil did. Instead, other factors led to the obsolescence of the Anglo-Spanish courts. The decline in the courts' cases began in the 1840s, when a new captain-general of Cuba arrived in 1842 and began enforcing the laws against the slave trade, and the open markets for newly imported slaves in Havana were shut down.[30] In 1845, the Spanish government passed stricter legislation for punishing illegal slave traders.[31] Following this new legislation, the court at Sierra Leone was directed to detain the captain and crew of Spanish ships until they could be carried to the Canary Islands for criminal trial by the Spanish government.[32] The decline in slave imports to Cuba continued in the mid- to late 1840s,[33] and the British attributed this decline to stricter enforcement by the Cuban authorities.[34] Enforcement actions had driven costs so high that, according to British officials in Havana, the trade was no longer profitable.[35] From the 1840s onward, the slavers became reluctant to fly the Spanish flag, evading the mixed courts' jurisdiction by sailing under the American flag or under no flag at all; only a handful of cases came before the Anglo-Spanish courts after that.

In 1851, with slave imports at a record low in both Brazil and Cuba, victory for the abolitionists seemed imminent. However, in the mid-1850s, the slave trade to Cuba began to increase once more. An increase in sugar prices led to increased demand for new slaves, even at the higher prices that prevailed because of enforcement of the 1845 act. In addition, the colonial Cuban authorities had somewhat relaxed enforcement.[36] Moreover, tense relations between Britain and the United States kept the British navy from engaging in the sort of aggressive action in Cuban waters that had triggered domestic suppression in Brazil.[37] The United States continued to object strenuously to the search of its ships, and British mercantile interests supportive of free oceans were more sympathetic to these claims. In addition, Britain did not want to give the United States any excuse to annex Cuba. By 1860, the British were doing very little to suppress the slave trade to Cuba.[38]

On the eve of the American Civil War, anything related to the institution of slavery might have been expected to be a delicate issue in the United States. Ironically, however, by this time the illegality of the transatlantic slave trade was a rare point of agreement between the North and the South. Indeed, the constitution of the Confederate States of America adopted in March 1861 actually banned the slave trade.[39] In the spring of 1860, the United States sent its own warships to Cuba, where they reportedly conducted searches of suspected Spanish and French slave vessels despite America's lack of mutual search treaties with those countries. Later that year, President Buchanan stated in his message to Congress:

> It is truly lamentable that Great Britain and the United States should be obliged to expend such a vast amount of blood and treasure for the

suppression of the African slave trade, and this when the only portions of the civilized world where it is tolerated and encouraged are the Spanish islands of Cuba and Porto Rico.[40]

But it was not until civil war broke out in the United States that a final turn in policy helped set the stage for the ultimate suppression of the transatlantic slave trade. In March 1862, Lincoln's secretary of state, William Seward, responded favorably to an approach by British diplomats eager to conclude finally an effective anti–slave trade treaty with the United States. The United States hoped to prevent Britain from intervening in the war on the side of the Confederacy and thus wanted to do what it could to foster goodwill in an otherwise tense relationship. Moreover, President Lincoln's administration viewed the extinction of the slave trade as a moral issue. Seward's one request was that the draft treaty appear to have come from the United States. The British readily agreed to the façade, manufacturing a fake correspondence to make it seem as if the proposal had come from the Americans. On April 25, 1862, the U.S. Senate unanimously ratified a treaty with Britain, which provided for mutual rights of search and the trial of slave ships in mixed courts.[41]

Other factors in Cuba—including changes in attitudes, the increased domestic enforcement of anti–slave trade laws, a decline in sugar prices and a concomitant drop in the value of slaves, and the perception that the institution of slavery itself might be doomed—also played a significant role in the final suppression of the Cuban slave trade in the 1860s.[42] But the abolitionists in Britain viewed the conclusion of the Anglo-American courts treaty as the final nail in the coffin of the slave trade. As one historian noted, "Henry Brougham, last survivor of the original British abolitionist group of 1807," spoke in the House of Lords about the new treaty, saying it was "'in many respects the most important event that had occurred during the period of his sixty years warfare against the African Slave Trade.'"[43]

The Anglo-American mixed courts never actually heard any cases, but that was in large part because no slave ships were willing to use the American flag once the treaty was signed. The network of treaties, begun forty-five years earlier, was complete. Finally, no flag existed under which the traffic could continue with impunity. The transatlantic slave trade was dead.

CHAPTER 8

A Bridge to the Future

Links to Contemporary International

Human Rights Law

W hy have contemporary scholars of international law largely forgotten the antislavery courts? The standard account of the development of international human rights law begins in earnest with the post–World War II era, with the Nuremberg trials and the drafting of foundational international human rights instruments such as the UN Charter, the Universal Declaration of Human Rights, and the Genocide Convention.[1] Likewise, most accounts of the history of international courts and tribunals describe the Permanent Court of Arbitration, established in 1899, and the Permanent Court of International Justice, created in 1921, as the first permanent international adjudicatory bodies,[2] and the International Military Tribunal at Nuremberg as the first international tribunal charged primarily with enforcing humanitarian norms.[3] The term "crimes against humanity" is said to have originated around 1915. Earlier developments in human rights law or international adjudication—like the ad hoc arbitrations for settlement of war claims between the United States and

Britain arising out of the Revolutionary War and the Civil War and the development of the humanitarian laws of war—are acknowledged, but generally receive only passing attention.

Indeed, as one scholar has noted, many historical accounts of human rights jump directly to 1945 from the American and French Revolutions in the late eighteenth century.[4] In so doing, these accounts attribute the sudden resurgence of human rights ideology as "a reaction to the atrocities committed during the Second World War."[5] They assume that the idea of human rights was largely dormant and underwent little further intellectual development during most of the nineteenth and early twentieth centuries, that it arose almost out of nowhere in the immediate aftermath of World War II, at which point it took form in the international legal arena for the first time.[6] This discontinuous story is simply wrong. Scholars are just beginning to fill in the missing pieces of the pre–World War II history of international law as a mechanism for the protection of human rights, and the anti–slave trade movement is a central part of that missing picture.[7]

As recounted in chapter 6, the conceptualization of the slave trade as a crime against humanity, and of slave traders as *hostis humani generis* helped lay the conceptual foundation for twentieth-century international human rights law. Legal actions against the slave trade introduced into modern international legal discourse the idea that violations of human rights were offenses of concern to humankind generally, and not just matters between a people and their sovereign. This is the key conceptual step that separates the contemporary world of international human rights law from the ideas of natural and universal rights that arose during the Enlightenment and took national legal form in documents like the Declaration of Independence, the U.S. Constitution, and the French Declaration of the Rights of Man (which focus on the relationship between individuals and the sovereign states where they reside). This is the idea that through treaties and international legal institutions nations can legally express the conviction that violations of human rights are of concern to all. This is the conceptual development that undergirds the words of the preambles of the Universal Declaration of Human Rights and the International Covenant on Civil and Political Rights, that "recognition of the inherent dignity and of the equal and inalienable rights of all members of the human family is the foundation of freedom, justice and peace in the world." This is also the development that lays the foundation for the idea that international cooperation can be necessary to eradicate human rights violations, a recognition reflected in the Genocide Convention's assertion that the crime of genocide "has inflicted great losses on humanity" and that, "in order to liberate mankind from such an odious scourge, international co-operation is required." It is precisely this blending of the idea of individual human rights with broader ideas of humanity and humanitarianism that allows for international legal institutions like the International Criminal Court, where nation-states take an interest in the protection of the human rights of people who are not their citizens. International human rights law is precisely not about the isolated, atomistic individual as rights bearer, but about a shared humanity in which we are concerned with the rights and dignity of others.

One potential objection to my characterization of the slave trade tribunals as the world's first international human rights courts is that the humans whose rights were being violated—the African captives—were not prime characters in the courts' operations. But this conflates the way individual rights are traditionally expressed in domestic legal fora—for example, in a national court on a claim of a constitutional rights violation—with the rather different modes in which international human rights claims are asserted. Certainly, under some international human rights treaties, individual persons have the right to go to court and raise claims, as before the European Court of Human Rights. But much of international human rights law in operation is not so individualistic and is instead focused on broader problems or issues—the report and investigations of a UN Special Rapporteur on Torture, the site visit of the Inter-American Commission on Human Rights to Ciudad Juarez to investigate violence against women,[8] or the trial in the International Criminal Tribunal for the former Yugoslavia of a criminal defendant for the genocidal massacre at Srebrenica. One of the frequent criticisms of court proceedings even today (whether criminal or civil, domestic or international) is that victims of rights violations are often given little voice in the proceedings. The post–World War II trials at Nuremberg and Tokyo, for example, relied primarily on documentary evidence, not live testimony of victim witnesses.[9] One commentator writing about the International Criminal Tribunal for Rwanda and the International Criminal Tribunal for the Former Yugoslavia, for example, noted that "victims do not play an autonomous role" and have no right to participate as independent parties in the proceedings, which means that for many victims, the international trials are experienced as "justice denied."[10] Indeed, one reason that some activists today suggest truth and reconciliation commissions as an alternative or supplement to other types of trials is that a nonjudicial format often allows victims greater participation and ownership of the proceedings. While the most recent international courts, like the International Criminal Court and the Extraordinary Chambers in the Courts of Cambodia, provide a greater role for victims in court proceedings, finding a way to give human rights victims a meaningful role in formal legal proceedings remains a persistent problem. The nineteenth-century slave trade tribunals are thus not atypical in the lack of voice they give to the individuals whose rights have been violated; rather, they are entirely typical of one unfortunate aspect of contemporary international human rights practice.

While contemporary international lawyers have largely forgotten the slave trade tribunals, those tribunals had not been entirely forgotten by those who were involved in setting up the post–World War II international legal framework. Some of those involved in the twentieth-century development of international human rights law were well aware of the role of international law and cooperation in the suppression of the slave trade in the previous century. At the founding convention of the United Nations in San Francisco in 1945, representatives of nongovernmental organizations (NGOs) were pivotal in pushing for references to human rights to be included in the UN Charter.[11] The great powers that had crafted the charter had not included any mention of human rights in the original draft. One of the nongovernmental representatives present at the convention was W. E. B. DuBois, there on behalf of the National Association for the Advancement of Colored People.[12] DuBois had written his doctoral dissertation on the suppression of the slave trade,[13] and through his attendance at several Pan-African Congresses in the early decades of the twentieth century he had coupled his work on behalf of African Americans with broader international efforts to promote human rights. Other NGOs active in the post–World War II period could likewise trace their genealogy to the nineteenth-century abolition campaign.[14]

More specifically, specialists writing about international courts and tribunals in the late nineteenth and early twentieth century remained aware of the nineteenth-century slave trade tribunals. John Bassett Moore's influential treatise, *International Adjudications: Ancient and Modern History*, recounts that the French writer Renault in 1879 had noted that "mixed courts" of an international nature "may be constituted in a permanent manner; this is rare, but it has sometimes been done in order to adjudicate prizes made in pursuance of conventions establishing the right of visit for the repression of the slave trade."[15]

In 1944, Judge Manley O. Hudson of the Permanent Court of International Justice and the Permanent Court of Arbitration wrote a book, *International Tribunals: Past and Future*, for the Brookings Institution and the Carnegie Endowment for International Peace.[16] The purpose of the book was to consider past experience with international courts and tribunals in deciding what should be done after World War II ended: "The problem of international organization now looms before the peoples of the world as one of the great responsibilities in our winning the war."[17] Hudson was aware of the details of the slave trade tribunals and discussed them in several places. To begin with, in recounting the history of international tribunals, Hudson notes, "Several tribunals of a continuing and more or less permanent nature were created under treaties for the suppression of the African slave trade" and briefly recounts the nature and structure of the mixed commissions. He notes that the commission in Sierra Leone "disposed of 535 cases in the period from 1819 to 1866" and "resulted in the emancipation of more than 55,000 slaves."[18] Later, in discussing the structure of international tribunals more generally, Hudson again refers to the slave trade tribunals and their structure.[19] Finally, in discussing proposals for a permanent international criminal court, Hudson explains, "If international law be conceived to govern the conduct of individuals, it becomes less difficult to project an individual penal law."[20] Describing the historical treatment of pirates as "enemies of all mankind" and of piracy as "an offense against the law of nations," he notes that "the conception of piracy as an offense against the law of nations has been seized upon, by way of analogy, for the service of other ends" and that "[v]arious treaties of the nineteenth century provided for the possibility of States' punishing persons engaged in the slave trade as pirates."[21] He adds, "Power to take cognizance of crimes committed by individuals has but rarely been conferred on international tribunals in the past"[22] and observes:

> The numerous tribunals set up by bipartite treaties concluded by Great Britain with other States in the earlier part of the nineteenth century, were given power to condemn and destroy or confiscate vessels engaged in the slave trade, but the masters and crews of such vessels were required to be delivered to certain States for punishment in accordance with their national laws.[23]

Although Hudson ultimately concludes that there was "little prospect for the establishment of a permanent international criminal court" at that moment,[24] this discussion—by a prominent international judge, just a year before the Nuremberg Trials—shows that the slave trade regime factored into considerations of the feasibility of holding individual persons internationally responsible for human rights violations (another one of the key innovations of Nuremberg).

Other supporters of proposals for international criminal courts both before and after World War II used the slave trade, along with piracy, as an example of a crime under the law of nations for which individuals could be held personally liable. An international congress that was held in 1926 supported the development of international criminal law, for example, and participants there mentioned the slave trade as an example of international crime.[25] The slave trade continued to be given as an example of an offense against international law in succeeding years.[26]

But though international lawyers do still talk about slave traders as *hostis humani generis* today, they do not remember that international courts played a significant role in suppressing the slave trade in the nineteenth century. There is not one simple, satisfactory explanation for the disappearance of the antislavery courts from the early twenty-first-century international law canon. Certainly, as Judge Hudson's 1944 report shows, there was still some memory of the courts among international lawyers at the time that the Nuremberg trials were planned. But in the years following World War II, they dropped out of mention. Perhaps the shameful complicity of so many nation-states in the institution of slavery makes this story less appealing than the Nuremberg narrative, which conveniently attributes responsibility for the Holocaust to a handful of individuals from a losing nation (Germany). The British abolitionist discourse contains embarrassing overtones of the "white man's burden," and the controversial history of colonialism extended for a hundred years after the abolition of slavery. For scholars in the United States, perhaps America's problematic (but eerily familiar) role as the reluctant outsider in the antislavery regime is less appealing than its starring turn at Nuremberg with Justice Jackson's eloquent speeches as chief prosecutor. Perhaps with so many of the records of the courts buried in handwritten archives, their story was simply forgotten.

Two things in particular seem evident from the immediate post–World War II period, the moment when knowledge and discussion of the slave trade courts seems to have fallen out of international legal discourse. First, many of the World War II–era architects of the new international legal regime felt the need to distance international human rights from European history to make it more globally legitimate. In December 1942, Hersch Lauterpacht (then a professor of law at Cambridge and later a judge on the International Court of Justice) delivered an essay before the Grotius Society titled "The Law of Nations, the Law of Nature and the Rights of Man."[27] Lauterpacht noted that the idea of an International Bill of the Rights of Man was "independent of any doctrine of natural law and natural rights," but argued that

> to eliminate the ideas of natural law and natural rights from the study of the question of the international protection of human rights is to renounce the faculty of understanding their growth in the course of history and their association with that law of nations which is now to become its ultimate sanction.[28]

In the course of creating the postwar human rights regime, and in particular in drafting the Universal Declaration of Human Rights, however, it became strategically advantageous to distance the contemporary international human rights project from the particularities of European history. This was necessary because of the ways in which arguments about human rights and humanitarian intervention had been deployed in past periods of world history as an excuse for European conquest and colonization. Dwelling extensively on the slave trade, which European international law had so long sanctioned, would hardly have advanced this goal of a fresh start.

Second, discussions of international courts and international criminal law in the era immediately before and after World War II were focused more on "crimes against peace" rather than "crimes against humanity," in ways that have almost been forgotten—though the recent review conference at which states participating in the International Criminal Court adopted a definition of the crime of aggression has revived interest in the central role played by "crimes against peace" at Nuremberg. The charter for the Nuremberg tribunal included "crimes against humanity," defined as "murder, extermination, enslavement, deportation, and other inhumane acts committed against any civilian population."[29] But these crimes were only treated as cognizable when committed in connection with the two other classes of crimes under the court's jurisdiction: war crimes and crimes against peace.

Discussions of international criminal law both immediately before and after Nuremberg focused on crimes against peace, or crimes that threatened peace. In the 1920s, there were proposals to create an international criminal court under the auspices of the League of Nations, and discussions mentioned the slave trade and piracy along with other offenses, such as war crimes.[30] The main focus, however, was on preventing warfare, and the proposal went nowhere. There was another proposal in 1937 for an international criminal tribunal to combat terrorism, which also focused on the potential for terrorist acts (specifically assassinations) to trigger wars. Although the treaty never entered into force, it was discussed throughout the years of the war, as in one 1942 article, "International Criminal Justice in Time of Peace."[31] Following the war, the issue was taken up again. As one article in 1950 on the possibility of a permanent international criminal court argued, international crimes could be divided into two categories: "crimes consisting of acts against the peace and security of mankind" and more ordinary crimes "such as piracy, slave trade, traffic in women and children."[32] The first group, it was argued, are internationally injurious . . . because they contribute to the preparation or conduct of a prohibited war, or to the violation of the laws and customs of war, or to the creation of situations likely to endanger peace, or finally because they conduce to the pursuit of a national policy revolting to the sentiments of mankind.[33]

The second group—things like the slave trade—the author believed were of less concern because they "do not prejudice international relations"[34] (a rather ironic conclusion if one takes into account the broad sweep of history). Thus, the author argued, with respect to these, "progress ought to take the form of generalization of the instances in which national courts already have extraterritorial jurisdiction in the direction of universal competence rather than in giving the international criminal court more jurisdiction than it can perhaps adequately handle."[35] In other words, international law ought to be primarily concerned with crimes that threatened to lead to international war, not other types of international offenses. Another article in 1952, "Proposal for an International Criminal Court," made a similar observation, distinguishing "piracy, banditry and breaches of the law of war and such offenses as slave-trading and cable-cutting" from "offenses against peace and humanity" such as "aggression, terrorism and genocide," which have a "political character" and are "initiated or stimulated by governments" and which are "the most important type of crime against the law of nations."[36] To put it bluntly, by the mid-twentieth century, the slave trade no longer seemed important. The millions killed by nation-states during the course of World War II seemed like a far bigger problem, and that was all anyone wanted to talk about. At the same time, the problem of decolonization in Africa likely made European countries reluctant to discuss the details of their past relations with the continent. The slave trade tribunals, and their contribution to the development of international law, were conveniently forgotten.

CHAPTER 9

International Human Rights Law and International Courts

Rethinking Their Origins and Future

At the dawn of the twenty-first century, international human rights law manages to generate both widespread support and deep skepticism. On the one hand, human rights are incredibly popular, even in unexpected quarters. In a 2008 survey of people in dozens of countries around the globe, more than 70 percent of respondents agreed that the United Nations should actively promote human rights in member states, notwithstanding concerns about national sovereignty, including large majorities in almost every country surveyed, which were as varied as Argentina, Russia, Kenya, China, Egypt, and the United States.[1] In the United States, even conservative Republicans celebrate Human Rights Day. In 2003, on the fifty-fifth anniversary of the adoption of the Universal Declaration of Human Rights by the UN General Assembly, then–U.S. President George W. Bush issued a proclamation in honor of Human Rights Day and stated, "Freedom is the right of mankind and the future of every nation. . . . It is God's gift to every man and woman who lives in this world."[2]

On the other hand, skepticism is unavoidable. Conservative radio talk show host Glenn Beck has argued that "anything with State Department and international law, they are all socialist, Marxist internationalists or a combination of all of them. . . . Once we sign our rights over to international law, the Constitution is officially dead."[3] More serious commentators express skepticism in equally strong if more measured terms; the title of one academic article summed up these critics by asking, "International Human Rights Law: Imperialist, Inept and Ineffective?"[4] Another article argues:

> international human rights treaties have had little or no impact on the actual practices of states. The Genocide Convention has not prevented genocides; the Torture Convention has not stopped torture. . . . States that already respect human rights join human rights treaties because doing so is costless for them. States that do not respect human rights simply ignore their treaty obligations.[5]

Others contend that the international human rights movement is "part of the problem"—Western, hegemonic, ineffective, hypocritical.[6]

One persistent criticism levied in American legal circles is that international human rights law is a novel and illegitimate invention of the twentieth century that is inconsistent with an originalist interpretation of the U.S. Constitution. For example, in a 2004 case concerning the use of the Alien Tort Statute of 1789 to bring civil lawsuits against human rights violators, Supreme Court Justice Antonin Scalia argued in his concurring opinion that:

> The notion that a law of nations, redefined to mean the consensus of states on *any* subject, can be used by a private citizen to control a sovereign's treatment of *its own citizens* within *its own territory* is a 20th-century invention of internationalist law professors and human rights advocates. . . . The Framers would, I am confident, be appalled by the proposition that, for example, the American peoples' democratic adoption of

the death penalty . . . could be judicially nullified because of the disapproving views of foreigners.[7]

Notwithstanding Justice Scalia's clairvoyant certainty that the Framers would be horrified by international human rights law, that body of law is not an "invention" of the mid-twentieth century but instead has deeper and more ancient roots. In part, it stems from the same ideas of natural rights that inspired and informed the American Revolution and the declaration by America's founders that all men were endowed "with certain unalienable Rights" that not only transcended the nation-state in which they found themselves but that entitled them to break free of a government that denied those rights. The same philosophers who posited the existence of a natural law that encompassed unalienable rights also saw the law of nations as part of that fabric of natural law transcending nation-states. During the nineteenth century, the United States and other nations agreed that they could voluntarily consent to make the behavior of their citizens on their ships the concern of other nations. And they accepted that the universal consent of all nations could make something a universally cognizable offense. To be sure, they were jealous of their sovereignty and emphasized the need for national consent to be bound by the international legal regime. But they accepted the legitimacy of international lawmaking focused on the rights of individuals and the shared interests of humanity in their protection; they did not consider human rights to be an illegitimate topic for treaty making.

The road from the *ius gentium* and *ius naturale* of ancient and medieval times through the laws of nations and natural rights of the Enlightenment to the international human rights law of the twentieth century crosses the path of slavery and the slave trade at numerous points in the nineteenth century, and these intersections are important for understanding the jurisprudential origins of international human rights law. Among other things, the history of the legal treatment of slavery sheds light on long-standing tensions between ideas of natural law and legal positivism (the idea that all laws must be traced to the formal acts of a sovereign), and between concepts of law that treat the nation-state as the primary (or even sole) source of law and concepts that include sources of law that potentially transcend individual nation-states.

The tension between ideas of natural law and legal positivism is one of the dominant, if deeply submerged, axes of debate in modern international law and international relations theory even today. International human rights law is sometimes still criticized for being too heavily based on natural law principles, which are seen as suspect in a secular, pluralistic world. What exactly is the source of the universality of the Universal Declaration of Human Rights? Defenders of international human rights will quickly point to that document's positivist credentials—its ratification without dissenting vote (though with a few abstentions) by the UN General Assembly in 1948. But to deny the Universal Declaration of Human Rights its moral underpinning is to deny it some of its force. The Universal Declaration of Human Rights is about right and wrong.

The secret puzzle of international law is that it is not just human rights law that has naturalistic underpinnings. Modern international law is strongly positivist in form, but once one goes beneath the surface, things become considerably more complex. The voluntary consent of sovereign states is said to be the basis of the international legal regime. The reason we have a United Nations is that almost every country in the world signed a treaty voluntarily creating the institution. Torture is illegal not because it is morally wrong nor because it is not useful, but rather because it is expressly outlawed in numerous treaties that have received nearly universal ratification and through the practice of states suggesting that they view torture as illegal. So too, with slavery and slave trafficking today. Certainly, the fact that national governments and the people who make them up believe torture and slavery are wrong or not useful may be one of the reasons why they have signed onto laws against these practices; but the moral (or utilitarian) arguments against them are said to have no legal force of their own. The authority of the Torture Convention is the authority of positive law.

Yet the emphasis on legal positivism conceals the normative choices underpinning the entire structure—for example, the decision to treat nation-states (rather than individual people or communities of people grouped in some other way) as the building blocks of the legal order, and to give those states certain rights, such as territorial exclusivity and absolute equality with other states in terms of their formal legal rights. To be sure, these foundational assumptions are "positive" in the sense that they track the world as it actually exists; despite loose talk about the end of sovereignty and the irrelevance of national borders in the age of jet travel, nuclear weapons, and the Internet, states are still the basic building blocks of the international community. But the argument that sovereign states have a right to torture people is just as normative as the argument that people have the right not to be tortured.

Given how central the tension between normative and positive argument is to modern international legal theory, it is illuminating to see how these tensions played out over centuries of philosophical development concerning the status of slavery and the slave trade. Moreover, giving the antislavery courts and treaties the central place they deserve in the international human rights law narrative changes that narrative in important ways. Compared to the post–World War II, Nuremberg-centric story, an understanding of international human rights law that begins with the antislavery movement places a much greater emphasis on nonstate actors—both the slave traders who were the human rights violators and the civil society leaders of the abolitionist movements in various countries. While Nuremberg was concerned with individual criminal liability, it was focused on crimes committed at the behest of nation-states; indeed, crimes against humanity were only recognized at Nuremberg to the extent they were perpetrated in connection with the crime of aggressive war that was the principal basis for the court's jurisdiction.

Modern international courts like the International Criminal Tribunals for the former Yugoslavia (ICTY) and Rwanda (ICTR) have likewise focused on crimes committed in armed conflict by individuals who are either affiliated with the state or who aspire to statehood. As shown by the work of these modern courts, the paradigmatic international trial is still based on the Nuremberg model: individual leaders are charged with responsibility for acts of mass slaughter and mistreatment of civilian populations in the context of warfare. Nuremberg is a powerful and important precedent, but it has a somewhat limiting effect on the scope of conduct that we imagine falls within the realm of international concern and redress.

Reviving the centrality of private transnational actors to the history of international human rights law's origins highlights the possibility of making international legal mechanisms a more central tool for addressing human rights violations by private actors today. What about nonstate terrorist organizations that commit war crimes and crimes against humanity, or individuals and businesses engaged in contemporary forms of forced labor trafficking? This would represent a dramatic shift in the focus of international human rights law and activism. Most of the debate about the International Criminal Court (ICC), for example, focuses on its role in preventing and punishing acts of state-sanctioned violence and the threat to state sovereignty posed by international prosecutions of national government officials.[8] Comparatively little attention has been given to the possibility of using an international court to address terrorism by nonstate actors,[9] human trafficking, or the role of corporations in grave human rights abuses. Indeed, as Philip Alston points out, nonstate actors have sometimes been viewed as falling outside the primary scope of international human rights law, which focuses on states themselves.[10] And yet, the antislavery story told here suggests that one of the most suitable uses for international courts may be combating illegal action by nonstate, transnational actors. Why not, for example, consider using an international court to address modern issues of slave labor and human trafficking with transnational dimensions?

Moreover, the history of the slave trade treaties casts doubt on the recent assertions by some commentators and courts that corporations are immune from international human rights law.[11] Joint stock companies, the earliest forms of corporations, played an important role in the early slave trade.[12] The involvement of joint stock companies in the slave trade dramatically declined after the trade was banned, and the trade shifted to smaller operators. At least one ship owned by a joint stock company was condemned by the international slave trade tribunals in the 1830s.[13] In that case, the judges noted that the joint stock company's willingness to engage in the trade was evidence of the slackness of local authorities in enforcing the slave trade ban. Joint stock companies clearly believed that the treaties banning the slave trade applied to them; otherwise, an easy way to avoid the ban would have been simply to incorporate.[14]

The history of the antislavery treaties also underscores the potential for the dissemination of human rights ideology across national borders, both through networks of nonstate actors and through the mediating force of international law and international legal institutions. In the nineteenth century, Quakers on both sides of the Atlantic spread the ideology of antislavery beyond their sect; in the twenty-first century, secular NGOs in conjunction with evangelical Christians seek to influence foreign policy on human rights issues such as genocide in the Sudan, sex trafficking, and the AIDS pandemic.[15]

Giving the antislavery courts their rightful place in the international human rights narrative also broadens the focus of that narrative beyond states' relationships with their own citizens to include the relationships between citizens of more developed and less developed countries. The principal conceptual innovation of Nuremberg and the postwar human rights regime was ostensibly to move international law beyond its preoccupation with state-to-state relations; the Nuremberg prosecutions pierced the veil of sovereignty and made a state's treatment of its own citizens a proper concern for international law.[16] This was certainly an important development. But many of the most pressing contemporary human rights problems do not involve states' treatment of their citizens, but rather the obligations, if any, of citizens in wealthy countries to those in less developed countries.[17] Forty-four percent of people in sub-Saharan Africa live on less than one dollar per day.[18] Some 824 million people in the developing world live with chronic hunger.[19] Roughly 2 million people in sub-Saharan Africa die of AIDS each year.[20] And each year half a million children worldwide still die of the measles, even though vaccination against that disease is one of the most cost-effective public health measures.[21]

To be sure, few if any of these problems are susceptible to resolution by international courts. But most will require some form of coordinated international action. To those who think that it is impossible that citizens of developed countries should ever care enough about people on the other side of the world to devote significant resources to these problems, the abolition of the slave trade stands as a stark counterexample. People did care. Nations did cooperate. And in the span of a human life, the transatlantic slave trade was extinguished.

In addition, close examination of the history of the abolition of the slave trade should cause international legal scholars to rethink the relationship between power, ideas, and international legal institutions. To the extent that the treaties against the slave trade and the mixed courts were effective, it was in no small part because Britain was willing to use its substantial economic and military power to support them. At the same time, the international legal regime gave Britain's use of its economic and military power a legitimacy that it would have otherwise lacked, and it amplified Britain's ability to influence other nations' conduct with regard to the slave trade. Once other nations had agreed in principle to the immorality of the slave trade, it was difficult for them to overtly oppose efforts to suppress that trade.

Moreover, Britain was able to project its momentary power at the end of the Napoleonic Wars far into the future by creating permanent international legal mechanisms that operated for decades to come in support of its abolitionist agenda. In the immediate aftermath of the Napoleonic Wars in 1817, Britain perhaps had the military power to seize Portuguese and Spanish slave ships whether or not those nations agreed. But because of the treaties, Britain was able to continue to seize their ships twenty years later in 1837, an exercise of power it might not otherwise have been willing or able to carry out in the absence of the treaties. Over time, Britain was even able to persuade more powerful countries like France and the United States to join in the increasingly universal international legal regime against the slave trade, something that might not have been possible without the initial treaties. Moreover, even when Britain subsequently engaged in somewhat dubious unilateral actions against the slave trade, it was at least able to argue that those actions were justified under the spirit of the treaties, forestalling a more vigorous opposition from the affected countries.

The potential for a mutually beneficial and reinforcing relationship between state power and international law is missing from many contemporary theories. Most theories of international adjudication assume that because of the absence of world government, international courts are by definition powerless institutions with no hard enforcement powers, dependent instead on the negative reputational consequences that noncompliance with the courts' decisions might have.[22] For proponents of international courts, this assumption leads to a tendency to discount the importance of state power and to focus instead on factors that magnify or reduce the reputational consequences of court decisions. For skeptics of international courts, this assumption causes doubt about the efficacy of international adjudication. Ironically, both arguments are wrong, or at least incomplete. Both sides overlook the possibility that powerful individual states might have the incentive and ability to enforce the judgments of international courts, and that such actions might be perceived as more acceptable and legitimate by other states than would unilateral action by those same powerful nations.[23]

The role of state power in supporting international courts does not appear to be entirely unique to the antislavery courts. Indeed, a similar lesson can be seen in the experience of the ICTY. After its creation by the UN Security Council, the ICTY indicted war criminals from the former Yugoslavia. The ICTY itself lacked enforcement power, but many of those war criminals were apprehended by NATO forces. Others, like Slobodan Milošević, were handed over to the tribunal in response to a combination of threats and bribes related to foreign aid.[24] Just as with the antislavery courts, the ICTY's success has been tied to the willingness of particular nations to use their economic and military power to support its legal work. In turn, the ICTY's legal mandate has given greater legitimacy to the involvement of NATO and the EU over many years in what would otherwise be considered the domestic affairs of the Balkan countries.

Certainly, national governments' use of economic and military powers to buttress international court judgments would not be effective or plausible for all international dispute resolution bodies. Moreover, such actions might be highly troubling in some circumstances, especially to the extent that they undermined the equality of nations by amplifying differences in state power. There is a fine line between using power to support international institutions and abusing power through international institutions.

But fraught as it is, the relationship between international courts and national economic and military enforcement powers is an area that deserves greater study by international legal academics, and greater consideration by policymakers.

The history of the antislavery courts is not only a story of military and economic power, however, but also a story about the power of ideas. Those who are realistic about state power often underestimate the extent to which ideology can affect human behavior and the behavior of the nation-states made up of those very same humans. Britain's multidecade campaign against the slave trade demonstrates the fact that nations can be influenced by moral ideas as well as material self-interest.

Constructivist international relations scholars, among others, have highlighted the potential of transnational networks and international legal regimes for influencing state behavior by influencing state perceptions of self-interest. Abolitionism appears to have taken hold in Britain largely as a result of domestic social and political forces, but abolitionism's spread to so many countries around the world in a short period of time is less well-explained.[25] A detailed analysis of the way in which the ideology of abolition took root in many disparate slave-holding societies requires in-depth study of social history that is beyond the scope of this book. But the narrative recounted here at least suggests the possibility that it was no mere coincidence of social conditions in different countries or even transnational networks of nonstate actors that fostered the spread of abolitionist ideology. Instead, at least some small role was played by international treaties and international courts themselves.

Certainly, those who were most closely involved in the negotiation and enforcement of the antislavery treaties thought so. Palmerston, for example, argued that "the efforts of this country to engage other governments in co-operating for the suppression of the slave trade have very much tended to awaken a moral feeling in other countries upon that subject."[26] When Britain bribed Spain, Portugal, and Brazil to sign the antislavery treaties, it is not clear that either elites or a majority of the population in each of these nations believed what the treaties said— that the traffic in slaves was unjust and inhumane.[27] Yet by the time the slave trade was finally suppressed some fifty years later, the Brazilian foreign minister felt that "'the whole of the civilised world'" was convinced of its immorality.[28] Changes in domestic attitudes were critical to the final suppression of the slave trade. The possibility that the universality of the antislavery treaty regime may have played some part in this shift in attitudes is at least worthy of further investigation.

In terms of academic theories of international law and relations, the slave trade abolition story presents something of a challenge to the major theoretical schools. Some elements support each theory, but they have difficulty explaining others. Realists and neorealists will tend to focus on the material self-interest of Britain; the fact that weak countries like Spain, Portugal, and Brazil joined the treaties while powerful countries like the United States and France did not for many years; Britain's use of its hegemonic military and economic power to achieve its goals; and the coincidence of the suppression of the slave trade with the national self-interest of each country that abolished it. In the realists' view, international law is a mere epiphenomenal artifact of the underlying power dynamics—though realists have a hard time explaining why nations go to the trouble of creating international law if that is true.[29] Those skeptical of the adequacy of the explanatory power of realism will point to the substantial evidence that Britain's actions harmed, rather than helped, its material position in the world. They will note that the cash payments and other benefits given by Britain to Spain, Portugal, and Brazil likely did not begin to compensate them for the total economic costs of the abolition of the slave trade and then slavery itself. And they will observe that the coercion Britain actually brought to bear—for example, a few shots fired by ships in Brazilian territorial waters, with no real commitment to war—was trivial compared to the change in policy it elicited. Institutionalists will likely see the treaties and the court system they created as rational, utility-maximizing mechanisms for cooperation.[30] In the absence of such mechanisms, even a state that wanted to abolish the slave trade would be tempted to defect to gain material advantage, but the regime created the opportunity for cooperation and thus mutual long-term gains for all participants.[31] Liberal international relations theorists will be more interested in the ways domestic politics and interest groups shaped British foreign policy. Constructivists, as I have noted, will be interested in the way in which state interests were constructed and reconstructed by their interactions.[32] Postcolonialists might view the entire enterprise as a by-product of European desire to establish economically viable colonies in Africa. And so forth.

There is some measure of truth in each of these theories, and yet each is necessarily reductionist. It is fashionable among legal academics to propound grand unified theories, and such theories have their value. Yet there remains a case to be made for thick descriptions of complex events and acknowledgment of the fact that no one theory can fully explain something as dramatic as the global abolition of the slave trade and then of slavery itself, let alone predict future changes in global society of a similar scale.[33] The history of the antislavery courts told purely through the lens of realism, neorealism, institutionalism, rational choice, institutional liberalism, constructivism, or any other "ism" would be an impoverished one, and so I do not claim that it entirely supports any one of these theories, or any novel grand unified theory of my own invention. But champions of existing theories do need to grapple with the complexities, and contradictions, presented by this history.

Beyond the realm of theory, one can find in the history of the abolition of the slave trade echoes of many contemporary debates in foreign policy, such as the efforts by some powerful countries to promote democracy and human rights in various societies around the world. Is it true, as Lord Castlereagh suggested, that "[m]orals were never well taught by the sword"?[34] Is it only the sword that works? Or is it possible, as Palmerston argued, that a combination of military force, international law, and moral persuasion is most effective?

The very different circumstances of the world two centuries ago cannot give us answers to these questions, but they provide food for thought as we contemplate them today. Palmerston's view suggests that instead of viewing international courts solely as a threat to their sovereignty and independence, powerful countries should consider the extent to which international courts can be a vital tool for adding legitimacy to their actions and entrenching norms they support. Why is it, for example, that the U.S. government has at times perceived the ICC primarily as a threat to its own independence rather than as a potentially valuable tool for advancing human rights, democracy, and the rule of law—goals that it has repeatedly characterized as the centerpiece of its current foreign policy? At a moment when U.S. military and economic power is at a peak (and a peak that seems unlikely to last forever as China's 1.3 billion people and India's 1.1 billion people move toward full economic development), the United States should consider projecting that power into the future by creating and supporting stable international legal institutions rather than fostering a world order based on power alone.

Finally, the history of the abolition of the slave trade suggests that the time horizon of many international legal scholars and practitioners is simply too short. Today, some observers of the ICC suggest that it is doomed to fail because the United States is not a participant. The same might have been said about the antislavery courts during the forty-five years before the United States finally joined the treaty regime. The analogy might seem not quite apt because the United States was not the global superpower in the 1800s that it is today. But though not yet a global hegemon, the United States was significant as a large slave-holding society with an important commercial and military maritime presence. Nor is the ICC the equivalent of the antislavery courts without the British; the ICC does, after all, enjoy the support of more than 100 countries, including the richest and most powerful countries in the European Union. For many of the international courts that were greeted with such fanfare in the post–cold war optimism of the 1990s, and that are now dismissed in the neorealist pessimism of the post–September 11 world, it may simply be too early to judge.

At the end of the day, the story of the abolition of the slave trade is a hopeful one for international law, for human rights, and for humanity. In 1762, Rousseau famously wrote, "Man was born free; and everywhere he is in chains."[35] A century later—after many statutes had been passed, many treaties had been signed, many cases had been adjudicated, several wars had been fought, and millions of minds had been changed on the morality of slavery and the slave trade—those chains were broken.

ACKNOWLEDGMENTS

Portions of several chapters of this book are based on Jenny S. Martinez, "Anti-Slavery Courts and the Dawn of International Human Rights Law," *Yale Law Journal* 117 (2008): 550, and portions of chapter 3 and to a lesser extent chapter 6 are based on Jenny S. Martinez, "International Courts and the Constitution: Reexamining the History," *University of Pennsylvania Law Review* 159 (2011): 1069. These portions are used pursuant to the author's publication agreements with those journals. I also thank the student editors at those journals for all their valuable comments.

I am grateful to so many people for their help in this project: my research assistants, including Jim Alexander, Marilie Coetsee, Hugh Gorman, Anne Hamilton, Kara Kapp, Sophia Lee, Sophia Lin Lakin, Nicolas Martinez, Alexander Weber, and D. J. Wolff; the amazing staff of the Stanford Law Library, including (but not limited to) Paul Lomio, Sonia Moss, Rich Porter, Sergio Stone, and Erica Wayne. Amy Applebaum, who secretly runs Stanford Law School, provided me with food and moral support at critical moments. My assistant Judy Dearing is a genius with manuscripts, and I am very grateful to her, and to Pat Adan and Ginny Turner for additional administrative support. I am also grateful to my dean, Larry Kramer, and to the Stanford University Presidential Fund for Innovation in International Studies, which provided research funding. In addition, I owe a debt to the many colleagues at Stanford and elsewhere who have commented on the project at various points. First and foremost are my coinvestigators on the Stanford Presidential fund grant for our project on courts, politics, and human rights: Josh Cohen, Terry Karl, and Helen Stacy. Other colleagues here and elsewhere who have provided invaluable advice and comments at various points include Curtis Bradley, Allison Danner, William Dodge, David Eltis, Lawrence Friedman, David Golove, Tom Grey, Laurence Helfer, Daniel Hulsebosch, Oona Hathaway, Chimene Keitner, Mark Kelman, Amalia Kessler, Harold Koh, David Luban, Martha Minow, Eric Posner, Jack Rakove, Judith Resnik, Deborah Rhode, Richard Steinberg, Priya Satia, Lisa Surwillo, Beth Van Schaack, Robert Weisberg, and John Witt. Thanks are also due to participants in the following conferences and workshops: the Newberry Library conference, The Law of Nations in the Early Modern Atlantic; the Omohundro Institute Conference, Domestic and International Consequences of the First Governmental Efforts to Abolish the Atlantic Slave Trade; the Stanford Division of Literatures, Cultures and Languages conference, Treating the Trata After 1808: The Historiography of Ignorance and the Spanish Slave Trade; the UCLA International Law Workshop; the Yale Law and Globalization Workshop; the Columbia Law and History Workshop; the Stanford Global Justice Workshop; and the Stanford Law School faculty workshop. The anonymous reviewers for Oxford University Press also provided valuable comments. Thanks are also due to my editor, David McBride, to Alexandra Dauler at Oxford University Press, and to the Strothman Agency.

But I am most grateful to my family. To my husband, David Graham, and my children Alyse, Patrice, and Nancy for their infinite patience with me (infinite!), and for making me coffee. I love you, my tribe. To my dad, Tomas Martinez, for his lively suggestions on title and artwork. To my mother-in-law, Sheila McCrea, and my Aunt Nancy for traveling with all of my small children and me to England on an archives trip (with a special medal of valor to Aunt Nancy for the flight home with us). And most of all to my mom, Susanne Martinez, who went to

England with me not once but twice and most memorably accompanied me to the archives in Kew Garden, outside London, while I was pregnant with Alyse. She sat beside me reading handwritten court records, just in case I went into labor. Since she is a very accomplished lawyer, I called her my most overqualified research assistant ever. But mostly, she is my hero and inspiration. I love you, Mom.

NOTES

CHAPTER 1

1. John Baker and John Evans, Statement, Being the Substance of a Conversation Held by the Undersigned, with Captain Kearney, Late of the Royal African Corps, and Now on Half-Pay, Residing Chiefly at Cape Shilling, on the Coast of Africa, 14 January 1820, in 2. *Further Papers Relating to the Suppression of the Slave Trade. Viz: A. Copies or Extracts of All Communications Received by the Lord Commissioners of the Admiralty, from the Naval Officers Stationed on the Coast of Africa, or in the West Indies, Since 1st of January 1820; Relative to the State of the Slave Trade; B. Copies or Extracts of All Instructions Issued by the Lords Commissioners of the Admiralty to Naval Officers, Since the 1st of January 1819; Relative to the Suppression of the Slave Trade,* 13, House of Commons Parliamentary Papers Online (2006), ProQuest (366) (hereafter cited as *Communications from and Instructions to Naval Officers, 1819–20*), http://gateway.proquest.com/openurl?url_ver=Z39.88-2004&res_dat=xri:hcpp-us&rft_dat=xri:hcpp:fulltext:1821-007497:13.

2. Hugh Thomas, *The Slave Trade: The Story of the Atlantic Slave Trade, 1440–1870* (New York: Simon and Schuster, 1997), 582–83 (discussing the use of Baltimore clippers in the slave trade); W. E. F. Ward, *The Royal Navy and the Slavers* (New York: Pantheon, 1969), 60–61. See also David Eltis, *Economic Growth and the Ending of the Transatlantic Slave Trade* (Oxford: Oxford University Press, 1987), 128–31 (discussing time trends in sizes of slave ships).

3. Ward, *The Royal Navy*, 101.

4. John Baker and John Evans, Statement, Being the Substance of a Conversation Held by the Undersigned, with Captain Kearney, Late of the Royal African Corps, and Now on Half-Pay, Residing Chiefly at Cape Shilling, on the Coast of Africa, 14 January 1820, in *Communications from and Instructions to Naval Officers, 1819–20*, 13.

5. Bernard Edwards, *Royal Navy Versus the Slave Traders: Enforcing Abolition at Sea 1808–1898* (Barnsley, UK: Pen and Sword Maritime, 2007), 85.

6. George William St. John Mildmay, Lieutenant of the H.M.S. Mildmay, to Commodore Sir. R. Mends, Kt., 16 April 1822, Enclosure in Commodore Sir. R. Mends, Kt. to John Wilson Croker, Esq., 17 April 1822, in *Further Papers Relating to the Slave Trade: Viz. Copies, Or Extracts, of Correspondence, from March 1822, Between the Board of Admiralty and Naval Officers, Relating to the Slave Trade*, 8, House of Commons Parliamentary Papers Online (2006), ProQuest (544) (hereafter cited as *Communications from and Instructions to Naval Officers, Relative to Suppression of Slave Trade: 1822–23*), http://gateway.proquest.com/openurl?url_ver=Z39.88-2004&res_dat=xri:hcpp-us&rft_dat=xri:hcpp:fulltext:1823-008706:7.
7. In some reports, the ship's name is spelled *Ycanam* or even *Yeanam*, and the *Vecua* is spelled *Becua*. I use the spelling from the court records.
8. See M. Ferrer to Mr. Aston, 16 February 1841, First Enclosure in Arthur Aston to Viscount Palmerston, 23 February 1841, in Class B. Correspondence with Spain, Portugal, Brazil, the Netherlands, Sweden, and the Argentine Confederation, Relative to the Slave Trade. From 1 January to 31 December 1841 Inclusive, pp. 10–12, House of Commons Parliamentary Papers Online (2005), ProQuest (403), http://gateway.proquest.com/openurl?url_ver=Z39.88-2004&res_dat=xri:hcpp-us&rft_dat=xri:hcpp:fulltext:1842-020663:32.
9. George William St. John Mildmay, Lieutenant of the H.M.S. Mildmay, to Commodore Sir. R. Mends, Kt., 16 April 1822, Enclosure in Commodore Sir. R. Mends, Kt. to John Wilson Croker, Esq., 17 April 1822, in *Communications from and Instructions to Naval Officers, Relative to Suppression of Slave Trade: 1822–23*, 7, http://gateway.proquest.com/openurl?url_ver=Z39.88-2004&res_dat=xri:hcpp-us&rft_dat=xri:hcpp:fulltext:1823-008706:7.
10. Herbert A. St. John Mildmay, *A Brief Memoir of the Mildmay Family* (London and New York: privately printed by John Lane the Bodley Head, 1908), 215–16.
11. Cases of the Spanish Schooners Vecua and Icanam, First Enclosure in E. Gregory and Edward Fitzgerald to the Marquess of Londonderry, 24 July 1822, in *Class B. Correspondence with the British Commissioners, at Sierra Leone, the Havannah, Rio de Janeiro, and Surinam, Relating to the Slave Trade, 1822, 1823*, 30, House of Commons Parliamentary Papers Online (2005), ProQuest (008), http://gateway.proquest.com/openurl?url_ver=Z39.88-2004&res_dat=xri:hcpp-us&rft_dat=xri:hcpp:fulltext:1823-008717:38.
12. George William St. John Mildmay, Lieutenant of the H.M.S. Mildmay, to Commodore Sir. R. Mends, Kt., 16 April 1822, Enclosure in

Commodore Sir. R. Mends, Kt. to John Wilson Croker, Esq., 17 April 1822, in *Communications from and Instructions to Naval Officers, Relative to Suppression of Slave Trade: 1822–23*, 8, http://gateway.proquest.com/openurl?url_ver=Z39.88-2004&res_dat=xri:hcpp-us&rft_dat=xri:hcpp:fulltext:1823-008706:8.

13. Commodore Sir. R. Mends, Kt. to John Wilson Croker, Esq., 17 April 1822, in *Communications from and Instructions to Naval Officers, Relative to Suppression of Slave Trade: 1822–23*, 7, http://gateway.proquest.com/openurl?url_ver=Z39.88-2004&res_dat=xri:hcpp-us&rft_dat=xri:hcpp:fulltext:1823-008706:7.

14. Ibid.

15. E. Gregory and Edward Fitzgerald to the Marquess of Londonderry, 24 July 1822, in *Class B. Correspondence with the British Commissioners, at Sierra Leone, the Havannah, Rio de Janeiro, and Surinam, Relating to the Slave Trade, 1822, 1823*, 61, House of Commons Parliamentary Papers Online (2005), ProQuest (008), http://gateway.proquest.com/openurl?url_ver=Z39.88-2004&res_dat=xri:hcpp-us&rft_dat=xri:hcpp:fulltext:1823-008717:69.

16. Ibid.

17. "The Slave Trade," *The Bury and Norwich Post*, August 14, 1822.

18. As noted, there is somewhat conflicting evidence about what happened to the French ships. One secondary source, relying on an article in the *Times* on August 26, 1822, suggests that all were released upon reaching England. Edwards, *Royal Navy Versus the Slave Traders*, 87–88. On the other hand, a publication from 1824 suggests at least some of them were condemned at Nantes. Committee Appointed by the Religious Society of Friends, to Aid in Promoting the Total Abolition of the Slave-Trade, *Statements Illustrative of the Nature of the Slave Trade. To Which Are Subjoined Some Particulars Respecting the Colony at Sierra Leone* (London: Harvey, Darton, & Co., 1824), 17–19. The Trans-Atlantic Slave Trade Database, relying on several sources, suggests that the *Ursule* was released by the vice-admiralty court in Sierra Leone, while the *Vigilante* and the *Petite Betsy* were condemned by a French tribunal in France. Given that the database relies on several primary sources, this seems most likely to be accurate. See Voyages Database, Trans-Atlantic Slave Trade Database, http://www.slavevoyages.org, s.v. "Voyage 2733, Ursule, 1822," "Voyage 2734, Vigilante, 1822," "Voyage 2735, Petite Betsy, 1822," all accessed February 21, 2011.

19. Abstract of the Case of the Portuguese Polacca, Esperanza Felix, Joaquim Jose Brito Lima, Master, 24 July 1822, Enclosure in E. Gregory and Edward Fitzgerald to the Marquess of Londonderry, 24 July 1822,

in *Class B. Correspondence with the British Commissioners, at Sierra Leone, the Havannah, Rio de Janeiro, and Surinam, Relating to the Slave Trade, 1822, 1823*, 62, House of Commons Parliamentary Papers Online (2005), ProQuest (008), http://gateway.proquest.com/openurl?url_ver=Z39.88-2004&res_dat=xri:hcpp-us&rft_dat=xri:hcpp:fulltext:1823-008717:70.

20. Ibid.
21. Ibid.
22. "A Second Narrative of Samuel Ajayi Crowther's Early Life," *Bulletin of the Society for African Church History* 2 (1965): 6 (transcription of letter from Samuel Crowther to Captain Bird Allen, 3 September 1841).
23. Ibid.
24. Ibid., 7.
25. Ibid., 9.
26. Ibid., 13.
27. Ibid.
28. Ibid., 14.
29. See "Consecration of Three Bishops in Canterbury Cathedral," *The Standard* (London, England), June 30, 1864.
30. Jesse Page, *Samuel Crowther: The Slave Boy Who Became Bishop of the Niger*, 4th ed. (New York: Fleming H. Revell, 1892), 118.
31. "The Late Admiral Sir Henry John Leeke, K.C.B., K.H.," *The Derby Mercury* (Derby, England), March 9, 1870.
32. "Local Topics, the Niger Mission," *The Derby Mercury* (Derby, England), April 23, 1873 (noting that Crowther said he was indebted to the "gallant" Leeke "not only for freedom from bodily slavery but from the slavery of sin and Satan").

CHAPTER 2

1. See generally David Brion Davis, *The Problem of Slavery in Western Culture* (Ithaca, NY: Cornell University Press, 1966).
2. Thomas Clarkson, *The History of the Rise, Progress, and Accomplishment of the Abolition of the African Slave Trade by the British Parliament* (London: Longman, Hurst, Reed, and Orme, 1808), 1:84 (quoting David Hartley).
3. *Substance of the Debates on a Resolution for Abolishing the Slave Trade* (London: Philips and Fardon, 1806), 99 (statement of Lord Grenville).
4. Thomas Jefferson, statement to Congress, 2 December 1806, in *A Compilation of the Messages and Papers of the Presidents*, ed. James D. Richardson, vol. 1 (New York: Bureau of National Literature, 1897), 396; see also W. E. Burghardt DuBois, *The Suppression of the African*

Slave-Trade to the United States of America, 1638–1870 (New York: Longmans, Green, 1896), 80 (quoting petitions for the abolition of the slave trade to the United States that describe the trade as "an outrageous violation of one of the most essential rights of human nature" and "degrading to the rights of man"); Executive Committee of the American Antislavery Society, *Slavery and the Internal Slave Trade in the United States of North America* (photo. repr., London: Thomas Ward, 1841), 162 (referring to "the cause of human rights"). This view of the slave trade as a human rights issue was carried on through the later part of the nineteenth century, as when Yale college president Theodore Dwight Woolsey's 1860 edition of *Introduction to the Study of International Law* explained that under the "correct views of human rights" slavery was a status unprotected by the law of nations and that "new views of men's rights" had led to the prohibition of the slave trade in international law. Theodore D. Woolsey, *Introduction to the Study of International Law* (Boston: James Munroe, 1860), 316–17.

5. See Robert M. Cover, *Justice Accused: Antislavery and the Judicial Process* (New Haven, CT: Yale University Press, 1975), 8–30. As Cover notes, jurists in England and the United States during the eighteenth and nineteenth centuries had sometimes conflicting and incompletely theorized views of the relationship between natural law, statutory law, the common law, and the law of nations. Slavery was a particularly complicated case, because although originally seen by some philosophers as a natural part of the order of the world (and perhaps even mandated by God), over time other philosophers came to view it as contrary to natural law. At the same time, slavery was sanctioned by the Roman predecessor of the law of nations, the *ius gentium*. As early as the third century, the Roman jurist Ulpian pointed out slavery as the sole example of a conflict between the *jus naturale* and the *jus gentium*, a contradiction that was later recognized by Justinian. Davis, *The Problem of Slavery in Western Culture*, 83.

6. Richard McKeon, ed., *The Basic Works of Aristotle* (New York: Random House, 1941), 1132.

7. Ibid., 1130–31.

8. Lloyd Weinreb, *Natural Law and Justice* (Cambridge, MA: Harvard University Press, 1987), 45; Francis Zulueta, trans., *The Institutes of Gaius* (Oxford: Clarendon Press, 1946), 1:3 ("the law that natural reason establishes among all mankind . . . is called *ius gentium* [law of nations]").

9. Davis, *The Problem of Slavery in Western Culture*, 83; Weinreb, *Natural Law*, 45–46. See, e.g., Florentinus, *The Digest of Justinian*, ed. Alan

Watson (Philadelphia: University of Pennsylvania Press, 1998), 1.5.4.1 ("Slavery is an institution of the *jus gentium*, whereby someone is against nature made subject to the ownership of another").

10. Hugo Grotius, *The Rights of War and Peace*, trans. A. C. Campbell (Washington: M. Walter Dunne, 1901), 346.
11. Ibid.
12. Ibid., 346–47.
13. Peter Laslett, *Locke's Two Treatises of Government: A Critical Edition with an Introduction and Apparatus Criticus*, 2nd ed. (Cambridge: Cambridge University Press, 1967), 159.
14. Davis, *The Problem of Slavery in Western Culture*, 119–20.
15. Baron de Montesquieu, *The Spirit of Laws*, trans. Thomas Nugent, ed. J. V. Prichard (Littleton, CO: Fred B. Rothman, 1991), 1:253.
16. Ibid., 1:257.
17. Jean Jacques Rousseau, *Rousseau's Political Writings*, trans. and ed. Julia Bondanella, and ed. Alan Ritter (New York: W. W. Norton, 1988), 88–91.
18. Ibid., 89.
19. Ibid.
20. Ibid., 91.
21. Emerich de Vattel, *The Law of Nations; or, Principles of the Law of Nature, Applied to the Conduct and Affairs of Nations and Sovereigns*, trans. and ed. Joseph Chitty (Philadelphia: T. & J. W. Johnson, 1852), 356.
22. Ibid.
23. Ibid.
24. David Brion Davis, *The Problem of Slavery in the Age of Revolution, 1770–1823* (Ithaca, NY: Cornell University Press, 1999), 485 (quoting Blackstone).
25. *Somerset v. Stewart*, (1772) 98 Eng. Rep. 499 (K.B.). For a discussion of similar cases in French courts, see Sue Peabody, *"There Are No Slaves in France": The Political Culture of Race and Slavery in the Ancien Régime* (New York: Oxford University Press, 1996).
26. Adam Hochschild, *Bury the Chains: Prophets and Rebels in the Fight to Free an Empire's Slaves* (Boston: Houghton Mifflin, 2005), 48–51 (describing the role of abolitionists in bringing Somerset's case).
27. *Somerset*, 98 Eng. Rep. at 502.
28. Ibid., 510. For a discussion of the natural law underpinnings of *Somerset* and other antislavery cases, see Cover, *Justice Accused*, 8–30.
29. *Somerset*, 98 Eng. Rep. at 509.
30. Hochschild, *Bury the Chains*, 233–34.
31. Ibid., 241–55.

32. See Act to Prevent the Importation of Slaves, 1806, 46 Geo. 3, c. 52 (Eng.).

33. Hochschild, *Bury the Chains*, 302–3; Seymour Drescher, "Whose Abolition? Popular Pressure and the Ending of the British Slave Trade," *Past and Present* no. 143 (1994): 141–42.

34. Drescher, "Whose Abolition?" 142.

35. Ibid., 142–44.

36. Ibid., 145–48.

37. Act for the Abolition of the Slave Trade, 1807, 47 Geo. 3, c. 36 (Eng.) (repealed 1824).

38. See David Eltis, "The Nineteenth-Century Transatlantic Slave Trade: An Annual Time Series of Imports into the Americas Broken Down by Region," *Hispanic American Historical Review* 67, no. 1 (1987): 136, table V.

39. Peabody, *"There Are No Slaves in France,"* 23–40, 88–93. Alarm about the number of blacks in Paris, however, led Louis XVI to enact a measure in 1777 prohibiting the entry of new blacks (free or slave) into France, requiring the registration of those already present, and prohibiting the admiralty court from hearing any further freedom petitions. The new law was not well enforced, and the admiralty court began granting freedom petitions again as early as 1778. See ibid., 120–33.

40. Davis, *The Problem of Slavery in the Age of Revolution*, 29.

41. Ibid., 29–31.

42. Warren S. Howard, *American Slavers and the Federal Law, 1837–1862* (Berkeley: University of California Press, 1963), 25–27.

43. Article I, Section 9 of the U.S. Constitution reflected a compromise between northern and southern states and provided that "[t]he Migration or Importation of such Persons as any of the States now existing shall think proper to admit, shall not be prohibited by the Congress prior to the Year one thousand eight hundred and eight."

44. See Eltis, "Nineteenth-Century Transatlantic Slave Trade," 136, table V.

45. DuBois, *Suppression of the African Slave-Trade*, 108–9.

46. Leslie Bethell, *The Abolition of the Brazilian Slave Trade* (Cambridge: Cambridge University Press, 1970), 6 (noting that the Portuguese foreign minister responded to British overtures about banning the slave trade in 1807 by saying it was "utterly impracticable" for Portugal even to discourage, let alone ban, the slave trade).

47. Tara Helfman, "Note, the Court of Vice Admiralty at Sierra Leone and the Abolition of the West African Slave Trade," *Yale Law Journal* 115 (2006): 1122.

48. *The Amedie*, (1810) 12 Eng. Rep. 92 (P.C.).

49. Ibid., 96.
50. Ibid.
51. Ibid.
52. Ibid., 96–97.
53. Ibid., 97.
54. Ibid., 92. Under prevailing practice in the nineteenth century, the proceeds from a ship condemned as a prize were shared between the government and the crew of the ship that made the capture. The precise division of the proceeds was set by statute and was changed from time to time.
55. For other cases, see, e.g., *Donna Marianna*, (1812) 165 Eng. Rep. 1244 (Adm. Ct.); *Fortuna*, (1811) 165 Eng. Rep. 1240 (Adm. Ct.); *Africa*, (1810) 12 Eng. Rep. 156 (P.C.); and *Anne*, (1810) 12 Eng. Rep. 158 (P.C.). See also Helfman, "Court of Vice Admiralty," 1122 (discussing cases tried before the vice-admiralty court in Sierra Leone).
56. Christopher Lloyd, *The Navy and the Slave Trade*, 2nd ed. (London: Frank Cass, 1968), 62–63 (describing Portuguese diplomatic protests in 1813 related to the capture of Portuguese-flagged slaving vessels off the coast of Africa).
57. Donald R. Hickey, *The War of 1812: A Forgotten Conflict* (Urbana: University of Illinois Press, 1989), 11–13.
58. Data on known slave voyages in table 2.1 and other tables in this book are derived from David Eltis et al., Trans-Atlantic Slave Trade Database, http://www.slavevoyages.org, accessed February 1, 2011. The online version of the database is a much-expanded version of the database that was published in 1999. David Eltis et al., *The Trans-Atlantic Slave Trade: A Database on CD-ROM* (Cambridge: Cambridge University Press, 1999), CD-ROM. Table 2.1 was created from the raw data by using the year of departure variable ("YEARDEP") for year and the variable describing the outcome of the voyage ("FATE") to count all voyages adjudicated in vice-admiralty courts each year as well as the total number of voyages of any outcome in that year. For a discussion of this data, and its limits, see Jenny Martinez, "Antislavery Courts and the Dawn of International Human Rights Law," *Yale Law Journal* 117 (2007): 597 nn. 208–10.
59. Howard, *American Slavers*, 4–6.
60. David Eltis, *Economic Growth and the Ending of the Transatlantic Slave Trade* (New York: Oxford University Press, 1987), 109. *Le Louis*, (1817) 165 Eng. Rep. 1464 (Adm. Ct.).
61. *Le Louis*, (1817) 165 Eng. Rep. 1464 (Adm. Ct.), 1473.
62. Ibid., 1475.

63. Ibid., 1482. For an interesting similar turnabout in American case law, compare Justice Story's decision upholding an American ship's capture of a French slave vessel on *Somerset*-type reasoning in *United States v. La Jeune Eugenie*, 26 F. Cas. 832, 846–48 (C.C.D. Mass. 1822) (No. 15,551) with Justice Marshall's invalidation of a similar seizure with *Le Louis*–type reasoning in *The Antelope*, 23 U.S. (10 Wheat.) 66, 122 (1825).

64. Drescher, "Whose Abolition?" 159; also see Additional Article to the Definitive Treaty of Peace Between Great Britain and France, Gr. Brit.–Fr., 30 May 1814, in *British and Foreign State Papers*, vol. 3 (London: James Ridgway and Sons, 1838), 890–91 (hereafter cited as *B.S.P.*, vol. 3) (acknowledging that slave trade is "repugnant to the principles of natural justice and the enlightened age in which we live" and pledging to cooperate with Britain at the upcoming Congress to induce agreement for abolition of the trade, as well as committing to abolish the trade in the course of five years, but preserving the right of France to engage in the trade in the interim).

65. Drescher, "Whose Abolition?" 159.

66. See ibid., 159–60; also see "House of Commons," *Times* (London), June 7, 1814 (describing the reaction to Lord Castlereagh's presentation of the peace treaty).

67. See Hochschild, *Bury the Chains*, 316–17; Drescher, "Whose Abolition?" 160; Bernard Nelson, "The Slave Trade as a Factor in British Foreign Policy, 1815–1862," *Journal of Negro History* 27, no. 2 (1942): 193–94 (noting that more than 600 petitions from various towns and associations were submitted to Parliament in July 1814).

68. See Drescher, "Whose Abolition?" 161.

69. See ibid., 164 (quoting Arthur Wellesley, Duke of Wellington, to Viscount Castlereagh, 17 June 1814; and Arthur Wellesley, Duke of Wellington, to Viscount Castlereagh, 6 July 1814).

70. Address of the House of Commons to the Prince Regent of Great Britain, 3 May 1814, Enclosed in Viscount Castlereagh to the Duke of Wellington, 6 August 1814, in *B.S.P.*, vol. 3, 893–94 (urging that "His Majesty's Government would employ every proper means to obtain a Convention of the Powers of Europe for the immediate and universal abolition of the African Slave Trade" at the Congress, which "afford[s] a most auspicious opportunity for interposing the good offices of Great Britain to accomplish the above noble purpose"); Nelson, "Slave Trade as a Factor," 194.

71. Bethell, *Abolition of the Brazilian Slave Trade*, 12.

72. Castlereagh was apparently quite susceptible to public opinion. He ended up committing suicide in 1822, partly in reaction to his

perception of his unpopularity. See generally J. A. R. Marriott, *Castlere-agh: The Political Life of Robert, Second Marquess of Londonderry* (London: Methuen, 1936).

73. Viscount Castlereagh to the Duke of Wellington, 6 August 1814, in *B.S.P.*, vol. 3, 891, 893.

74. The Duke of Wellington to Viscount Castlereagh, 25 August 1814, in *B.S.P.*, vol. 3, 901, 902.

75. Viscount Castlereagh to the Duke of Wellington, 4 October 1814, in *B.S.P.*, vol. 3, 907.

76. The Duke of Wellington to Viscount Castlereagh, 5 November 1814, in *B.S.P.*, vol. 3, 913.

77. Convention Between Great Britain and the Netherlands Relative to the Dutch Colonies; Trade with the East and West Indies, art. VIII, Gr. Brit.–Neth., 13 August 1814, in *British and Foreign State Papers*, vol. 2 (London: James Ridgway and Sons, 1839), 370, 374–75 (hereafter cited as *B.S.P.*, vol. 2) (promising to forbid subjects from "taking any share whatsoever in such inhuman Traffic"). Sweden, too, was per-suaded to enter into a treaty banning the trade, but Sweden was not a major maritime power.

78. Act of March 2, 1807, ch. 22, 2 Stat. 426.

79. Treaty of Peace and Amity, Between His Britannic Majesty and the United States of America, art. X, Gr. Brit.–U.S., 24 December 1814, in *B.S.P.*, vol. 2, 357, 364.

80. Sir Henry Wellesley to Viscount Castlereagh, 17 June 1814, in *B.S.P.*, vol. 3, 920.

81. Sir Henry Wellesley to Viscount Castlereagh, 6 July 1814, in *B.S.P.*, vol. 3, 920.

82. Sir Henry Wellesley to Viscount Castlereagh, 25 August 1814, in *B.S.P.*, vol. 3, 926.

83. Sir Henry Wellesley to Viscount Castlereagh, 20 September 1814, in *B.S.P.*, vol. 3, 931.

84. Sir Henry Wellesley to Viscount Castlereagh, 23 October 1814, in *B.S.P.*, vol. 3, 932.

85. Earl Bathurst to Sir Henry Wellesley, 11 November 1814, in *B.S.P.*, vol. 3, 934.

86. See Bethell, *Abolition of the Brazilian Slave Trade*, 7–9.

87. Convention Between Great Britain and Portugal, Relative to the Indemnification of Portuguese Subjects for Certain Detained Slave-Trade Vessels, Gr. Brit.–Port., 21 January 1815, in *B.S.P.*, vol. 2, 345–48.

88. Treaty Between Great Britain and Portugal, for the Restriction of the Portuguese Slave Trade; and for the Annulment of the Convention of

Loan of 1809, and Treaty of Alliance of 1810, Gr. Brit.–Port., 22 January 1815, in *B.S.P.*, vol. 2, 348–55.

89. See generally Jerome Reich, "The Slave Trade at the Congress of Vienna—a Study in English Public Opinion," *Journal of Negro History* 53, no. 2 (1968): 129.

90. See Charles K. Webster, ed., *British Diplomacy, 1813–1815: Select Documents Dealing with the Reconstruction of Europe* (London: G. Bell and Sons, 1921); Viscount Castlereagh, *Correspondence, Dispatches, and Other Papers*, vol. 10, ed. Charles W. Vane (London: William Shoberl, 1852), 213–61; Hilde Spiel, ed., *The Congress of Vienna: An Eyewitness Account*, trans. Richard H. Weber (Philadelphia: Chilton, 1968).

91. See Tim Chapman, *The Congress of Vienna: Origins, Processes and Results* (London: Routledge, 1998), 60–61.

92. Ibid., 61.

93. Viscount Castlereagh to the Earl of Liverpool, 28 September 1815, in Webster, *British Diplomacy*, 383 (internal quotation marks omitted).

94. Chapman, *Congress of Vienna*, 60–62.

95. Viscount Castlereagh to the Earl of Liverpool, 21 November 1814, in Webster, *British Diplomacy*, 233–35; Reich, "Slave Trade," 135–36.

96. Reich, "Slave Trade," 139–40 (quoting delegates to the Declaration of the Powers on the Abolition of the Slave Trade, 8 February 1815, in *Parliamentary Debates*, ed. T. C. Hansard, vol. 32 (1816), 200–201).

97. See Martha Putney, "The Slave Trade in French Diplomacy from 1814 to 1815," *Journal of Negro History* 60, no. 3 (1975): 424–25.

98. Ibid., 426.

99. Ibid., 427. As noted in the British press, the treaty was implemented by way of a French ordinance prohibiting the slave trade and providing for confiscation of any vessels importing slaves into the French West Indian possessions. "French Papers," *Times* (London), February 7, 1817.

100. Answers from Sierra Leone to the Queries of Viscount Castlereagh, April 1817, in *British and Foreign State Papers*, vol. 6 (London: James Ridgway, 1835), 38, 45 (hereafter cited as *B.S.P.*, vol. 6).

101. Ibid. (emphasis added).

102. Treaty of Amity, Commerce and Navigation, U.S.-U.K., November 19, 1794, 8 Stat. 116.

103. See Convention Relative to the Claims of the Subjects of the Allied Powers upon France, art. V, 20 November 1815, in *B.S.P.*, vol. 3, 315, 321–26; also see Viscount Castlereagh to the Duke de Richelieu, 27 October 1818, in *B.S.P.*, vol. 6, 59 (noting that the provisions for judge and arbitrator were like those in a previous convention between Great

Britain and France for adjudicating private claims); British Government, memorandum, enclosed in Viscount Castlereagh to Earl Bathurst, 28 November 1818, in *B.S.P.*, vol. 6, 65, 77, 79 (similar).

104. Additional Convention Between Great Britain and Portugal for the Prevention of the Slave Trade, Gr. Brit.–Port., 28 July 1817, 67 Consol. T.S. 398 (1817) (hereafter cited as Anglo-Portuguese Treaty of 1817); Treaty Between Great Britain and Spain for the Abolition of the Slave Trade, Gr. Brit.–Spain, 23 September 1817, 68 Consol. T.S. 45 (1817–18) (hereafter cited as Anglo-Spanish Treaty of 1817); Treaty Between His Britannic Majesty and His Majesty the King of the Netherlands, for Preventing Their Subjects from Engaging in Any Traffic in Slaves, Gr. Brit.–Neth., 4 May 1818, in *British and Foreign State Papers*, vol. 5 (London: James Ridgway and Sons, 1837), 125.

105. This would be the equivalent of roughly £20 million today.

106. Anglo-Spanish Treaty of 1817, arts. III–IV. Not everyone in London was thrilled with this concession. "Why," asked one newspaper writer, "should England pay Spain for performing an act of humanity and justice?" *Times* (London), October 13, 1817.

107. British diplomats would not let their Spanish and Portuguese counterparts soon forget about the cash payments; for years to come, when Spain and Portugal were less than enthusiastic about enforcing the treaties, the British would remind them that they had been paid in advance for their cooperation. See, e.g., Draft of a Note to Be Presented by Lord Howard de Walden to the Portuguese Government, Enclosed in Viscount Palmerston to Lord Howard de Walden, 20 April 1839, in *Correspondence with Foreign Powers Relating to the Slave Trade*, class B, 71, 76–78, in *British Parliamentary Papers*, vol. 17 (1839; photo. repr., Shannon: Irish University Press, 1968).

108. Anglo-Spanish Treaty of 1817, art. I.

109. Ibid., art. II.

110. Anglo-Portuguese Treaty of 1817, art. II.

111. Anglo-Spanish Treaty of 1817, art. XII. The presence of Spanish and Portuguese judges under instructions from their governments did not render the courts cheap talk. At most, this would have meant acquittal in half the cases, given the system for breaking tie votes, which is discussed in greater detail in chapter 4.

112. Regulation for the Mixed Commissions, Which Are to Reside on the Coast of Africa, and in a Colonial Possession of His Catholic Majesty, art. I (hereafter cited as Regulation for the Mixed Commissions), Appended to Anglo-Spanish Treaty of 1817.

113. Ibid., preamble.

114. Viscount Palmerston to the Baron de Moncorvo, 30 April 1836, in *Correspondence with Foreign Powers, Relating to the Slave Trade*, class B, 83, in *British Parliamentary Papers*, vol. 14 (1839; photo. repr., Shannon: Irish University Press, 1968).

CHAPTER 3

1. Gordon S. Wood, *Empire of Liberty: A History of the Early Republic, 1789–1815* (Oxford: Oxford University Press, 2009), 517–19.
2. Ibid., 522.
3. Keith L. Dougherty and Jac C. Heckelman, "Voting on Slavery at the Constitutional Convention," *Public Choice* 136 (2008): 293, 295; John P. Kaminski, ed., *A Necessary Evil?: Slavery and the Debate over the Constitution* (Madison, WI: Madison House, 1995), 1.
4. See Susan L. Boyd, "A Look into the Constitutional Understanding of Slavery," *Res Publica* 6, no. 1 (1995), http://www.ashbrook.org/publicat/respub/v6n1/boyd.html.
5. U.S. Const. art. IV, § 2.
6. U.S. Const. art. I, § 9.
7. Boyd, "A Look into the Constitutional Understanding of Slavery."
8. Const. of the Confederate States of America, art. I, § 9, cl. 1 (1861).
9. Merrill Jensen, et al., eds., "The Pennsylvania Convention: Monday, 3 December 1787," in *The Documentary History of the Ratification of the Constitution: Ratification by the States: Pennsylvania*, vol. 2 (Madison: Wisconsin Historical Society, 1976), 463 (statement of James Wilson).
10. Doughtery and Heckelman, "Voting on Slavery," 294–95.
11. W. E. Burghardt DuBois, *The Suppression of the African Slave-Trade to the United States of America, 1638–1870* (New York: Longmans, Green, 1896), 80.
12. Act of March 22, 1794, ch. 11, 1 Stat. 347, 349; Charles Rappleye, *Sons of Providence: The Brown Brothers, the Slave Trade and the American Revolution* (New York: Simon and Schuster, 2006), 299.
13. Rappleye, *Sons of Providence*, 305.
14. Actually, many slave ships had strangely optimistic names like *Liberty, Fraternité,* and *Egalité*. Voyages Database, Trans-Atlantic Slave Trade Database, http://www.slavevoyages.org, s.v. "Liberty, 1700–1824," s.v. "Fraternite, 1700–1824," s.v. "Egalite, 1700–1824," all accessed February 21, 2011.
15. Rappleye, *Sons of Providence*, 310.
16. Ibid., 311–12.
17. *United States v. Schooner Sally*, 6 U.S. (2 Cranch) 406 (1805). The 1794 act prohibited Americans from engaging in the trade to foreign

countries; the importation of slaves could not constitutionally be banned until 1808.

18. Act of May 10, 1800, ch. 51, 2 Stat. 70, 70–71.
19. DuBois, *The Suppression of the African Slave-Trade*, 82 (internal quotation marks omitted).
20. Ibid., 84.
21. *Brig Caroline, William Broadfoot v. United States*, 11 U.S. (7 Cranch) 496, 498–99 (1813); *The Marianna Flora*, 24 U.S. (11 Wheat.) 1, 38 (1826) (upholding the introduction of a new count while the case was on appeal because such amendments were allowed in admiralty actions); *The Mary Ann*, 21 U.S. (8 Wheat.) 380, 390 (1823) (reversing "the sentence of the District Court of Louisiana" in a slave trade case "for these defects in the libel; but as there is much reason to believe, that the offence for which the forfeiture is claimed has been committed, the cause is remanded to the District Court of Louisiana, with directions to permit the libel to be amended"); *The Josefa Segunda*, 18 U.S. (5 Wheat.) 338, 343 (1820) (describing the district court's condemnation of the ship under the slave trade acts); *The Josefa Segunda*, 23 U.S. (10 Wheat.) 312, 322 (1825) (noting, in subsequent proceeding of the case under the 1807 slave trade act, that "the District Court has jurisdiction over seizures made under the latter act. The principal proceedings are certainly to be against the vessel, and the goods and effects found on board").
22. *United States v. Vickery*, 28 F. Cas. 374, 374 (C.C.D. Md. 1803) (No. 16, 619).
23. Thomas Jefferson, Sixth Annual Presidential Message to Congress, 2 December 1806, in *Presidential Messages and State Papers*, vol. 2, ed. Julius W. Muller (New York: Review of Reviews, 1917), 390.
24. See figure 3.1, at p. 40.
25. William Wilberforce to James Monroe, 6 June 1804, 21 August 1806, quoted in Betty Fladeland, *Men and Brothers* (Urbana: University of Illinois Press, 1972), 108; Robert Isaac Wilberforce and Samuel Wilberforce, *The Life of William Wilberforce*, vol. 3 (London: John Murray, 1838), 374.
26. Treaty of Peace and Amity Between His Britannic Majesty and the United States of America, art. X, Gr. Brit.–U.S., December 24, 1814, in *British and Foreign State Papers*, vol. 2 (London: James Ridgway and Sons, 1839), 357, 364.
27. Fladeland, *Men and Brothers*, 113.
28. Memorandum of the British Government, Enclosure 5 in Viscount Castlereagh to Earl Bathurst, 23 November 1818, in *British and Foreign*

State Papers, vol. 6, *1818–1819* (London: James Ridgway, 1835) (hereafter cited as *B.S.P.*, vol. 6), 79.

29. Ibid., 79 (spelling as in original).
30. Ibid., 77, 79. See also "Protocole de la Conference entre les Plénipoten-tiaires des 5 Cours," 4 November 1818, Enclosure in Viscount Castlere-agh to Earl Bathurst, 12 November 1818, in *B.S.P.*, vol. 6, 64.
31. Marcus Niehbur Tod, *International Arbitration Amongst the Greeks* (Oxford: Clarendon, 1913), 170–75; Jonathan I. Charney, "Is Interna-tional Law Threatened by Multiple International Tribunals?" in *Recueil Des Cours*, vol. 271 (The Hague: Martinus Nijhoff, 1999), 118 n. 8; John Bassett Moore, ed., *International Adjudications: Ancient and Modern: History and Documents Together with Mediatorial Reports, Advisory Opinions, and the Decisions of Domestic Commissions, on International Claims*, vol. 1 (New York: Oxford University Press, 1929), xi–xii.
32. Peter Malanczuk, *Akehurst's Modern Introduction to International Law*, 7th ed. (London: Routledge, 1997), 20; Charney, "Is International Law Threatened," 118.
33. Interestingly enough, constitutional objections were raised to the Jay Treaty at the time of its ratification on the grounds that the foreign commissions would not have been appointed in accordance with the Constitution and that it was an impermissible delegation of Article III authority to a non–Article III tribunal. These objections were not accepted, and the treaty was adopted. See generally David Golove, "The New Confederalism: Treaty Delegations of Legislative, Executive, and Judicial Power," *Stanford Law Review* 55 (2003), 1697, 1745–46.
34. Treaty of Amity, Commerce and Navigation, U.S.–Gr. Brit., art. VII, November 19, 1794, 8 Stat. 116.
35. Charles H. Brower, "The Functions and Limits of Arbitration and Judicial Settlement under Private and Public International Law," *Duke Journal of Comparative and International Law* 18 (2008), 259, 268–69.
36. John Quincy Adams, 6 June 1817, in *Memoirs of John Quincy Adams Comprising Portions of His Diary from 1795 to 1848*, ed. Charles Francis Adams, vol. 3 (1874–77; repr., Freeport, ME: Books for Libraries Press, 1969), 557.
37. John Quincy Adams, 30 October 1818, in *Memoirs of John Quincy Adams*, vol. 4 (hereafter cited as *Adams Memoirs*, vol. 4), 148–49.
38. Ibid., 149.
39. Ibid., 148.
40. Ibid.
41. Ibid., 151–52.

42. Ibid.

43. Ibid.

44. Ibid.

45. For a detailed discussion of the constitutional law issues, compare Jenny S. Martinez, "International Courts and the U.S. Constitution: Reexamining the History," *University of Pennsylvania Law Review* 159, no. 3 (2011), 1069; with Eugene Kontorovich, "The Constitutionality of International Courts: The Forgotten Precedent of Slave-Trade Tribunals," *University of Pennsylvania Law Review* 158, no. 1 (2009), 39, 75–81, 87–88.

46. Daniel Walker Howe, *What Hath God Wrought: The Transformation of America 1815–1848* (Oxford: Oxford University Press, 2007), 91.

47. Ibid., 91, 93.

48. Stratford Canning to George Canning, 6 June 1823, NA, FO 5, no. 176, cited in John T. Noonan Jr., *The Antelope: The Ordeal of the Recaptured Africans in the Administrations of James Monroe and John Quincy Adams* (Berkeley: University of California Press, 1977), 86.

49. Howe, *What Hath God Wrought*, 112.

50. See generally Henry M. Dowling, "William Wirt," *Green Bag* 10, no. 11 (1898), 453.

51. John Quincy Adams, 28 April 1818, in *Adams Memoirs*, vol. 4, 82.

52. Noonan, *The Antelope*, 85.

53. An Act of Mar. 3, 1819, ch. 101, 3 Stat. 532.

54. An Act of Mar. 3, 1819, ch. 77, 3 Stat. 510.

55. *United States v. Smith*, 18 U.S. (5 Wheat.) 153 (1820).

56. Ibid., 160–61.

57. An Act of May 15, 1820, ch. 113, § 4, 3 Stat. 600.

58. H.R. Rep. No. 17–92, at 5–6 (1821), cited in DuBois, *Suppression of the African Slave Trade*, 126.

59. Bernard Edwards, *Royal Navy Versus the Slave Traders: Enforcing Abolition at Sea 1808–1898* (Barnsley, Yorkshire: Pen and Sword Maritime, 2007), 78–79.

60. John Quincy Adams, 3 March 1820, in *Memoirs of John Quincy Adams*, vol. 5 (hereafter cited as *Adams Memoirs*, vol. 5), 11–12.

61. 37 Annals of Cong. 2216, 2235 (1820).

62. John Quincy Adams, 14 March 1819, in *Adams Memoirs*, vol. 4, 335.

63. Ibid., 335–36.

64. Ibid.

65. Ibid.

66. Fladeland, *Men and Brothers*, 125.

67. John Quincy Adams, 2 October 1820, in *Adams Memoirs*, vol. 5, 182.
68. Ibid.
69. Ibid.
70. Ibid., 182–83.
71. Ibid., 183.
72. Ibid.
73. John Quincy Adams, 20 October 1820, in *Adams Memoirs*, vol. 5, 189–91.
74. Ibid. at 190.
75. John Quincy Adams, 26 October 1820, in *Adams Memoirs*, vol. 5, 191–92.
76. Ibid. at 193.
77. Ibid., 192.
78. John Quincy Adams, 29 June 1822, in *Memoirs of John Quincy Adams*, vol. 6 (hereafter cited as *Adams Memoirs*, vol. 6), 37.
79. John Quincy Adams, 12 June 1823, in *Adams Memoirs*, vol. 6, 147.
80. James Monroe to Daniel Brent, 17 September 1821, quoted in *The Political Writings of James Monroe*, ed. James P. Lucier (Washington, DC: Regnery, 2001), 323.
81. *United States v. La Jeune Eugenie*, 26 F. Cas. 832 (C.C.D. Ma. 1822) (No. 15,551).
82. Ibid.
83. Ibid.
84. Ibid.
85. Noonan, *The Antelope*, 70.
86. Ibid.
87. Ibid., 71.
88. *La Jeune Eugenie*, 26 F. Cas. at 832, 841.
89. Ibid., 845.
90. Noonan, *The Antelope*, 73.
91. *La Jeune Eugenie*, 26 F. Cas. at 846.
92. Ibid., 847.
93. Ibid., 849–50.
94. *The Antelope*, 23 U.S. (Wheat.) 66 (1825).
95. Ibid., 68.
96. James Monroe to John Quincy Adams, 3 August 1820, quoted in Noonan, *The Antelope*, 37.
97. Ibid.
98. Ibid., 52–53.
99. Ibid., 41 ("a suit in admiralty was a request that the federal judge, William Davies, decide a claim for compensation arising at sea").

100. Ibid., 59. A small group of the slaves, who had been taken by the *Antelope* from an American ship illegally engaged in the slave trade, were assigned to the government of the United States. Ibid.

101. Ibid., 62 (internal quotation marks omitted).

102. Ibid., 62–63.

103. Secretary George Canning to the Duke of Wellington, 1 October 1822, in *British and Foreign State Papers*, vol. 20 (London: James Ridgway and Sons, 1850), 94–110; DuBois, *The Suppression of the African Slave-Trade*, 138.

104. 40 Annals of Cong. 928 (1823). The resolution passed 131–9. 40 Annals of Cong. 1155 (1823).

105. 40 Annals of Cong. 1147 (1823).

106. Howe, *What Hath God Wrought*, 113–15; James Monroe, Seventh Annual Message, 2 December 1823, in *Presidential Messages and State Papers*, vol. 2, ed. Julius W. Muller (New York: Review of Reviews, 1917), 712, 721–22.

107. John Quincy Adams to Viscount Stratford Canning, 31 March 1823, First Enclosure in Viscount Stratford Canning to Secretary George Canning, 31 March 1823, in *British and Foreign State Papers*, vol. 10 (London: James Ridgeway and Sons, 1850), 262.

108. John Quincy Adams to Viscount Stratford Canning, 24 June 1823, in *Writings of John Quincy Adams*, vol. 7, ed. Worthington Chauncey Ford (New York: Macmillan, 1917) (hereafter cited as *Adams Writings*, vol. 7), 501–2.

109. Ibid.

110. 42 Annals of Cong. 3001–02 (1823).

111. John Quincy Adams, 23 December 1820, in *Adams Memoirs*, vol. 5, 217.

112. John Quincy Adams to Viscount Stratford Canning, 24 June 1823, in *Adams Writings*, vol. 7, 502.

113. James Monroe, Message from the President of the United States, 21 May 1824, 1 Reg. Deb. 20 (1825).

114. Ibid.

115. See Letter from John Quincy Adams to Richard Rush (May 29, 1824), in *American State Papers: Foreign Relations*, vol. 5, ed. Asbury Dickins and James C. Allen (Washington, DC: Gales and Seaton, 1858), 362–63.

116. Extracts of Letter from Mr. Rush to Mr. Adams, 9 August 1824, Document Accompanying the Message of the President of the United States to Both Houses of Congress, 7 December 1824, 1 Reg. Deb. app. 24 (1824).

117. *The Antelope*, 23 U.S. (10 Wheat.) 66, 114 (1825).

118. Ibid., 115.

119. Ibid., 118.
120. Ibid.
121. Ibid., 118–19.
122. Ibid., 120.
123. Ibid., 121.
124. Ibid.
125. Ibid., 122.
126. Ibid.
127. Ibid., 122–23.
128. James Kent, *Commentaries on American Law*, vol. 1 (New York: O. Halsted, 1826), 180.
129. Ibid., 185.
130. Ibid., 174.
131. Ibid., 182.
132. Ibid., 186.

CHAPTER 4

1. Commodore Sir G. R. Collier to J. W. Croker, Esq., 13 January 1820, in *2. Further Papers Relating to the Suppression of the Slave Trade. Viz: A. Copies or Extracts of All Communications Received by the Lords Commissioners of the Admiralty from the Naval Officers Stationed on the Coast of Africa, or in the West Indies, Since the 1st of January 1820; Relative to the State of the Slave Trade. B. Copies or Extracts of All Instructions Issued by the Lords Commissioners of the Admiralty to Naval Officers, Since the 1st of January 1819; Relative to the Suppression of the Slave Trade*, p. 5, House of Commons Parliamentary Papers Online (2006), ProQuest (366) (hereafter cited as *Communications from and Instructions to Naval Officers, 1819–20*), http://gateway.proquest.com/openurl?url_ver=Z39.88-2004&res_dat=xri:hcpp-us&rft_dat=xri:hcpp:fulltext:1821-007497:5.
2. Ibid., p. 6, http://gateway.proquest.com/openurl?url_ver=Z39.88-2004&res_dat=xri:hcpp-us&rft_dat=xri:hcpp:fulltext:1821-007497:6.
3. Letter from Lieutenant R. Hagan to the Commissary Judges and the Commissioners of the Arbitration, 10 November 1819, in *Communications from and Instructions to Naval Officers, 1819–20*, p. 7, http://gateway.proquest.com/openurl?url_ver=Z39.88-2004&res_dat=xri:hcpp-us&rft_dat=xri:hcpp:fulltext:1821-007497:7.
4. Ibid.; also see Lieutenant R. Hagan to the Commissary Judges and the Commissioners of the Arbitration, 22 November 1819, in *Communications from and Instructions to Naval Officers, 1819–20*, pp. 8–9, http://gateway.proquest.com/openurl?url_ver=Z39.88-2004&res_dat=xri:hcpp-us&rft_dat=xri:hcpp:fulltext:1821-007497:8; Commodore Sir G. R. Collier to J. W. Croker, Esq., 14 February 1820, in *Communications from and*

Instructions to Naval Officers, 1819–20, p. 16, http://gateway.proquest.com/openurl?url_ver=Z39.88-2004&res_dat=xri:hcpp-us&rft_dat=xri:hcpp:fulltext:1821-007497:16.

5. First Enclosure in Commodore Sir Geo. R. Collier to J. W. Croker, Esq., 21 February 1820, in *Communications from and Instructions to Naval Officers, 1819–20*, p. 24, http://gateway.proquest.com/openurl?url_ver=Z39.88-2004&res_dat=xri:hcpp-us&rft_dat=xri:hcpp:fulltext:1821-007497:24.

6. See Thomas Gregory and Edward Fitzgerald, His Majesty's Commissioners, to Viscount Castlereagh, 27 November 1819, in (1821) *Papers Relative to the Slave Trade. Class A. Correspondence with His Majesty's Commissioners at Sierra Leone. Class B. Correspondence with Foreign Courts Relative to the Execution of Treaties Contracted by Them with Great Britain for the Prevention of Illicit Traffic in Slaves, and Correspondence with His Majesty's Commissioners in the Colonies of Those Powers. Class C. Correspondence with France Relative to the Slave Trade. Class D. Correspondence with the United States of America Relative to the Slave Trade*, p. 68, House of Commons Parliamentary Papers Online (2006), ProQuest (003) (hereafter cited as *Correspondence Relative to the Slave Trade, 1821*), http://gateway.proquest.com/openurl?url_ver=Z39.88-2004&res_dat=xri:hcpp-us&rft_dat=xri:hcpp:fulltext:1821-007486:76.

7. Commodore Sir G. R. Collier to J. W. Croker, Esq., 13 January 1820, in *Communications from and Instructions to Naval Officers, 1819–20*, p. 6, http://gateway.proquest.com/openurl?url_ver=Z39.88-2004&res_dat=xri:hcpp-us&rft_dat=xri:hcpp:fulltext:1821-007497:6.

8. See Thomas Gregory and Edward Fitzgerald, His Majesty's Commissioners, to Viscount Castlereagh, 27 November 1819, in *Correspondence Relative to the Slave Trade, 1821*, p. 68, http://gateway.proquest.com/openurl?url_ver=Z39.88-2004&res_dat=xri:hcpp-us&rft_dat=xri:hcpp:fulltext:1821-007486:76.

9. In terms of structure, the anti–slave trade treaty regime cannot be neatly characterized as bilateral or multilateral. Formally, the courts were bilateral institutions. But they functioned as part of a de facto multilateral treaty network, organized as a hub-and-spoke system with Britain at the center. Some nations had more effective bilateral treaties with Britain than others, but many were simultaneously party to multilateral agreements against the slave trade such as the agreement at the Congress of Vienna.

10. Regulation for the Mixed Commissions, Which Are to Reside on the Coast of Africa, and in a Colonial Possession of His Catholic Majesty art. II (hereafter cited as Regulation for the Mixed Commissions),

Appended to Treaty Between Great Britain and Spain for the Abolition of the Slave Trade, Gr. Brit.–Spain, 23 September 1817, 68 Consol. T.S. 45 (1817–18) (hereafter cited as Anglo-Spanish Treaty of 1817).

11. Ibid., art. III.

12. See, e.g., Oct. Temple and H. W. Macauley, Commissioners at Sierra Leone, to Viscount Palmerston, 30 June 1834, in *Correspondence with the British Commissioners at Sierra Leone, the Havana, Rio de Janeiro, and Surinam, Relating to the Slave Trade*, class A, 63, in *British Parliamentary Papers*, vol. 14 (1835–36; photo. repr., Shannon: Irish University Press, 1968) (hereafter cited as *B.P.P.*, vol. 14) (reporting the death of a Brazilian judge); H. W. Macaulay, Commissioner at Sierra Leone, to Viscount Palmerston, 14 August 1834, in ibid., 8 ("informing your Lordship of another loss which the Courts of Mixed Commission and his Majesty's service have sustained" in the death of the lieutenant-governor of the colony and commissary judge ad interim); J. de Aranjo Ribeiro to the Duke of Wellington, 18 December 1834, in *Correspondence with Foreign Powers Relating to the Slave Trade*, class B, 37, in *B.P.P.*, vol. 14 (reporting the appointment of a new Brazilian judge at Sierra Leone, approximately six months after the death of the preceding judge); W. Fergusson and M. L. Melville, Commissioners at Sierra Leone, to Earl of Aberdeen, 23 January 1842, in *Correspondence with British Commissioners Relating to the Slave Trade*, class A, 10, in *British Parliamentary Papers*, vol. 23 (1843; photo. repr., Shannon: Irish University Press, 1969) (hereafter cited as *B.P.P.*, vol. 23) (reporting the death of a judge); Jos. T. Crawford, Acting Commissioner at Havana, to Viscount Palmerston, 17 July 1847, in *Correspondence with British Commissioners at Sierra Leone, Havana, Rio de Janeiro, Surinam, Cape of Good Hope, Jamaica, Loanda, and Boa Vista, Proceedings of British Vice-Admiralty Courts, and Reports of Naval Officers, Relating to the Slave Trade*, class A, 88, in *British Parliamentary Papers*, vol. 34 (1847–48; photo. repr., Shannon: Irish University Press, 1969) (hereafter cited as *B.P.P.*, vol. 34) (reporting the death of a judge).

13. See Return of Vessels Adjudicated in the British and Brazilian Court of Mixed Commission at Sierra Leone, Enclosed in James Hook and N. W. MacDonald, Commissioners at Sierra Leone, to Viscount Palmerston, 6 April 1847, in *Correspondence with British Commissioners at Sierra Leone, Havana, Rio de Janeiro, Surinam, Cape of Good Hope, Jamaica, Loanda, and Boa Vista, Proceedings of British Vice-Admiralty Courts, and Reports of Naval Officers, Relating to the Slave Trade*, 1847–48, class A, 22–30, in *B.P.P.*, vol. 34. The Brazilian judges' absences were intermittent, as was the court's caseload. Brazilian judges did not

participate in decisions from September 1828 through April 1829, February 1837 through January 1842, September 1843 through May 1844, and April 1845 through the close of the commission in July 1845. In many years when judges were present, however, no cases were decided at all. Compare ibid. with Oct. Temple and H. W. Macaulay, Commissioners at Sierra Leone, to Viscount Palmerston, 30 June 1834, in *Correspondence with the British Commissioners at Sierra Leone, the Havana, Rio de Janeiro, and Surinam, Relating to the Slave Trade, 1835*, class A, 63, in *B.P.P.*, vol. 14 (reporting the death of a Brazilian judge who had served for six years, in which few cases were decided).

14. George Canning, Secretary, to Commissioners at Sierra Leone, 26 November 1822, in *Correspondence with the British Commissioners at Sierra Leone, the Havannah, Rio de Janeiro, and Surinam Relating to the Slave Trade, 1822–23*, class B, 5, in *British Parliamentary Papers*, vol. 9 (1823–24; photo. repr., Shannon: Irish University Press, 1969).

15. For example, some of the Spanish judges at the court in Havana were prominent landowners and businessmen. See Luis Martinez-Fernández, *Fighting Slavery in the Caribbean: The Life and Times of a British Family in Nineteenth-Century Havana* (Armonk, NY: M.E. Sharpe, 1998), 47.

16. M. L. Melville, Commissioner at Sierra Leone, to the Earl of Aberdeen, 2 February 1842, in *Correspondence with British Commissioners Relating to the Slave Trade*, class A, 10, in *B.P.P.*, vol. 23 (recording the swearing in of the governor of the colony as acting commissioner following death of incumbent); H. W. Macaulay, Commissioner at Sierra Leone, to Viscount Palmerston, 14 August 1834, in *Correspondence with the British Commissioners at Sierra Leone, the Havana, Rio de Janeiro, and Surinam, Relating to the Slave Trade*, class A, 8, in *B.P.P.*, vol. 14 (describing how the lieutenant-governor had replaced the British judge— who was on leave for health reasons—until the lieutenant-governor died, at which time he was replaced by the colonial secretary, who simultaneously became acting governor and acting commissary judge).

17. Anglo-Spanish Treaty of 1817, art. IX.

18. Regulation for the Mixed Commissions, art. V ("Instructions for the British and Spanish Ships of War Employed to Prevent the Illicit Traffic in Slaves").

19. Ibid., art. IX. One of the major changes later made to the treaties was an amendment of this clause to allow the detention of ships that did not have slaves onboard but were outfitted for the slave trade.

20. Leslie Bethell, "The Mixed Commissions for the Suppression of the Transatlantic Slave Trade in the Nineteenth Century," *Journal of African History* 7, no. 1 (1966): 83.

21. Christopher Lloyd, *The Navy and the Slave Trade*, 2nd ed. (London: Frank Cass, 1968), 83 (describing payments made to the crew of one "fast and successful" ship between 1839 and 1843 as including £2,628 for the commander, £1,359 for the flag officer, and more than £2,000 shared among other crew members).

22. House of Commons, "First Report from the Select Committee on Slave Trade," p. 102, in *British Parliamentary Papers*, vol. 4 (1847–48; photo. repr., Shannon: Irish University Press, 1968) (hereafter cited as First Commons Report) (testimony of Commander Henry James Matson).

23. "Select Committee of the House of Lords to Consider the Best Means Which Great Britain Can Adopt for the Final Extinction of the African Slave Trade," p. 321, in *British Parliamentary Papers*, vol. 6 (1850; photo. repr., Shannon: Irish University Press, 1968) (hereafter cited as B.P.P., vol. 6) (testimony of Captain Joseph Denman). Denman was also the son of the lord chief justice, who was an influential abolitionist member of the House of Lords.

24. Copy of Declaration of Captors of the Spanish Schooner "Anna Maria," Detained by His Majesty's Ship Tartar, in March 1821, in the River Bonny, on the Coast of Africa, 26 March 1821, in (1822) *Further Papers Relating to the Slave Trade: viz. Copies of Papers Relating to the Portuguese Brig "Gaviao," and the Spanish Schooner "Anna Maria,"* p. 25, House of Commons Parliamentary Papers Online (2006), ProQuest (600), http://gateway.proquest.com/openurl?url_ver=Z39.88-2004&res_dat=xri:hcpp-us&rft_dat=xri:hcpp:fulltext:1822-008134:25.

25. Regulations for the Guidance of the Commissions Appointed for Carrying into Effect the Treaties for the Abolition of the Slave Trade (1819), 6 (on file with British National Archives, F.O. 313/1) (hereafter cited as Commission Regulations) ("It is not absolutely necessary that the Affidavit should be made by the Commander of the capturing ship, the Officer in charge of the ship captured is equally competent thereto"); also see the Earl of Aberdeen to Commissioners at Havana, 18 September 1828, in *Correspondence with the British Commissioners at Sierra Leone, the Havana, Rio de Janeiro, and Surinam, Relative to the Slave Trade*, class A, 128, in *British Parliamentary Papers*, vol. 12 (1829–31; photo. repr., Shannon: Irish University Press, 1968) (hereafter cited as B.P.P., vol. 12) (instructing that the captain of the captor ship need not be present at the adjudication).

26. See, e.g., Report of the Case of the Portuguese Barque "Maria da Gloria," Enclosed in Wm. Smith and H. W. Macaulay, Commissioners at Sierra Leone, to Viscount Palmerston, 31 March 1834, in *Correspondence with*

the British Commissioners at Sierra Leone, the Havana, Rio de Janeiro, and Surinam, Relating to the Slave Trade, class A, 32, 37, in B.P.P., vol. 14 (describing the removal of sick Africans from a captured slave vessel and their treatment by a British ship's surgeon).

27. Ibid.

28. First Commons Report, 156–57 (testimony of Commander Thomas Francis Birch).

29. Instructions for the British and Spanish Ships of War Employed to Prevent the Illicit Traffic in Slaves art. VI, Appended to Anglo-Spanish Treaty of 1817; also see Commission Regulations, 5 ("Form of Certificate of the Necessity of Disembarking Slaves from a Captured Vessel").

30. See, e.g., Return of Portuguese Vessels Adjudicated by the British and Portuguese Court of Mixed Commission, Established at Sierra Leone, Between the 30th Day of June and the 31st Day of December, 1838, Enclosed in H. W. Macaulay and R. Doherty, Commissioners at Sierra Leone, to John Backhouse, 31 December 1838, in Correspondence with the British Commissioners at Sierra Leone, the Havana, and Rio de Janeiro, Relating to the Slave Trade, class A, 93–94, in British Parliamentary Papers, vol. 17 (1839; photo. repr., Shannon: Irish University Press, 1968) (hereafter cited as B.P.P., vol. 17) (noting that some slaves died on all ten ships brought in for adjudication, with death tolls ranging from two to thirty-one).

31. Captain Keith Stewart to James Kennedy, 1 January 1841, in Correspondence with the British Commissioners at Sierra Leone, the Havana, Rio de Janeiro, and Surinam, Relating to the Slave Trade, class A, 178, in British Parliamentary Papers, vol. 21 (1842; photo. repr., Shannon: Irish University Press, 1968) (hereafter cited as B.P.P., vol. 21). See also, e.g., G. Shee to Commissioners at Sierra Leone, 9 December 1830, in Correspondence with the British Commissioners at Sierra Leone, the Havana, Rio de Janeiro, and Surinam, Relating to the Slave Trade, class A, 11, in B.P.P., vol. 12 (relaying that the Admiralty Office had ordered captains to place a medical officer when possible onboard captured slave ships on their way to adjudication in Sierra Leone); Robert Hasketh and Frederick Grigg, Commissioners at Rio, to Hamilton, 6 December 1841, in Correspondence with Spain, Portugal, Brazil &c &c, Relative to the Slave Trade, class B, 306, in B.P.P., vol. 23 (describing concern for expediting proceedings when a ship was captured with slaves onboard).

32. E. Gregory and Edward Fitzgerald to Viscount Castlereagh, 6 June 1821, in (1822) III. Further Papers Relating to the Slave Trade: Viz.

Correspondence with Foreign Powers, and with His Majesty's Commissioners, p. 61, House of Commons Parliamentary Papers Online (2006), ProQuest (175), http://gateway.proquest.com/openurl?url_ver=Z39.88-2004&res_dat=xri:hcpp-us&rft_dat=xri:hcpp:fulltext:1822-008131:69.

33. See, e.g., William Hamilton to Commissioners at Sierra Leone, 13 November 1821, in *Further Papers Relating to the Slave Trade Viz. Correspondence with Foreign Powers and with His Majesty's Commissioners, 1821, 1822,* p. 72, in *British Parliamentary Papers,* vol. 64 (photo. repr., Shannon: Irish University Press, 1969) (advising commissioners to "request the assistance of the Governor of Sierra Leone, in all cases in which any delay in landing the slaves might be attended with fatal consequences to those suffering individuals").

34. George Villiers to Viscount Palmerston, 14 October 1835, in *Foreign Powers, Relating to the Slave Trade,* class B, 10, in B.P.P., vol. 14 (noting the opinion of the Spanish government that "the great number of liberated negroes at the Havana are considered to be dangerous to the tranquility of the slave population of Cuba").

35. See J. Kennedy and Campbell J. Dalrymple, Commissioners at Havana, to Viscount Palmerston, 1 July 1841, in *Correspondence with the British Commissioners at Sierra Leone, the Havana, Rio de Janeiro, and Surinam Relating to the Slave Trade, 1842,* class A, 229, in B.P.P., vol. 21 (describing captured slaves put onboard the HMS *Romney* in conjunction with commission trials); George Jackson and Frederick Grigg, Commissioners at Rio, to Viscount Palmerston, 12 February 1839, in *Correspondence with the British Commissioners,* class A, 144, in B.P.P., vol. 17 (acknowledging that a British vessel would be sent to Rio to house Africans from ships awaiting trial).

36. Regulation for the Mixed Commissions, art. I.

37. See George Jackson and Fred. Grigg, Commissioners at Rio, to Viscount Palmerston, 5 June 1841, in *Correspondence with the British Commissioners at Sierra Leone, the Havana, Rio de Janeiro, and Surinam Relating to the Slave Trade, 1843,* class A, 333, in B.P.P., vol. 21 (discussing delays in adjudication, based on observance of Brazilian holidays); H. S. Fox to Viscount Palmerston, 24 July 1834, in *Correspondence with Foreign Powers, 1835,* class B, 28, in B.P.P., vol. 14 (discussing negotiations with the Brazilian government about speeding up operation of the courts); W. Fergusson and M. L. Melville, Commissioners at Sierra Leone, to the Earl of Aberdeen, 8 January 1842, in *Correspondence with British Commissioners Relating to the Slave Trade, 1842,* class A, 65, 68, in B.P.P., vol. 23 (noting that "in no one of the several Mixed

Commissions has there been a more prompt adjudication of cases than in the Courts at Sierra Leone").

38. Commission Regulations, 5.

39. See, e.g., Interrogatories for the Use of the British Commissioners, to Be Administered to Witnesses Belonging to the Vessel Taken (1819) (on file with the British National Archives, F.O. 313/1); W. Fergusson and M. L. Melville, Commissioners at Sierra Leone, to the Earl of Aberdeen, 8 January 1842, in *Correspondence with British Commissioners Relating to the Slave Trade, 1842*, class A, 65–68, in *B.P.P.*, vol. 23 (describing disagreement with new Brazilian judges about whether to continue the practice of having the registrar take the depositions).

40. Commodore George R. Collier to J. W. Croker, Esq., 14 February 1820, in *Communications from and Instructions to Naval Officers, 1819–20*, p. 16, http://gateway.proquest.com/openurl?url_ver=Z39.88-2004&res_dat=xri:hcpp-us&rft_dat=xri:hcpp:fullt ext:1821-007497:16.

41. In their use of written depositions rather than live testimony in front of the judges, the commissions' procedures were more similar to those of British admiralty courts than to those of ordinary common law courts. See W. Fergusson and M. L. Melville, Commissioners at Sierra Leone, to the Earl of Aberdeen, 8 January 1842, in *Correspondence with the British Commissioners, 1842*, class A, 65, 67, in *B.P.P.*, vol. 23 (noting that the "intention of the parties who framed the Treaties and the 'Regulations' . . . being, as is understood, and indeed stated, in the latter document, to assimilate the practice of these Courts as nearly as possible to that of the High Court of Admiralty, the mode of taking examinations in use in that Court was adopted in the Mixed Commissions"). However, the courts declined to borrow other domestic judicial procedures that were deemed incompatible with the treaties, such as Spanish and Brazilian modes of appeal. See, e.g., George Jackson and Frederick Grigg, Commissioners at Rio de Janeiro, to Viscount Palmerston, 22 January 1839, in *Correspondence with the British Commissioners, 1839*, class A, 138, in *B.P.P.*, vol. 17 (discussing a disagreement with Brazilian judges about availability of "embargoes," a form of appeal allowed under local law, in cases heard by the commission); Marques Lisboa, to Viscount Palmerston, 8 April 1839, in *Correspondence with Foreign Powers, 1838–39*, class B, 128, in *B.P.P.*, vol. 17 (announcing the decision of the Brazilian government not to allow "embargoes" in mixed commission cases).

42. Enclosure No. 3, in G. R. Collier to J. W. Croker, 21 February 1820, in *Communications from and Instructions to Naval Officers, 1819–20*, p. 26,

http://gateway.proquest.com/openurl?url_ver=Z39.88-2004&res_
dat=xri:hcpp-us&rft_dat=xri:hcpp:fulltext:1821-007497:26 (describing testimony of two Africans on board one of the ships).

43. See W. Fergusson and M. L. Melville, Commissioners at Sierra Leone,
to the Earl of Aberdeen, 8 January 1842, in *Correspondence with British
Commissioners, 1842*, class A, 65, in *B.P.P.*, vol. 23.

44. See, e.g., Alex Finley and Wm. Smith, Commissioners at Sierra Leone,
to the Earl of Aberdeen, 4 May 1830, in *Correspondence with the British
Commissioners at Sierra Leone, the Havana, Rio de Janeiro, and Surinam,
Relating to the Slave Trade, 1830*, class A, 59–60, in *B.P.P.*, vol. 12
(reporting the agreement of British and Brazilian judges in the case of
the *Emilia*).

45. Captain Henry J. Leeke to Commodore G. R. Collier, on board His
Majesty's Ship Myrmidon, 15 December 1819, Enclosed in Commodore G. R. Collier to J. W. Croker, Esq., 23 January 1820, in *Communications from and Instructions to Naval Officers, 1819–20*, p. 6, http://
gateway.proquest.com/openurl?url_ver=Z39.88-2004&res_
dat=xri:hcpp-us&rft_dat=xri:hcpp:fulltext:1821-007497:6.

46. See Judgment Given in the Case of the Spanish Brig *Diligente*, 12
October 1838, Enclosed in H. W. Macaulay and R. Doherty to
Viscount Palmerston, 20 October 1838, in *Correspondence with the
British Commissioners, 1838–39*, class A, 17–24, in *B.P.P.*, vol. 17
(discussing case law); Viscount Palmerston to George Jackson and
Frederick Grigg, Commissioners at Rio, 8 October 1834, in *Corre-
spondence with British Commissioners, 1835*, class A, 147, in *B.P.P.*, vol.
14 (noting that "it is a principle of the Law of Nations, that the
national character of a merchant is to be taken from the place of his
residence of his mercantile establishment, and not from the place of
his birth," and instructing them to apply this rule in future cases);
George Jackson and Fred. Grigg, Commissioners, to Viscount
Palmerston, 10 November 1835, in *Correspondence with the British
Commissioners, 1836*, class A, 309–10, in *B.P.P.*, vol. 14 (reporting the
agreement of the Brazilian government on this point).

47. See, e.g., Report of the Case of the Spanish Schooner "Opposiçao,"
Enclosed in H. W. Macaulay and R. Doherty, Commissioners at Sierra
Leone, to Viscount Palmerston, 15 August 1838, in *Correspondence
with the British Commissioners, 1838–39*, class A, 6, 9, in *B.P.P.*, vol. 17
(condemning as Spanish a ship with a Portuguese flag and papers that
was equipped for the slave trade, based on the principle that "the
national character of a merchant is to be taken from the place of his
residence, and of his mercantile establishment, and not from the place

of his birth"); Report of the Case of the Brig *Diligente*, 12 October 1838, Enclosed in H. W. Macaulay and R. Doherty, Commissioners at Sierra Leone, to Viscount Palmerston, 20 October 1838, in *Correspondence with the British Commissioners, 1838–39*, class A, 13, in *B.P.P.*, vol. 17 (condemning as Spanish a Portuguese-flagged ship); Report of the Case of the Schooner *Sirse*, Enclosed in H. W. Macaulay and R. Doherty, Commissioners at Sierra Leone, to Viscount Palmerston, 22 December 1838, in *Correspondence with the British Commissioners, 1838–39*, class A, 26, in *B.P.P.*, vol. 17 (same, based on the course-of-trade test).

48. Compare Anglo-Spanish Treaty of 1817, art. I, with Additional Convention Between Great Britain and Portugal for the Prevention of the Slave Trade art. II, Gr. Brit.–Port., 28 July 1817, 67 Consol. T.S. 398 (1817) (hereafter cited as Anglo-Portuguese Treaty of 1817); also see, e.g., Wm. Smith and H. W. Macauley, Commissioners at Sierra Leone, to Viscount Palmerston, 22 March 1834, in *Correspondence with the British Commissioners*, class A, 31, in *B.P.P.*, vol. 14 (noting that court was "reluctantly compelled" to restore the Portuguese ship, the *Maria da Gloria*, because it was captured south of the equator).

49. Treaty Between Great Britain and Spain, for the Abolition of the Slave Trade art. X, Gr. Brit.–Spain, 28 June 1835, 85 Consol. T.S. 177 (1834–36) (hereafter cited as Anglo-Spanish Treaty of 1835); Treaty Between Great Britain and Portugal, for the Suppression of the Traffic in Slaves art. V, 30 July 1842, in *British and Foreign State Papers*, vol. 30 (London: James Ridgway and Sons, 1858), 527 (hereafter cited as Anglo-Portuguese Treaty of 1842).

50. See, e.g., H. W. Macauley and R. Doherty, Commissioners at Sierra Leone, to Viscount Palmerston, 22 December 1838, in *Correspondence with the British Commissioners, 1838–39*, class A, 26, in *B.P.P.*, vol. 17 (noting that "[o]f illegal equipment for the Slave Trade there could be no doubt: but this fact could only avail in the case of a Spanish vessel" and reporting that the commission found the *Sirse* to be Spanish based on its course of trade, notwithstanding its Portuguese flag and papers); M. L. Melville, Commissioner at Sierra Leone, to the Earl of Aberdeen, 31 December 1841, in *Correspondence with British Commissioners, 1842*, class A, 29–32, in *B.P.P.*, vol. 23 (reporting the cases of the *Recurso, San Paulo de Loando, Boa Uniao, Josephina, Erculos,* and *Paz*, all of which bore a Portuguese flag and papers but were found to be Spanish and condemned); M. L. Melville, Commissioner at Sierra Leone, to the Earl of Aberdeen, 31 December 1841, in *Correspondence with British Commissioners, 1842*, class A, 60, 61, in *B.P.P.*, vol. 23 (reporting case of

the *Bellona,* condemned and found to be Brazilian despite its Portuguese flag).

51. Explanatory and Additional Articles to the Treaty Between Great Britain and Spain, for the Prevention of the Traffic in Slaves, Gr. Brit.–Spain, 10 December 1822, in *British and Foreign State Papers,* vol. 10 (London: James Ridgway and Sons, 1850), 87; Additional Articles Between Great Britain and Portugal, Gr. Brit.–Port., 15 March 1823, in *British and Foreign State Papers,* vol. 11 (London: James Ridgway and Sons, 1843), 23.

52. Anglo-Spanish Treaty of 1835; Anglo-Portuguese Treaty of 1842. Although the Anglo-Brazilian Treaty was not amended to include an equipment clause, it was reinterpreted by the judges to allow the condemnation of such ships. See, e.g., Return of Vessels Adjudicated by the British and Brazilian Court of Mixed Commission, Established at Sierra Leone, Between the 1st Day of July and the 31st Day of December, 1840, Enclosed in H. W. Macauley and R. Doherty, Commissioners at Sierra Leone, to Viscount Palmerston, 15 November 1839, in *Correspondence with British Commission Relative to the Slave Trade,* class A, 123, in *British Parliamentary Papers,* vol. 20 (1841; photo. repr., Shannon: Irish University Press, 1969) (hereafter cited as *B.P.P.,* vol. 20) (reporting several cases of condemnation of ships with no slaves onboard at the time of capture).

53. See, e.g., Report of the Case of the *Paquete do Sul,* Enclosed in George Jackson and Fred. Grigg to Viscount Palmerston, 30 January 1834, in *Correspondence with the British Commissioners, 1835,* class A, 133, in *B.P.P.,* vol. 14.

54. See, e.g., Report of the Case of the Schooner *Sirse,* Enclosed in H. W. Macaulay and R. Doherty to Viscount Palmerston, 22 December 1838, in *Correspondence with the British Commissioners, 1838–39,* class A, 26–32, in *B.P.P.,* vol. 17.

55. See, e.g., George Jackson and Fred. Grigg, Commissioners at Rio, to Viscount Palmerston, 15 January 1839, in *Correspondence with the British Commissioners,* class A, 132, in *B.P.P.,* vol. 17 ("the Brazilian Commissary Judge joined Her Majesty's Judge, without any difficulty, in this sentence [of condemnation]"); George Jackson and Fred. Grigg, Commissioners at Rio, to Viscount Palmerston, 30 June 1841, in *Correspondence with the British Commissioners at Sierra Leone, the Havana, Rio de Janeiro, and Surinam Relating to the Slave Trade,* class A, 344–45, in *B.P.P.,* vol. 21 (noting that the judges were unanimous that a ship captured in a territorial creek was not within the court's jurisdiction).

56. See note 13.

57. See, e.g., George Jackson and Fred. Grigg, Commissioners at Rio, to Viscount Palmerston, 31 October 1840, in *Correspondence with the British Commissioners at Sierra Leone, the Havana, Rio de Janeiro, and Surinam Relating to the Slave Trade,* class A, 279, 281, in *B.P.P.,* vol. 21 (reporting a case in which the British arbitrator sided with the Brazilian judge).

58. See, e.g., H. T. Kilbee, Commissioner at Havana, to George Canning, Secretary, 31 July 1824, in *Correspondence with the British Commissioners,* class A, 68, in *British Parliamentary Papers,* vol. 10 (1825–26; photo. repr., Shannon: Irish University Press, 1968) (hereafter cited as *B.P.P.,* vol. 10); also see Bethell, "Mixed Commissions," 85–86.

59. W. G. Ouseley to Viscount Palmerston, 25 February 1839, in *Correspondence with Foreign Powers Relating to the Slave Trade,* class B, 139, in *B.P.P.,* vol. 17 (describing the removal of Senhor Joaquim Feliciano Gomez). The Portuguese judges at Loanda in 1844–45 were also notorious participants in the slave trade. David Eltis, *Economic Growth and the Ending of the Transatlantic Slave Trade* (New York: Oxford University Press, 1987), 114. Some British judges were also less than effective. One critic said of the British judges at Havana that one spent "his whole time" studying ornithology and the other was a "*poor man* . . . too simple to do good, and too innocent to do harm." Martínez-Fernández, *Fighting Slavery in the Caribbean,* 47. One British commissioner at Rio was also criticized for incompetence and possible corruption. Leslie Bethell, *The Abolition of the Brazilian Slave Trade* (New York: Cambridge University Press, 1970), 201–2.

60. Martínez-Fernández, *Fighting Slavery in the Caribbean,* 47.

61. These numbers were calculated from the Revised Trans-Atlantic Slave Trade Database using the "FATE" variable. David Eltis et al., Trans-Atlantic Slave Trade Database, http://www.slavevoyages.org, accessed February 1, 2010.

62. Bethell, *Abolition of the Brazilian Slave Trade,* 194–98.

63. See, e.g., Regulation for the Mixed Commissions, art. VII. The allocation of prize money to crews was an important way for the navy to increase the pay for naval officers without draining the national treasury.

64. See Bethell, "Mixed Commissions," 88 n. 33.

65. See Lloyd, *Navy and the Slave Trade,* 83. The amount of prize money offered to British ships varied over the years. Other countries did not always offer prize money to their naval officers.

66. Ibid.

67. See Viscount Palmerston to Lord Howard de Walden, 14 February 1839, in *Correspondence with Foreign Powers*, class B, 42, 43, in *B.P.P.*, vol. 17 (discussing the *Diligente*, which had been captured by the British and condemned at Sierra Leone, and whose crew had been sent to Lisbon to be tried under Portuguese law); the Earl of Aberdeen to Commissioners at Rio, 21 September 1841, in *Correspondence with the British Commissioners at Sierra Leone, the Havana, Rio de Janeiro, and Surinam Relating to the Slave Trade*, class A, 355–56, in *B.P.P.*, vol. 21 (discussing the acquittal by Brazilian criminal courts of crew members declared by the mixed commission to have been engaged in piracy). For example, in one letter the commissioners at Sierra Leone related that Lord Palmerston had rejected their suggestion that slave crews be held in custody at Sierra Leone until they could be sent to their own countries for punishment, on the grounds that there was no legal authority for such detention. The commissioners reiterated their suggestion that punishment of slave crews would be likely to check the slave trade and that crews "at present are invariably thrown loose on the coast, and help to man many a vessel which otherwise would be unable to carry off her human cargo for want of hands." W. Fergusson and M. L. Melville, Commissioners at Sierra Leone, to Viscount Palmerston, 23 September 1841, in *Correspondence with the British Commissioners at Sierra Leone, the Havana, Rio de Janeiro, and Surinam Relating to the Slave Trade*, class A, 31, in *B.P.P.*, vol. 21. Later, the mixed courts were authorized to hold slave crews in custody until they could be transferred to national authorities for trial. See George Frere and Frederic R. Surtees, Commissioners at Cape of Good Hope, to Viscount Palmerston, 31 October 1846, in *Correspondence with the British Commissioners at Sierra Leone, Havana, Rio de Janeiro, Surinam, Cape of Good Hope, Jamaica, Loanda, and Boa Vista, Proceedings of British Vice-Admiralty Courts, and Reports of Naval Officers, Relating to the Slave Trade*, class A, 113, in *B.P.P.*, vol. 34 (acknowledging the opinion of British law officers that under Article XII of the Anglo-Portuguese Treaty of 1842, slave crews could be detained in custody by the mixed commission until they could be turned over to their own governments for trial); Ildefonso Leopoldo Bayard to Alfredo Duprat, Portuguese Commissioner, 22 May 1847, in *Correspondence with the British Commissioners at Sierra Leone, Havana, Rio de Janeiro, Surinam, Cape of Good Hope, Jamaica, Loanda, and Boa Vista, Proceedings of British Vice-Admiralty Courts, and Reports of Naval Officers, Relating to the Slave Trade*, class A, 130, in *B.P.P.*, vol. 34 (instructing the Portuguese commissioner that slave crews should be sent to Loanda or Cape Verde and "delivered to the respective Governor-Generals, to be dealt with according to law").

68. See First Commons Report, 15–16 (testimony of Viscount Palmerston).
69. See *Registry of Slaves: Sierra Leone* (on file with the British National Archives, F.O. 315/31) (original logbooks).
70. See, e.g., John Samo and Fred. Grigg, Commissioners at Rio, to the Earl of Aberdeen, 23 September 1842, in *Correspondence with British Commissioners Relating to the Slave Trade*, class A, 291–94, in *B.P.P.*, vol. 23 (describing a case in which British and Brazilian judges disagreed about whether the claimant was entitled to indemnity).
71. See Bethell, *Abolition of the Brazilian Slave Trade*, 130 ("British commissioners were specifically instructed that in reaching a verdict they should never lose sight of their judicial character, and that they should 'uniformly endeavor to combine a fair and conscientious zeal for the prevention of the illegal traffic in slaves with the maintenance of the strictest justice towards the parties concerned'") (quoting letter from Viscount Castlereagh to Thomas Gregory, 19 February 1819).
72. See, e.g., Commission Regulations, 6.
73. See, e.g., Viscount Palmerston to Commissioners at Rio, 22 March 1839, in *Correspondence with the British Commissioners at Sierra Leone, the Havana, and Rio de Janeiro Relating to the Slave Trade, 1839*, class A, 136, in *B.P.P.*, vol. 17 (requesting that the commissioners send more detailed information about every case, including "translation in full of the deposition made by each witness" and "copies or translations of every paper," "a statement of the argument which may have been given by each member of the Court," so that the government could "form a sure opinion upon the merits of each case respectively"); the Earl of Aberdeen to Commissioners at Sierra Leone, 28 December 1828, in *Correspondence with the British Commissioners at Sierra Leone, the Havana, Rio de Janeiro, and Surinam Relative to the Slave Trade, 1829*, class A, 19, in *B.P.P.*, vol. 12 (similar); Foreign Office to Commissioners at Sierra Leone, 6 December 1837 (on file with the British National Archives, F.O. 315/4), 573 ("I am directed by Viscount Palmerston to observe to you that your Dispatches and Reports should be copied in Black Ink, and I am to desire, that you will not give his Lordship occasion to make this remark again").
74. See, e.g., George Lansing, Commissioner at Sierra Leone, to the Foreign Office, 25 September 1822 (on file with the British National Archives, F.O. 315/1), 241 (disapproving of the court's decision in the case of the Spanish schooner *Rosalia*); Viscount Palmerston to Commissioners at Rio, 8 October 1834, in *Correspondence with the British Commissioners at Sierra Leone, the Havana, Rio de Janeiro, and Surinam, Relating to the Slave Trade, 1834*, class A, 147, in *B.P.P.*, vol. 14 (stating

that the commission was wrong to release the *Maria da Gloria* because, although it had a Portuguese flag and papers, it was owned by a merchant resident in Rio and "it is a principle of the Law of Nations, that the national character of a merchant is to be taken from the place of his residence and of his mercantile establishment, and not from the place of his birth," and instructing them to so rule in future cases).

75. See, e.g., George Canning, Secretary, to Commissioners at Sierra Leone, 29 May 1824, in *Correspondence with the British Commissioners at Sierra Leone, the Havannah, Rio de Janeiro, and Surinam, Relating to the Slave Trade, 1824–25*, class A, 27, in B.P.P., vol. 10 (transmitting the opinion of the King's Advocate on what the commissioners ought to do in the case of the *Fabiana*); Viscount Palmerston to Commissioners at Rio de Janeiro, 26 March 1836, in *Correspondence with British Commissioners Relating to the Slave Trade at Sierra Leone, the Havana, Rio de Janeiro, and Surinam, 1835*, class A, 314, in B.P.P., vol. 14 (transmitting the opinion of the king's advocate-general on issues in two cases); John Samo and Fred. Grigg, Commissioners at Rio de Janeiro, to the Earl of Aberdeen, 20 September 1842, in *Correspondence with the British Commissioners at Sierra Leone, the Havana, Rio de Janeiro, and Surinam Relating to the Slave Trade, 1842*, class A, 291, in B.P.P., vol. 23 (asking for instructions).

76. See Bethell, "Mixed Commissions," 87 (noting that the Brazilian commissioners "on instructions from their government" objected to the seizures of ships equipped for the slave trade but without slaves onboard).

77. See, e.g., Viscount Palmerston to Commissioners at Havana, 11 August 1841, in *Correspondence with the British Commissioners Relating to the Slave Trade, 1841*, class A, 217, in B.P.P., vol. 21 ("With reference to your Despatches of the 22nd of January and of the 15th of February last, reporting the state of the Slave Trade at the Havana . . . I herewith transmit to you, for your information, a Copy of a Communication, which I have received from Her Majesty's Commissioners at Sierra Leone, containing some Observations upon our Despatches above mentioned").

78. See, e.g., George Canning, Secretary, to Commissioners at Sierra Leone, 16 March 1825, in *Correspondence with the British Commissioners at Sierra Leone, the Havannah, Rio de Janeiro, and Surinam, Relating to the Slave Trade, 1824–25*, class A, 57, in B.P.P., vol. 10 (transmitting "[t]wo dispatches from the Consul General at Rio de Janeiro, on the subject of the Brazilian Government regulations on the tonnage of slave ships").

79. See, e.g., Viscount Palmerston to G. W. F. Villiers, 6 October 1834, in *Correspondence with Foreign Powers Relating to the Slave Trade, 1834,* class B, 12, in *B.P.P.,* vol. 14 (transmitting reports from courts at Havana and Sierra Leone to a British diplomat in Madrid).

80. See, e.g., W. G. Ouseley to Captain Herbert, R.N., 24 January 1839, in *Correspondence with Spain, Portugal, and Brazil, Relative to the Slave Trade, 1839,* class B, 130, in *B.P.P.,* vol. 17 (communicating information, via the local British consul, from commissioners to captains about the interpretation of a treaty regarding captures of ships without slaves onboard).

81. See generally the correspondence between Britain and other nations, which runs to hundreds of pages a year in each of the annual sets of *British Parliamentary Papers* on the slave trade.

82. See Howard Hazen Wilson, "Some Principal Aspects of British Efforts to Crush the African Slave Trade, 1807–1929," *American Journal of International Law* 44 (1950): 505, 509 n. 22.

83. See Bethell, "Mixed Commissions," 82.

84. See ibid., 83.

85. See ibid.

86. See Bethell, *Abolition of the Brazilian Slave Trade,* 92.

87. See, e.g., Henry T. Kilbee, Commissioner at Havana, to George Canning, 30 December 1824, in *Correspondence with the British Commissioners, at Sierra Leone, the Havannah, Rio de Janeiro, and Surinam, Relating to the Slave Trade, 1824–25,* class A, 140, in *B.P.P.,* vol. 10 (reporting that the emancipation of the slaves by the mixed commission had "excited considerable sensation among the inhabitants of this place" who had demanded that the local government invalidate the commission's verdict); also see Bethell, "Mixed Commissions," 83–84.

88. See Bethell, "Mixed Commissions," 84.

89. *Registry of Slaves: Sierra Leone* (on file with the British National Archives, F.O. 315/31) (original logbooks).

90. See Bethell, "Mixed Commissions," 89.

91. See Figures 4.1 and 4.2, infra.

92. The average percentage of known voyages of all fates that ended up in the mixed courts from 1830 to 1845 is 18.8 percent. These calculations from the online Trans-Atlantic Slave Trade Database were calculated using the year of departure variable ("YEARDEP") for the year, and the variable describing the outcome of each voyage ("FATE") to count ships adjudicated in mixed commissions as well as the total known voyages for each year. These estimates are consistent with those of other scholars. See Eltis, *Economic Growth,* 97–99 (calculating that one

in five ships involved in the traffic were intercepted and condemned in either the mixed courts or in national courts); Lloyd, *Navy and the Slave Trade*, 117 (estimating that one in four slaving vessels was captured).

93. These reports appear in the annual volumes of *British and Foreign State Papers* and the *British Parliamentary Papers: Slave Trade Series*. See Eltis, Trans-Atlantic Slave Trade Database.

94. Such a study would require imputation of missing data about slave voyages, as well as information about a number of variables, including commodity prices, crop failures, weather, tariffs, free labor costs, elasticity of demand, and other factors in the interdependent markets for slaves and the commodities produced by plantation slave labor.

95. See "Report from the Select Committee of the House of Lords, Appointed to Consider the Best Means Which Great Britain Can Adopt for the Final Extinction of the African Slave Trade, 1850," p. 1, in *B.P.P.*, vol. 6 (hereafter cited as Lords Report 1850); "Report from the Select Committee of the House of Lords, Appointed to Consider the Best Means Which Great Britain Can Adopt for the Final Extinction of the African Slave Trade, 1849," p. 1, in *B.P.P.*, vol. 6 (hereafter cited as Lords Report 1849).

96. See First Commons Report, 2–3 (testimony of Viscount Palmerston) (stating that suppression efforts had not increased the cruelty of the slave trade); ibid., 23 (testimony of Joseph Denman) (stating that they had).

97. See ibid., 95 (questions of William Hutt, chairman of the Select Committee).

98. House of Commons, "Second Report from the Select Committee on Slave Trade, 1848," p. 15, in *British Parliamentary Papers*, vol. 4 (1847–48; photo. repr., Shannon: Irish University Press, 1968) (hereafter cited as Second Commons Report) (testimony of William Smith). Smith did believe that entering into treaties with local chiefs to increase legitimate commerce in Africa would reduce the supply of slaves. Ibid., 18. He also believed that it would be necessary to keep some warships on the coast to enforce the treaties and protect legitimate commerce. Ibid., 20.

99. See Lords Report 1849, 128 (testimony of Commodore Charles Hotham); see also Lloyd, *Navy and the Slave Trade*, 120–22. There appears to be some basis for the criticism of Hotham. When asked about his knowledge of Africa before taking up command of the squadron, he answered, "None whatever; I am almost ashamed to say that I had never even directed my attention to the subject." Lords Report 1849, 110 (testimony of Commodore Charles Hotham).

Moreover, once in command, he did not consult officers of longer experience on the African coast about the best way to carry out the suppression mission. Almost with pride, he stated, "During the time of my commanding the African station, I consulted no one who happened to be serving under my orders at the time" and that, in general, commodores did not seek the opinions of their inferior officers. Ibid., 115–16.

100. Lloyd, *Navy and the Slave Trade*, 112–13.
101. First Commons Report, 4 (testimony of Viscount Palmerston).
102. Ibid., 10. This figure included ships condemned by British vice-admiralty courts as well as the mixed commissions.
103. See Eltis, *Economic Growth*, 262.
104. See Second Commons Report, 66 (testimony of Captain George Manuel); ibid., 99 (testimony of Thomas Berry Horsfall); ibid., 162 (testimony of John Bramley Moore).
105. Ibid., 99 (testimony of Thomas Berry Horsfall).
106. During his stay in Havana, Turnbull was reportedly involved with plans by free blacks for insurrection. Eltis, *Economic Growth*, 118.
107. Lords Report 1850, 71 (testimony of David Turnbull) ("In the beginning of my residence in Cuba [the slave trade] was not on the increase; and I think that a great deal has been done in the way of prevention").
108. First Commons Report, 52–53 (testimony of Captain Edward Harris Butterfield). Many of Butterfield's prizes, however, were taken to the vice admiralty court in St. Helena. Ibid., 57–58.
109. Ibid., 58–59.
110. Second Commons Report, 2 (testimony of Captain Christopher Wyvill).
111. First Commons Report, 95 (testimony of Commander Henry James Matson).
112. Ibid., 2–3 (testimony of Viscount Palmerston); ibid., 23 (testimony of Captain Joseph Denman).
113. Even prior to the treaty, British crews did occasionally board French ships. See List of French Slave-Vessels Boarded by the British Squadron Employed on the Western Coast of Africa, Between the 1st of June and the 14th of December 1827, Enclosed in the Earl of Dudley to Viscount Granville, 25 January 1828, in *Correspondence with Foreign Powers, Relating to the Slave Trade*, class B, 123–24, in *B.P.P.*, vol. 12 (listing twelve boardings).
114. A. Taylor Milne, "The Lyon-Seward Treaty of 1862," *American Historical Review* 38, no. 3 (1933): 511–14.

115. See David Eltis, "The Nineteenth-Century Transatlantic Slave Trade: An Annual Time Series of Imports into the Americas Broken Down by Region," *Hispanic American Historical Review* 67, no. 1 (1987): 136, table V.

116. See figure 4.3, infra; also see Lawrence C. Jennings, "France, Great Britain and the Repression of the Slave Trade, 1841–1845," *French Historical Studies* 10, no. 1 (1977): 101, 105, 123 (discussing France's suspension of the "right to search").

117. See Betty Fladeland, *Men and Brothers: Anglo-American Antislavery Cooperation* (Urbana: University of Illinois Press, 1972), 125–44.

118. Viscount Palmerston to Earl Granville, 3 June 1834, in *Correspondence with Foreign Powers Relating to the Slave Trade*, class B, 52–53, in *B.P.P.*, vol. 14 (discussing negotiations with the United States on the treaty, including U.S. objections to a clause regarding searches on the coast of America, which the British and French then offered to remove); Sir Charles Vaughan to Viscount Palmerston, 28 August 1834, in *Correspondence with Foreign Powers Relating to the Slave Trade*, class B, 88, in *B.P.P.*, vol. 14 (reporting on negotiations).

119. See, e.g., Return of Vessels Adjudicated by the British and Spanish Mixed Court of Justice, Established at Sierra Leone, Between July 1 and December 31, 1840, Enclosed in John Jeremie and Walter W. Lewis, Commissioners at Sierra Leone, to John Backhouse, 31 December 1840, in *Correspondence with the British Commissioners at Sierra Leone, the Havana, Rio de Janeiro, and Surinam Relating to the Slave Trade*, class A, 57–58, in *B.P.P.*, vol. 21 (noting the condemnation of the *Plant* and the *Clara* as Spanish ships, despite their flying of American colors).

120. See Viscount Palmerston to A. Stevenson, 5 August 1841, in *Correspondence with Foreign Powers, Relating to the Slave Trade*, class D, 255–57, in *B.P.P.*, vol. 21 (describing an agreement entered into between the British and American commanding officers off the coast of Africa); Agreement Between Commander William Tucker of the HMS *Wolverene* and Lieutenant John S. Paine of the USS *Grampus*, 11 March 1840, in *Correspondence with Foreign Powers Not Parties to Conventions Giving Right of Search of Vessels Suspected of the Slave Trade*, class D, 76–77, in *B.P.P.*, vol. 20.

121. See, e.g., *United States v. Morris*, 39 U.S. (14 Pet.) 464 (1840) (discussing an American criminal prosecution arising out of the capture of the *Butterfly* by the HMS *Dolphin*); Consul James Buchanan to Viscount Palmerston, 10 June 1841, in *Correspondence with Foreign Powers, Relating to the Slave Trade*, class D, 319, in *B.P.P.*, vol. 21 (discussing the case of the *Butterfly*); the Earl of Aberdeen to Consul James Buchanan,

30 September 1841, in *Correspondence with Foreign Powers, Relating to the Slave Trade*, class D, 323, in *B.P.P.*, vol. 21 (discussing American courts' condemnation of the *Butterfly* and the *Catherine*).

122. See John Jeremie and Walter W. Lewis, Commissioners at Sierra Leone, to Viscount Palmerston, 31 December 1840, in *Correspondence with the British Commissioners at Sierra Leone, the Havana, Rio de Janeiro, and Surinam, Relating to the Slave Trade*, class A, 51–57, in *B.P.P.*, vol. 21.

123. See Commander William Tucker to More O'Ferrall, HMS *Wolverene*, 16 March 1841, in *Correspondence with Foreign Powers, Relating to the Slave Trade*, class D, 246, in *B.P.P.*, vol. 21 (reporting a meeting with the USS *Cyane*, and noting, "I still more and very deeply regret that the American men-of-war remain so very short a time on the coast" though Tucker believed, "The American men-of-war, I am convinced, have been of service on this coast, inasmuch as the knowledge of it has prevented many vessels from raising their flag" and citing examples).

124. See A. Stevenson to Viscount Palmerston, 9 August 1841, in *Correspondence with Foreign Powers, Relating to the Slave Trade*, class D, 258, in *B.P.P.*, vol. 21 (noting, in relation to the agreement between the British and American commanders to which Palmerston alluded, that he had no official information and "had no reason to suppose that such authority had been confided by the American Government to any of its naval officers").

125. See, e.g., A. Stevenson to the Earl of Aberdeen, 10 September 1841, in *Correspondence with Foreign Powers, Relating to the Slave Trade*, class D, 263, 266, in *B.P.P.*, vol. 21.

126. See, e.g., Viscount Palmerston to A. Stevenson, 5 August 1841, in *Correspondence with Foreign Powers, Relating to the Slave Trade, 1842*, class D, 255, in *B.P.P.*, vol. 21; A. Stevenson to Viscount Palmerston, 9 August 1841, in *Correspondence with Foreign Powers, Relating to the Slave Trade, 1842*, class D, 258, in *B.P.P.*, vol. 21; Viscount Palmerston to A. Stevenson, 27 August 1841, in *Correspondence with Foreign Powers, Relating to the Slave Trade, 1842*, class D, 260, in *B.P.P.*, vol. 21; A. Stevenson to the Earl of Aberdeen, 10 September 1841, in *Correspondence with Foreign Powers, Relating to the Slave Trade, 1842*, class D, 263, 266, in *B.P.P.*, vol. 21; the Earl of Aberdeen to A. Stevenson, 13 October 1841, in *Correspondence with Foreign Powers, Relating to the Slave Trade, 1842*, class D, at 267, 269, in *B.P.P.*, vol. 21 (arguing that the "rights which have been mutually conceded to each other by the Governments of Great Britain and France, can scarcely be incompatible with the honour and independence of any State upon the face of the earth").

127. See Sir John Barrow to the Commanders in Chief and Senior Officers at the Cape of Good Hope, Coast of Africa, West Indies, and Brazil, 7 December 1841, in *Correspondence with Foreign Powers, Relating to the Slave Trade, 1842*, class D, 279, in *B.P.P.*, vol. 21 (ordering naval officers "neither to capture nor interfere with, nor even to visit United States' vessels, whether they shall have slaves on board or not," yet noting that "it is not intended to allow vessels of other nations to escape visit and examination by merely hoisting an United States flag" and suggesting that if there was reason to suspect a vessel was not truly American, a British ship would be justified in boarding it to examine its papers, but ordering immediate reports of all such boardings to be sent to London). In the Treaty of 1845, France reportedly agreed with Britain on the right of visit to verify the flag, and one navy captain argued before Parliament that, with France's backing on this principle of the law of nations, British ships would be justified in boarding American-flagged slave ships on the inference that they were really Portuguese, Spanish, or Brazilian. First Commons Report, 23 (testimony of Captain Joseph Denman).

128. See Webster-Ashburton Treaty, U.S.–Gr. Brit., August 10, 1842, 8 Stat. 572.

129. Warren S. Howard, *American Slaves and the Federal Law, 1837–1863* (Berkeley: University of California Press, 1963), 202, 214–35.

130. See, e.g., Commissioners at Sierra Leone to Viscount Palmerston, 24 January 1842, in *Correspondence with British Commissioners Relating to the Slave Trade, 1842*, class A, 33, *in B.P.P.*, vol. 23.

131. See First Commons Report, 8 (testimony of Viscount Palmerston); Arthur F. Corwin, *Spain and the Abolition of Slavery in Cuba, 1817–1886* (Austin: University of Texas Press, 1967), 96; also see Rear-Admiral Campbell to Mr. Wood, 14 December 1835, in *Correspondence with Foreign Powers, Relating to the Slave Trade, 1835*, class B, 40, in *B.P.P.*, vol. 14 (noting that traffic is carried on "to a most extraordinary extent" by Spanish and Portuguese vessels).

132. First Commons Report, 6 (testimony of Viscount Palmerston); also see, e.g., Lord Stuart de Rothesay to Viscount Palmerston, 26 November 1830, in *Correspondence with Foreign Powers, Relating to the Slave Trade, 1829–31*, class B, 165, in *B.P.P.*, vol. 12 (reporting criminal sentences against slave traders by the French court in Guadaloupe).

133. First Commons Report, 17 (testimony of Viscount Palmerston).

134. Ibid., 6.

135. Ibid., 7. However, other witnesses, including Sir Charles Hotham, who had commanded the African squadron, viewed the nonparticipation of

the United States as a more significant problem. Ibid. (responding to Hotham's testimony).

136. Figure 4.3 was compiled from the Revised Trans-Atlantic Slave Trade Database using the YEARDEP variable for the year of departure for the voyage and the NATIONAL variable for the country in which the ship was registered, if known. The imputed nationality variable was not used, as it might not accurately reflect what this figure is concerned with.

137. In addition, some ships carried multiple flags. Thus, the number of ships that carried American or French flags onboard may be seriously underrepresented in the database.

138. J. P. Van Niekerk, "British, Portuguese, and American Judges in Adderley Street: The International Legal Background to and Some Judicial Aspects of the Cape Town Mixed Commissions for the Suppression of the Transatlantic Slave Trade in the Nineteenth Century (pt. 3)," *Comparative and International Law Journal of Southern Arica* 37 (2004): 413.

139. Ibid., 432. For the history of the negotiations behind the 1862 treaty, see Milne, "Lyon-Seward Treaty," 511.

140. See First Commons Report, 32 (testimony of Captain Joseph Denman).

141. W. M. Smith and H. W. Macaulay, Commissioners at Sierra Leone, to Viscount Palmerston, 9 April 1834, in *Correspondence with the British Commissioners, at Sierra Leone, the Havana, Rio de Janeiro, and Surinam, Relating to the Slave Trade*, class A, 45–46, in *B.P.P.*, vol. 14. In this case, the British commissioners sat alone, due to the vacancy of the Portuguese seats on the commission. Viscount Palmerston to Lord Howard de Walden, 7 October 1834, in *Correspondence with Foreign Powers, Relating to the Slave Trade*, class B, 18, in *B.P.P.*, vol. 14.

142. W. M. Smith and H. W. Macaulay, Commissioners at Sierra Leone, to Viscount Palmerston, 9 April 1834, in *Correspondence with the British Commissioners, at Sierra Leone, the Havana, Rio de Janeiro, and Surinam, Relating to the Slave Trade*, class A, 45–46, in *B.P.P.*, vol. 14.

143. Viscount Palmerston to Lord Howard de Walden, 7 October 1834, in *Correspondence with Foreign Powers, Relating to the Slave Trade*, class B, 18, 19, in *B.P.P.*, vol. 14; also see Viscount Palmerston to Commissioners at Rio, 8 October 1834, in *Correspondence with the British Commissioners at Sierra Leone, the Havana, Rio de Janeiro, and Surinam, Relating to the Slave Trade*, class A, 147, in *B.P.P.*, vol. 14 (stating that commission misapplied the law to the facts in releasing the *Maria da Gloria*).

144. W. M. Smith and Edward W. H. Schenbey, Commissioners at Sierra Leone, to Viscount Palmerston, 6 January 1834, in *Correspondence with the British Commissioners, at Sierra Leone, the Havana, Rio de Janeiro, and Surinam, Relating to the Slave Trade*, class A, 1, in *B.P.P.*, vol. 14.

145. On Spain's resistance, see the Earl of Aberdeen to Commissioners at Havana, 24 April 1830, in *Correspondence with the British Commissioners, at Sierra Leone, the Havana, Rio de Janeiro, and Surinam, Relating to the Slave Trade*, class A, 91, in *B.P.P.*, vol. 12 (reporting Spain's refusal of a proposed equipment clause). On the treaty revision, see George Villiers to Viscount Palmerston, 9 September 1834, in *Correspondence with Foreign Powers, Relating to the Slave trade*, class B, 11, in *B.P.P.*, vol. 14. On the signing, George Villiers to Viscount Palmerston, 28 June 1835, in *Correspondence with the Foreign Powers, Relating to the Slave Trade*, class B, 8, in *B.P.P.*, vol. 14. On the news reaching Havana, W. S. Macleay and Edward W. H. Schenbey, Commissioners at Havana, to Viscount Palmerston, 10 January 1836, in *Correspondence with the British Commissioners, at Sierra Leone, the Havana, Rio de Janeiro, and Surinam, Relating to the Slave Trade*, class A, 212, in *B.P.P.*, vol. 14.

146. Viscount Palmerston to the Baron de Moncorvo, 30 April 1836, in *Correspondence with Foreign Powers, Relating to the Slave Trade*, class B, 46–54, in *B.P.P.*, vol. 14; Viscount Palmerston to Lord Howard de Walden, 20 April 1839, in *Correspondence with Foreign Powers Relating to the Slave Trade*, class B, 71, in *B.P.P.*, vol. 17.

147. See Bethell, *Abolition of the Brazilian Slave Trade*, 166–79; also see H. W. Macaulay and R. Doherty, Commissioners at Sierra Leone, to Viscount Palmerston, 2 September 1839, in *Correspondence with the British Commissioners Relating to the Slave Trade, 1839–40*, class A, 111–12, in *British Parliamentary Papers*, vol. 18 (1839–40; photo. repr., Shannon: Irish University Press, 1968) (hereafter cited as *B.P.P.*, vol. 18) (enclosing a "Report of the Case of the Brig *Emprehendedor*"); George Jackson and Frederick Grigg, Commissioners at Rio, to Viscount Palmerston, 23 September 1839, in *Correspondence with the British Commissioners Relating to the Slave Trade*, class A, 258, in *B.P.P.*, vol. 18 (enclosing a report on the case of the *Maria Carlota*).

148. For the suggestion about jurisdiction over slaves on land, see Lords Report 1850, 71 (testimony of David Turnbull). For suggestions of criminal punishment, either in national courts or in mixed courts, see, e.g., First Commons Report, 5 (testimony of Viscount Palmerston); ibid.,122 (testimony of John Carr, chief justice of Sierra Leone); ibid., 34–35 (testimony of Captain Joseph Denman); ibid., 166 (testimony of Commander Thomas Francis Birch).

149. Compare W. Fergusson and M. L. Melville, Commissioners at Sierra Leone, to Viscount Palmerston, 23 September 1841, in *Correspondence with the British Commissioners at Sierra Leone, the Havana, Rio de Janeiro, and Surinam, Relating to the Slave Trade*, class A, 31, in *B.P.P.*, vol. 21 (acknowledging Palmerston's instruction that there was no legal authority for the detention of crews), with Geo. Frere, Jr. and Frederic R. Surtees, Commissioners at Cape of Good Hope, to Viscount Palmerston, 31 October 1846, in *Correspondence with the British Commissioners at Sierra Leone, Havana, Rio de Janeiro, Surinam, Cape of Good Hope, Jamaica, Loanda, and Boa Vista, Proceedings of British Vice-Admiralty Courts, and Reports of Naval Officers, Relating to the Slave Trade*, class A, 113, in *B.P.P.*, vol. 34 (acknowledging the opinion of British law officers that under Article XII of the Anglo-Portuguese Treaty of 1842, slave crews could be detained in custody by the mixed commission until they could be turned over to their own governments for trial), and Ildefenso Leopoldo Bayard to Alfredo Duprat, Portuguese Commissioner, 22 May 1847, in *Correspondence with the British Commissioners at Sierra Leone, Havana, Rio de Janeiro, Surinam, Cape of Good Hope, Jamaica, Loanda, and Boa Vista, Proceedings of British Vice-Admiralty Courts, and Reports of Naval Officers, Relating to the Slave Trade*, class A, 130, in *B.P.P.*, vol. 34 (instructing the Portuguese commissioner that slave crews should be sent to Loanda or Cape Verde and "delivered to the Governor-Generals, to be dealt with according to law").

150. See the text accompanying notes 55–62 of this chapter for a more thorough discussion of the rates of condemnation and acquittal in the various courts of mixed commission.

151. Oct. Temple and H. W. Macauley, Commissioners at Sierra Leone, to Viscount Palmerston, 30 June 1834, in *Correspondence with the British Commissioners, at Sierra Leone, the Havana, Rio de Janeiro, and Surinam, Relating to the Slave Trade*, class A, 63, in *B.P.P.*, vol. 14.

152. H. T. Kilbee, Commissioner at Havana, to George Canning, Secretary, 31 July 1824, in *Correspondence with the British Commissioners at Sierra Leone, the Havannah, Rio de Janeiro, and Surinam, Relating to the Slave Trade*, class A, 74, in *B.P.P.*, vol. 12.

153. George Jackson and Frederick Grigg, Commissioners at Rio, to Viscount Palmerston, 16 January 1839, in *Correspondence with the British Commissioners at Sierra Leone, the Havana, and Rio de Janeiro, Relating to the Slave Trade*, class A, 135–36, in *B.P.P.*, vol. 17.

154. See, e.g., First Commons Report, 161–62 (testimony of Commander Thomas Francis Birch).

155. Viscount Palmerston to Commissioners at Havana, 31 July 1841, in *Correspondence with the British Commissioners at Sierra Leone, the Havana, Rio de Janeiro, and Surinam, Relating to the Slave Trade*, class A, 206, in *B.P.P.*, vol. 21.

156. Walter W. Lewis and L. Hook, Commissioners at Sierra Leone, to Viscount Palmerston, 10 April 1841, in *Correspondence with the British Commissioners at Sierra Leone, the Havana, Rio de Janeiro, and Surinam, Relating to the Slave Trade*, class A, 78, in *B.P.P.*, vol. 21.

157. George Villiers to Don Juan Alvarez y Mendizabal, 10 March 1836, Enclosed in Mr. Villiers to Viscount Palmerston, 12 March 1836, in *Correspondence with Foreign Powers, Relating to the Slave Trade, 1836*, class B, 20–21, *in B.P.P.*, vol. 14.

158. The Earl of Aberdeen to Commissioners at Havana, 15 December 1841, in *Correspondence with the British Commissioners and with Foreign Powers, Relating to the Slave Trade*, class A, 249, in *B.P.P.*, vol. 21.

159. See, e.g., Chris Edwd. Lefroy to the Earl of Dudley, 13 December 1827, in *Correspondence with the British Commissioners at Sierra Leone, the Havana, Rio de Janeiro, and Surinam, Relating to the Slave Trade*, class A, 172, in *B.P.P.*, vol. 12 (discussing the lack of Dutch cruisers assigned to suppress the slave trade in Surinam).

160. See, e.g., W. S. Macleay to the Earl of Aberdeen, 19 August 1828, in *Correspondence with the British Commissioners at Sierra Leone, the Havana, Rio de Janeiro, and Surinam, Relative to the Slave Trade*, class A, 147, in *B.P.P.*, vol. 12 (reporting the acquittal of a slave vessel by the Spanish Court of Admiralty in Havana).

161. See, e.g., the Earl of Aberdeen to Commissioners at Rio de Janeiro, 21 September 1841, in *Correspondence with the British Commissioners and with Foreign Powers, Relating to the Slave Trade*, class A, 355–56, in *B.P.P.*, vol. 21 (discussing the acquittal by Brazilian criminal courts of crew members declared by the mixed commission to have been engaged in piracy relating to the slave trade).

162. See generally, First Commons Report.

163. See Governor Doherty to Lord John Russel, 7 December 1840, in *Correspondence Relative to Slave Trade at the Gallinas*, pp. 3–4, House of Commons Parliamentary Papers Online (2005), ProQuest (300), http://gateway.proquest.com/openurl?url_ver=Z39.88-2004&res_dat=xri:hcpp-us&rft_dat=xri:hcpp:rec:1841-019917.

164. *Buron v. Denman*, (1848) 154 Eng. Rep. 450, 455–56 (Exch. Div.).

165. See First Commons Report, 32 (testimony of Captain Joseph Denman).

166. See Lords Report 1850, 59–60 (testimony of David Turnbull).

167. See Bethell, *Abolition of the Brazilian Slave Trade*, 185.

168. See ibid.; also see First Commons Report, 84 (testimony of Commander Henry James Matson).

169. Denman later testified that this strategy of destruction of barracoons and close blockade of ports of embarkation would have been much more effective than the strategy of more distant offshore cruising pursued by the navy for many years. First Commons Report, 22 (testimony of Captain Joseph Denman). Several other naval officers agreed. See, e.g., ibid., 154 (testimony of Commander Thomas Francis Birch). On the other hand, some witnesses were skeptical. See Lords Report 1849, 114–17 (testimony of Commodore Charles Hotham); Second Commons Report, 16 (testimony of William Smith).

170. This case, *Buron v. Denman*, (1848) 154 Eng. Rep. 450 (Exch. Div.), is famous in its own right in international law for establishing the "act of state" doctrine.

171. For a list of forty treaties entered into with local chiefs, see House of Commons, "Third Report from the Select Committee on Slave Trade, 1848," pp. 224–25, in *British Parliamentary Papers*, vol. 4 (1847–48; photo. repr., Shannon: Irish University Press, 1968).

CHAPTER 5

1. W. Fergusson and M. L. Melville, Commissioners at Sierra Leone, to Viscount Palmerston, 20 September 1841, in *Correspondence with the British Commissioners at Sierra Leone, the Havana, Rio de Janeiro, and Surinam, Relating to the Slave Trade*, class A, 31, in *British Parliamentary Papers*, vol. 21 (1842; photo. repr., Shannon: Irish University Press, 1969) (hereafter cited as *B.P.P.*, vol. 21).

2. *First Report from the Select Committee on Slave Trade; Together with the Minutes of Evidence, and Appendix, House of Commons*, 16 (testimony of Viscount Palmerston), in *British Parliamentary Papers*, vol. 4 (1847–48; photo. repr., Shannon: Irish University Press, 1968) (hereafter cited as *First Commons Report*).

3. H. S. Fox to Viscount Palmerston, 15 October 1834, in *Correspondence with Foreign Powers, Relating to the Slave Trade*, class B, 34, in *British Parliamentary Papers*, vol. 14 (1835–36; photo. repr., Shannon: Irish University Press, 1968) (hereafter cited as *B.P.P.*, vol. 14).

4. Ibid.

5. W. G. Ouseley to George Jackson and Frederick Grigg, Commissioners at Rio, 2 July 1841, First Enclosure in George Jackson and Frederick Grigg, Commissioners at Rio, to Viscount Palmerston, 7 July 1841, in *Correspondence with the British Commissioners at Sierra Leone, the*

Havana, Rio de Janeiro, and Surinam, Relating to the Slave Trade, class A, 354–55, in *B.P.P.*, vol. 21.

6. See, e.g., Mr. Turnbull to the Earl of Aberdeen, 24 December 1841, in *Correspondence with Spain, Portugal, Brazil, et al., Relative to the Slave Trade*, class B, 85–86, in *British Parliamentary Papers*, vol. 23 (1843; photo. repr., Shannon: Irish University Press, 1969) (hereafter cited as *B.P.P.*, vol. 23) (describing the cases of "two individual emancipados, Gavino and Matilda, both of whom have been subjected to long periods of uncompensated compulsory servitude").

7. See David R. Murray, *Odious Commerce: Britain, Spain and the Abolition of the Cuban Slave Trade* (Cambridge: Cambridge University Press, 1980), 134–35, 141–42.

8. Ibid., 134.

9. David Turnbull, *Travels in the West. Cuba; with Notices of Porto Rico and the Slave Trade* (London: Longman, Orme, Brown, Green, and Longmans, 1840). See M. Ferrer to Mr. Aston, 16 February 1841, First Enclosure in Arthur Aston to Viscount Palmerston, 23 February 1841, in *Class B. Correspondence with Spain, Portugal, Brazil, the Netherlands, Sweden, and the Argentine Confederation, Relative to the Slave Trade. From January 1 to December 31, 1841 Inclusive*, pp. 10–12, House of Commons Parliamentary Papers Online (2005), ProQuest (403), http://gateway.proquest.com/openurl?url_ver=Z39.88-2004&res_dat=xri:hcpp-us&rft_dat=xri:hcpp:fulltext:1842-020663:32.

10. Report of Don Wenceslao de Villa Urrutia on the Draft Treaty Proposed to Spain by Great Britain, 21 October 1841, First Enclosure in Mr. Turnbull to the Earl of Aberdeen, 25 November 1841, in *Class B. Correspondence with Spain, Portugal, Brazil, the Netherlands, Sweden, and the Argentine Confederation, Relative to the Slave Trade*, pp. 392–93, House of Commons Parliamentary Papers Online (2005), ProQuest (403), http://gateway.proquest.com/openurl?url_ver=Z39.88-2004&res_dat=xri:hcpp-us&rft_dat=xri:hcpp:fullt ext:1842-020663:414.

11. Murray, *Odious Commerce*, 138.

12. Ibid., 138–39.

13. Ibid., 137.

14. Ibid., 141.

15. Ibid.

16. Ibid.

17. Ibid.

18. M. Ferrer to Mr. Aston, 16 February 1841, First Enclosure in Arthur Aston to Viscount Palmerston, 23 February 1841, in *Class B.*

Correspondence with Spain, Portugal, Brazil, the Netherlands, Sweden, and the Argentine Confederation, Relating to the Slave Trade, p. 11, House of Commons Parliamentary Papers Online (2005), ProQuest (403), http://gateway.proquest.com/openurl?url_ver=Z39.88-2004&res_dat=xri:hcpp-us&rft_dat=xri:hcpp:fulltext:1842-020663:33.

19. Murray, *Odious Commerce,* 151–52.
20. Ibid., 154–55.
21. Mr. Aston to M. de Ferrer, Madrid, 22 March 1841, Enclosure in Mr. Aston to Viscount Palmerston, 4 April 1841, in *Class B. Correspondence with Spain, Portugal, Brazil, the Netherlands, Sweden, and the Argentine Confederation, Relative to the Slave Trade,* pp. 61–62, House of Commons Parliamentary Papers Online (2005), ProQuest (403), http://gateway.proquest.com/openurl?url_ver=Z39.88-2004&res_dat=xri:hcpp-us&rft_dat=xri:hcpp:fulltext:1842-020663:83.
22. Ibid., 62.
23. Ibid.
24. Ibid.
25. Ibid.
26. Certificate of the Baptism of Matilda, 29 October 1841, First Enclosure in Mr. Turnbull to the Earl of Aberdeen, 14 December 1841, in *Correspondence with Spain, Portugal, Brazil, &c., &c., Relative to the Slave Trade,* class B, 55, in *B.P.P.,* vol. 23.
27. Paul E. Lovejoy, "Ethnic Designations of the Slave Trade and the Reconstruction of the History of Trans-Atlantic Slavery," in *Trans-Atlantic Dimension of Ethnicity in the African Diaspora,* ed. Paul E. Lovejoy and David Vincent Trotman (London: Continuum, 2003), 17; Renee Soulodre-La France, "'I, Francisco Castañeda, Negro Esclavo Caravali,' Caravali Ethnicity in Colonial New Granada," in ibid., 101.
28. List of Spanish Vessels That Have Sailed from the Port of Havana for the Coast of Africa, Enclosure in Henry T. Kilbee and W. S. Macleay to the Earl of Dudley, 11 February 1828, in *Correspondence with the British Commissioners at Sierra Leone, the Havana, Rio de Janeiro, and Surinam, Relative to the Slave Trade,* class A, 116, in *British Parliamentary Papers,* vol. 12 (1829–31; photo. repr., Shannon: Irish University Press, 1968) (hereafter cited as *B.P.P.,* vol. 12).
29. Abstract of the Evidence in the Case of the Spanish Schooner "Xerxes," Fifth Enclosure in W. S. Macleay, Esq. to the Earl of Dudley, 30 July 1828, in *Correspondence with the British Commissioners at Sierra Leone, the Havana, Rio de Janeiro, and Surinam, Relative to the Slave Trade,* class A, 140, in *B.P.P.,* vol. 12.

30. For the crew, see Declaration of the Captor of the Spanish Schooner "Xerxes," Second Enclosure in W. S. Macleay, Esq. to the Earl of Dudley, 30 July 1828, in *Correspondence with the British Commissioners at Sierra Leone, the Havana, Rio de Janeiro, and Surinam, Relative to the Slave Trade*, in class A, 139, in *B.P.P.*, vol. 12. For the number of slaves onboard, W. S. Macleay, Esq. to the Earl of Dudley, 11 July 1828, in *Correspondence with the British Commissioners at Sierra Leone, the Havana, Rio de Janeiro, and Surinam, Relative to the Slave Trade*, class A, 128, in *B.P.P.*, vol. 12.

31. W. S. Macleay, Esq. to the Earl of Dudley, 30 July 1828, in *Correspondence with the British Commissioners at Sierra Leone, the Havana, Rio de Janeiro, and Surinam, Relative to the Slave Trade*, class A, 136, in *B.P.P.*, vol. 12.

32. For the sick children, see Declaration of the Captor of the Spanish Schooner "Xerxes," Second Enclosure in W. S. Macleay, Esq. to the Earl of Dudley, 30 July 1828, in *Correspondence with the British Commissioners at Sierra Leone, the Havana, Rio de Janeiro, and Surinam, Relative to the Slave Trade*, class A, 139, in *B.P.P.*, vol. 12. For crew deaths, The Captain General to the Mixed Commission, 8 July 1828, Sixth Enclosure in W. S. Macleay, Esq. to the Earl of Dudley, 30 July 1828, in *Correspondence with the British Commissioners at Sierra Leone, the Havana, Rio de Janeiro, and Surinam, Relative to the Slave Trade*, class A, 142, in *B.P.P.*, vol. 12.

33. Ibid., 143.

34. W. S. Macleay, Esq. to the Earl of Dudley, 30 July 1828, in *Correspondence with the British Commissioners at Sierra Leone, the Havana, Rio de Janeiro, and Surinam, Relative to the Slave Trade*, class A, 136, in *B.P.P.*, vol. 12.

35. W. S. Macleay, Esq. to the Earl of Dudley, 24 July 1828, in *Correspondence with the British Commissioners at Sierra Leone, the Havana, Rio de Janeiro, and Surinam, Relative to the Slave Trade*, class A, 129, in *B.P.P.*, vol. 12.

36. Abstract of the Evidence in the Case of the Spanish Schooner "Xerxes," 30 July 1828, Fifth Enclosure in W. S. Macleay, Esq. to the Earl of Dudley, 30 July 1828, in *Correspondence with the British Commissioners at Sierra Leone, the Havana, Rio de Janeiro, and Surinam, Relative to the Slave Trade*, class A, 140, in *B.P.P.*, vol. 12.

37. W. S. Macleay, Esq. to the Earl of Dudley, 30 July 1828, in *Correspondence with the British Commissioners at Sierra Leone, the Havana, Rio de Janeiro, and Surinam, Relative to the Slave Trade*, class A, 136, *B.P.P.*, vol. 12.

38. Ibid., 137–38; Abstract of the Evidence in the Case of the Spanish Schooner "Xerxes," 30 July 1828, Fifth Enclosure in W. S. Macleay, Esq. to the Earl of Dudley, 30 July 1828, in *Correspondence with the British Commissioners at Sierra Leone, the Havana, Rio de Janeiro, and Surinam, Relative to the Slave Trade*, class A, 142, in *B.P.P.*, vol. 12.

39. The Mixed Commission to the Captain General, 14 July 1828, Seventh Enclosure in W. S. Macleay, Esq. to the Earl of Dudley, 30 July 1828, in *Correspondence with the British Commissioners at Sierra Leone, the Havana, Rio de Janeiro, and Surinam, Relative to the Slave Trade*, class A, 143, in *B.P.P.*, vol. 12.

40. W. S. Macleay, Esq. to the Earl of Dudley, 30 July 1828, in *Correspondence with the British Commissioners at Sierra Leone, the Havana, Rio de Janeiro, and Surinam, Relative to the Slave Trade*, class A, 138, in *B.P.P.*, vol. 12.

41. Ibid.

42. Ibid.

43. Certificate of the Baptism of Matilda, 29 October 1841, First Enclosure in Mr. Turnbull to the Earl of Aberdeen, 14 December 1841, in *Correspondence with Spain, Portugal, Brazil, &c., &c., Relative to the Slave Trade*, class B, 55, in *B.P.P.*, vol. 23.

44. David Turnbull to the Earl of Aberdeen, 14 December 1841, in *Correspondence with Spain, Portugal, Brazil, &c., &c., Relative to the Slave Trade*, class B, 52, in *B.P.P.*, vol. 23.

45. Certificate of the Baptism of Marina, 15 November 1841, Second Enclosure in Mr. Turnbull to the Earl of Aberdeen, 14 December 1841, in *Correspondence with Spain, Portugal, Brazil, &c., &c., Relative to the Slave Trade*, class B, 56, in *B.P.P.*, vol. 23.

46. David Turnbull to the Earl of Aberdeen, 14 December 1841, in *Correspondence with Spain, Portugal, Brazil, &c., &c., Relative to the Slave Trade*, class B, 52, in *B.P.P.*, vol. 23.

47. Murray, *Odious Commerce*, 139.

48. Ibid.

49. Ibid., 55.

50. Ibid., 52.

51. David Turnbull to the Earl of Aberdeen, 14 December 1841, in *Correspondence with Spain, Portugal, Brazil, &c., &c., Relative to the Slave Trade*, class B, 52, in *B.P.P.*, vol. 23.

52. Ibid., 53.

53. Ibid.

54. Ibid.

55. Ibid.

56. Ibid.
57. Ibid., 54.
58. Ibid., 55.
59. J. Kennedy and Campbell J. Dalrymple, Her Majesty's Commissioners, to Mr. Turnbull, 18 May 1842, Second Enclosure in J. Kennedy and Campbell J. Dalrymple to the Earl of Alberdeen, 12 May 1842, in *Correspondence with British Commissioners Relating to the Slave Trade*, class A, 163, in *B.P.P.*, vol. 23.
60. Ibid., 155.
61. Mr. Turnbull to Kennedy and Campbell J. Dalrymple, Her Majesty's Commissioners, 19 May 1842, Third Enclosure in J. Kennedy and Campbell J. Dalrymple to the Earl of Alberdeen, 12 May 1842, in *Correspondence with British Commissioners Relating to the Slave Trade*, class A, 163, in *B.P.P.*, vol. 23.
62. Murray, *Odious Commerce*, 155.
63. Ibid., 156.
64. Ibid., 159, 162.
65. Ibid., 158.
66. J. Kennedy and Campbell J. Dalrymple, Her Majesty's Commissioners, to the Captain-General, 22 August 1842, First Enclosure in J. Kennedy and Campbell J. Dalrymple to the Earl of Alberdeen, 29 August 1842, in *Correspondence with British Commissioners Relating to the Slave Trade*, class A, 199, in *B.P.P.*, vol. 23.
67. J. Kennedy and Campbell J. Dalrymple, Her Majesty's Commissioners, to the Earl of Aberdeen, 29 August 1842, in *Correspondence with British Commissioners Relating to the Slave Trade*, class A, 198–99, in *B.P.P.*, vol. 23.
68. Ibid.; J. Kennedy and Campbell J. Dalrymple, Her Majesty's Commissioners, to the Captain-General, 22 August 1842, in *Correspondence with British Commissioners Relating to the Slave Trade*, class A, 199, in *B.P.P.*, vol. 23.
69. See J. Kennedy and Campbell J. Dalrymple, Commissioners at Havana, to Viscount Palmerston, 4 December 1846, in *Correspondence with British Commissioners*, class A, 61, in *British Parliamentary Papers*, vol. 34 (photo. repr., Shannon: Irish University Press, 1969) (1847–48) (discussing further removal of *emancipados* to Jamaica); Viscount Palmerston to Commissioners at Havana, 15 March 1841, in *Correspondence with the British Commissioners at Sierra Leone, the Havana, Rio de Janeiro, and Surinam, Relating to the Slave Trade*, class A, 166, in *B.P.P.*, vol. 21 (similar); Mr. Stephen to Viscount Canning, 25 January 1842, in *Correspondence with Foreign Powers*, class B, 310, in *B.P.P.*, vol. 23 (discussing plan to remove emancipated Africans from Rio).

70. *First Commons Report*, 23–24 (testimony of Captain Joseph Denman).

71. W. M. Smith and H. W. Macaulay, Commissioners at Sierra Leone, to Viscount Palmerston, 31 March 1834, in *Correspondence with the British Commissioners, Relating to the Slave Trade*, class A, 32, in *B.P.P.*, vol. 14.

72. Report of the Case of the Portuguese Barque, "Maria da Gloria," 31 March 1834, First Enclosure in W. M. Smith and H. W. Macaulay, Commissioners at Sierra Leone, to Viscount Palmerston, 31 March 1834, in *Correspondence with the British Commissioners, Relating to the Slave Trade*, class A, 36, in *B.P.P.*, vol. 14.

73. Ibid., 37.

74. W. M. Smith and H. W. Macaulay, Commissioners at Sierra Leone, to Viscount Palmerston, 22 March 1834, in *Correspondence with the British Commissioners, Relating to the Slave Trade*, class A, 31, in *B.P.P.*, vol. 14.

75. George Jackson and Fred. Grigg, Commissioners at Rio, to Viscount Palmerston, 26 December 1833, in *Correspondence with the British Commissioners, Relating to the Slave Trade*, class A, 122, in *B.P.P.*, vol. 14.

76. Report of the Case of the Portuguese Barque, "Maria da Gloria," 31 March 1834, First Enclosure in W. M. Smith and H. W. Macaulay, Commissioners at Sierra Leone, to Viscount Palmerston, 31 March 1834, in *Correspondence with the British Commissioners, Relating to the Slave Trade*, class A, 37, in *B.P.P.*, vol. 14.

77. Ibid.

78. W. M. Smith and H. W. Macaulay, Commissioners at Sierra Leone, to Viscount Palmerston, 22 March 1834, in *Correspondence with the British Commissioners, Relating to the Slave Trade*, class A, 31–32, in *B.P.P.*, vol. 14.

79. W. M. Smith and H. W. Macaulay, Commissioners at Sierra Leone, to Viscount Palmerston, 31 March 1834, in *Correspondence with the British Commissioners, Relating to the Slave Trade*, class A, 32, in *B.P.P.*, vol. 14.

80. Ibid., 34.

81. Ibid.

82. Ibid., 35.

83. See *First Commons Report*, 32 (testimony of Captain Joseph Denman).

84. W. M. Smith and H. W. Macaulay, Commissioners at Sierra Leone, to Viscount Palmerston, 9 April 1834, in *Correspondence with the British Commissioners, Relating to the Slave Trade*, class A, 45–46, in *B.P.P.*, vol. 14. In this case, the British commissioners sat alone, due to the vacancy of the Portuguese seats on the commission. Viscount Palmerston to Lord Howard de Walden, 7 October 1834, in *Correspondence with Foreign Powers, Relating to the Slave Trade*, class B, 18, in *B.P.P.*, vol. 14.

85. Report of the Case of the Portuguese Barque, "Maria da Gloria," 31 March 1834, First Enclosure in W. M. Smith and H. W. Macaulay, Commissioners at Sierra Leone, to Viscount Palmerston, 31 March 1834, in *Correspondence with the British Commissioners, Relating to the Slave Trade*, class A, 43, in *B.P.P.*, vol. 14.

86. W. M. Smith and H. W. Macaulay, Commissioners at Sierra Leone, to Viscount Palmerston, 9 April 1834, in *Correspondence with the British Commissioners, Relating to the Slave Trade*, class A, 45–46, in *B.P.P.*, vol. 14.

87. See Voyages Database, Trans-Atlantic Slave Trade Database, http://www.slavevoyages.org, s.v. "Voyage 1327, Maria da Gloria, 1833," accessed February 21, 2011.

88. *First Commons Report*, 32 (testimony of Captain Joseph Denman).

CHAPTER 6

1. Antonio Cassese, *International Criminal Law* (New York: Oxford University Press, 2003), 67.

2. M. Cherif Bassiouni, *Crimes Against Humanity in International Criminal Law*, 2nd rev. ed. (The Hague: Kluwer Law International, 1999), 62.

3. Ibid., 60–61.

4. See ibid., 44–60.

5. Henry Wheaton, *Enquiry into the Validity of the British Claim to a Right of Visitation and Search of American Vessels Suspected to Be Engaged in the African Slave-Trade* (Philadelphia: Lea and Blanchard, 1842), 4, 16.

6. Henry Wheaton, *History of the Law of Nations in Europe and America; from the Earliest Times to the Treaty of Washington, 1842* (New York: Gould, Banks, 1845), 594 (emphasis added).

7. Quoted in W. E. Burghardt DuBois, *The Suppression of the African Slave-Trade to the United States of America, 1638–1870* (New York: Longmans, Green, 1904), 110 (emphasis added).

8. *Filartiga v. Pena-Irala*, 630 F.2d 876, 890 (2d Cir. 1980).

9. Theodor Meron, "Editorial Comment, Common Rights of Mankind in Gentili, Grotius and Suarez," *American Journal of International Law* 85, no. 1 (1991): 114, quoting A. Gentili, *De jure belli libri tres*, vol. 2, trans. J. C. Rolfe (Oxford: Clarendon Press, 1933), 122.

10. Gentili, *De jure belli*, 122.

11. Ibid., 122; Meron, "Rights of Mankind," 114.

12. Gentili, *De jure belli*, 75; Meron, "Rights of Mankind," 115.

13. Gentili, *De jure belli*, 74; Meron, "Rights of Mankind," 115.

14. Gentili, *De jure belli*, 123; Meron, "Rights of Mankind," 114.

15. Gentili, *De jure belli*, 257; Meron, "Rights of Mankind," 116.

16. Gentili, *De jure belli*, 124; also see Meron, "Rights of Mankind," 114.
17. Alfred P. Rubin, *The Law of Piracy* (Newport, RI: Naval War College Press, 1988), 97, 102–3.
18. William Blackstone, *Commentaries on the Laws of England*, 13th ed. (London: A Strahan, 1800), 71.
19. See Rubin, *Law of Piracy*, 100–105.
20. Act of Apr. 30, 1790, 1 Cong. ch. 9 s. 8; 1 Stat. 112, 113–14 (1790).
21. *United States v. Palmer*, 16 U.S. 610, 630–32 (U.S. 1818).
22. Ibid., 632–33.
23. See Edwin D. Dickinson, "Is the Crime of Piracy Obsolete?" *Harvard Law Review* 38, no. 3 (1925): 345–46.
24. Act of Mar. 3, 1819, 15 Cong. ch. 77 s. 5; 3 Stat. 510, 513–14 (1819).
25. *U.S. v. Klintock*, 18 U.S. 144 (U.S. 1820).
26. Ibid., 151.
27. Ibid., 152.
28. *U.S. v. Smith*, 18 U.S. 153, 160–163 (U.S. 1820).
29. *U.S. v. Furlong, alias Hobson*, 18 U.S. 184, 193 (1820).
30. Ibid., 197.
31. Ibid., 198.
32. DuBois, *Suppression of the African Slave-Trade*, at 135–36, 136 n. 1.
33. 40 Annals of Cong. 928 (1823), 1155 (the resolution passed 131–9).
34. See Message from the President of the United States Transmitting the Information Required by a Resolution of the House of Representatives, of 27th February last, in Relation to the Suppression of the African Slave Trade, 20 March 1824, 18th Cong., 1st Session, 119 (Washington: Gales and Seaton, 1824) (hereafter cited as Message from the President, 20 March 1824).
35. Mr. Canning to Mr. Adams, 8 April 1823, in Message from the President, 20 March 1824, 11 (emphasis added).
36. Message from the President of the United States, to Both Houses of Congress, at the Commencement of the Second Session of the Eighteenth Congress, 7 December 1824, 18th Cong., 2nd Session (Washington: Gales and Seaton, 1824), 5.
37. Ibid., 5 (emphasis added).
38. Mr. Adams to Mr. Canning, 24 June 1823, in Message from the President, 20 March 1824, 17.
39. Ibid., 16–17.
40. Ibid., 19 (emphasis added).
41. Mr. Adams to Mr. Rush, 24 June 1823, in Message from the President, 20 March 1824, 25.

42. Ibid.
43. A Bill for the More Effectual Suppression of the African Slave Trade, 16 March 1824, House of Commons Parliamentary Papers Online (2006), ProQuest (136), http://gateway.proquest.com/openurl?url_ver=Z39.88-2004&res_dat=xri:hcpp-us&rft_dat=xri:hcpp:fullt ext:1824-008845.
44. Suppression of the Slave Trade: A Convention for the Suppression of Piracy, Committed by the African Slave Trade, art. 1, in Message from the President, 20 March 1824, 27.
45. See Betty Fladeland, *Men and Brothers: Anglo-American Antislavery Cooperation* (Urbana: University of Illinois Press, 1972), 125–44.
46. Convention Between Brazil and Great Britain for the Abolition of the African Slave Trade, art. I, Gr. Brit.–Brazil, 23 November 1826, 76 Consol. T.S. 491 (1825–26).
47. Slave Trade Treaty Between Chile and Great Britain, art. II, Gr. Brit.–Chile, 19 January 1839, 88 Consol. T.S. 231 (1838–39).
48. Treaty Between Great Britain and Texas, for the Suppression of the African Slave Trade, art. I, Gr. Brit.–Tex., 16 November 1840, 91 Consol. T.S. 153 (1840–41).
49. Loi sur la Répression de la Traite (Law on the Suppression of the (Slave) Trade), art. I, Port-au-Prince, 19 November 1839, Enclosure no. 40 in Captain Courtenay to Viscount Palmerston, 6 December 1839, in *House of Commons Accounts and Papers, Class D: Correspondence with Foreign Powers, Not Parties to Conventions Giving Right of Search of Vessels Suspected of the Slave Trade*, vol. 47 (London: Clowes and Sons, 1840), 16–17.
50. Treaty Between Great Britain, Austria, France, Prussia, and Russia, for the Suppression of the African Slave Trade, art. I, 20 December 1841, 92 Consol. T.S. 437 (1841–42).
51. Dodson to the Earl of Aberdeen, 2 July 1845, reprinted in *Law Officers' Opinions to the Foreign Office, 1793–1860*, vol. 73 (1970), 527, F.O. 83.2352; see also Dodson, et al., to the Earl of Aberdeen, 30 May 1845, reprinted in ibid., 510, F.O. 83.2352.
52. Bill Intitled "An Act to Amend an Act Intitled 'An Act to Carry into Execution a Convention Between His Majesty and the Emperor of Brazil, for the Regulation and Final Abolition of the African Slave Trade,'" reprinted in *Law Officers' Opinions to the Foreign Office, 1793–1860*, vol. 73 (1960), 367, F.O. 83.2352.
53. The Earl of Aberdeen to M. Lisboa, Foreign Office, 6 August 1845, in *British and Foreign State Papers*, vol. 34 (London: Harrison and Sons, 1860), 710–11.

54. Debate before the House of Lords, 7 July 1845, reprinted in *Parliamentary Debates, Third Series*, vol. 82, ed. T. C. Hansard (1845).

55. Senhor d'Abreu to Mr. Hamilton, Rio de Janeiro, Foreign Office, 22 October 1845, Enclosure no. 1 in Mr. Hamilton to the Earl of Aberdeen, 11 November 1845, in *British and Foreign State Papers*, vol. 34 (London: Harrison and Sons, 1860), 760–61.

56. Ibid., 761.

57. Ibid., 763.

58. Ibid.

59. Ibid., 766.

60. House of Commons, "First Report from the Select Committee on Slave Trade," in *British Parliamentary Papers*, vol. 4 (1847–48; photo. repr., Shannon: Irish University Press, 1968) (hereafter cited as First Commons Report), 22.

61. Ibid., 23.

62. Ibid., 31.

63. Wheaton, *Right of Visitation and Search*, 16.

64. Ibid., 143.

65. Ibid., 144.

66. Ibid.

67. Henry Wheaton, *Elements of International Law* (Boston: Little, Brown, 1866), 199.

68. Robert Phillimore, *Commentaries upon International Law*, vol. 1, 2nd ed. (Philadelphia: T. & J. W. Johnson, 1854), 246–47.

69. Ibid., 250.

70. Ibid., 253.

71. I would not have noticed these provisions of the Lieber Code but for John Witt's forthcoming book on the relationship between the Lieber Code and Emancipation. See generally John Fabian Witt, "Lincoln's Laws of War," *Slate* (February 11, 2009).

72. Instructions for the Government of Armies of the United States in the Field, arts. 42–43 (emphases added), prepared by Francis Lieber, LL.D., Originally Issued as General Orders No. 100, Adjutant General's Office, 1863, Washington 1898: Government Printing Office.

73. J. T. Abdy, ed., *Kent's Commentary on International Law* (Cambridge: Deighton, Bell, 1878), 398.

74. Theodore D. Woolsey, *Introduction to the Study of International Law*, 5th ed. (New York: Charles Scribner's Sons, 1878), 379 (emphasis added).

75. Ibid.

76. Theodore D. Woolsey, *Introduction to the Study of International Law* (Boston: James Munroe, 1860), 316–17.

77. Executive Committee of the American Antislavery Society, *Slavery and the Internal Slave Trade in the United States of North America* (photo. repr., London: Thomas Ward, 1841), 162.

78. Thomas Jefferson, Statement to Congress, 2 December 1806, in *A Compilation of the Messages and Papers of the Presidents*, vol. 1, ed. James D. Richardson (New York: Bureau of National Literature, 1897), 396; see also DuBois, *Suppression of the African Slave-Trade*, 80.

79. Jerome Reich, "The Slave Trade at the Congress of Vienna—a Study in English Public Opinion," *Journal of Negro History* 53, no. 2 (1968): 139–40.

80. *Cambridge Dictionaries Online* (Advanced Learner's ed.), http://dictionary.cambridge.org/dictionary/british/humanity_1, http://dictionary.cambridge.org/dictionary/british/humanity_2, accessed March 2, 2011.

81. *Webster's Revised Unabridged Dictionary* (1828), http://machaut.uchicago.edu/?resource=Webster%27s&word=humanity&use1828=on, accessed March 2, 2011.

82. David Luban, "Folktales of International Justice," *Proceedings of the Annual Meeting (American Society of International Law)* 98 (2004): 183; see also David Luban, "A Theory of Crimes Against Humanity," *Yale Journal of International Law* 29 (2004): 85.

83. Arthur Nussbaum, *A Concise History of the Law of Nations* (New York: Macmillan, 1950), 18–19.

84. Lloyd Weinreb, *Natural Law and Justice* (Cambridge, MA: Harvard University Press, 1987), 45; Francis Zulueta, trans., *The Institutes of Gaius* (Oxford: Clarendon Press, 1946), 1:3 ("the law that natural reason establishes among all mankind . . . is called *ius gentium* [law of nations]").

85. Weinreb, *Natural Law*, 45 (quoting Zulueta, *The Institutes of Gaius*, 1:3).

86. Francisco Suarez, *Selections from Three Works of Francisco Suarez: De legibus, ac deo legislatore* (Oxford: Clarendon Press, 1944), 347 (emphasis added).

87. *Webster's Revised Unabridged Dictionary* (1913), 712, http://machaut.uchicago.edu/?action=search&word=humanitarian&resource=Webster%27s&quicksearch=on, accessed March 2, 2011.

88. *Cambridge Dictionaries Online* (Advanced Learner's ed.), http://dictionary.cambridge.org/dictionary/british/humanitarian, accessed March 2, 2011.

89. Ibid.

90. See, e.g., Theodor Meron, "The Humanization of Humanitarian Law," *American Journal of International Law* 94, no. 2 (2000): 242–43.
91. Hague Convention (II) with Respect to the Laws and Customs of War on Land, pmbl., 29 July 1899, 187 Consol. T.S. 429.
92. See, e.g., Bassiouni, *Crimes Against Humanity*, 61–62.
93. First Commons Report, 19 (testimony of Viscount Palmerston).
94. Ibid.
95. Ibid.

CHAPTER 7

1. See Lord Howard de Walden to Viscount Palmerston, 28 April 1839, in *British and Foreign State Papers*, vol. 27 (London: Harrison and Sons, 1856), 588 (enclosing list of twenty-five pieces of correspondence between Britain and Portugal between 1837 and 1839 on negotiations for a new treaty).
2. Viscount Palmerston to Lord Howard de Walden, 27 April 1839, in *Correspondence with Foreign Powers*, class B, 91–100, in *British Parliamentary Papers*, vol. 17 (1839; photo. repr., Shannon: Irish University Press, 1968) (hereafter cited as *B.P.P.*, vol. 17).
3. Draft of a Note to Be Presented by Lord Howard de Walden to the Portuguese Government, Enclosure in Viscount Palmerston to Lord Howard de Walden, 20 April 1839, in *Correspondence with Foreign Powers*, class B, 71, 78, in *B.P.P.*, vol. 17; see also Howard Hazen Wilson, "Some Principal Aspects of British Efforts to Crush the African Slave Trade, 1807–1929," *American Journal of International Law* 44 (1950): 513.
4. Leslie Bethell, *The Abolition of the Brazilian Slave Trade* (Cambridge: Cambridge University Press, 1970), 155.
5. Ibid.
6. Palmerston's Act, 1839, 2 & 3 Vict., c. 73 (Eng.).
7. Bethell, *Abolition of the Brazilian Slave Trade*, 161.
8. Ibid., 162–63.
9. Ibid., 164–65.
10. For examples of ships condemned as Spanish, see, e.g., H. W. Macauley and R. Doherty, Commissioners at Sierra Leone, to Viscount Palmerston, 22 December 1838, in *Correspondence with British Commissioners, 1838–39*, class A, 26, in *B.P.P.*, vol. 17 (noting, "Of illegal equipment for the Slave Trade there could be no doubt: but this fact could only avail in the case of a Spanish vessel" and reporting that the commission found the *Sirse* to be Spanish based on its course of trade, notwithstanding its Portuguese flag and papers); M. L. Melville, Commissioner

at Sierra Leone, to the Earl of Aberdeen, 31 December 1841, in *Correspondence with British Commissioners, 1842*, class A, 29–32, in *British Parliamentary Papers*, vol. 23 (1842; photo. repr., Shannon: Irish University Press, 1968) (hereafter cited as *B.P.P.*, vol. 23) (reporting the cases of the *Recurso, San Paulo de Loando, Boa Uniao, Josephina, Erculos*, and *Paz*, all of which bore a Portuguese flag and papers but were found to be Spanish and condemned); M. L. Melville, Commissioner at Sierra Leone, to the Earl of Aberdeen, 31 December 1841, in *Correspondence with British Commissioners, 1842*, class A, 60–61, in *B.P.P.*, vol. 23 (reporting the case of the *Bellona*, condemned and found to be Brazilian despite its Portuguese flag).

11. See Treaty Between Great Britain and Portugal, for the Suppression of the Traffic in Slaves, art. 5, 30 July 1842, 30 B.S.P. 257.

12. See George Frere, Jr., and Frederic R. Surtees, Commissioners at Cape of Good Hope, to Viscount Palmerston, 31 October 1846, in *Correspondence with the British Commissioners at Sierra Leone, Havana, Rio de Janeiro, Surinam, Cape of Good Hope, Jamaica, Loanda, and Boa Vista, Proceedings of British Vice-Admiralty Courts, and Reports of Naval Officers, Relating to the Slave Trade*, class A, 113, in *British Parliamentary Papers*, vol. 34 (1847–48; photo. repr., Shannon: Irish University Press, 1969) (hereafter cited as *B.P.P.*, vol. 34); Senhor Bayard to Alfredo Duprat, Portuguese Commissioner, 22 May 1847, Enclosure in George Frere, Jr., and Frederic R. Surtees, Commissioners at Cape of Good Hope, to Viscount Palmerston, 11 November 1847, in *Correspondence with the British Commissioners at Sierra Leone, Havana, Rio de Janeiro, Surinam, Cape of Good Hope, Jamaica, Loanda, and Boa Vista, Proceedings of British Vice-Admiralty Courts, and Reports of Naval Officers, Relating to the Slave Trade*, class A, 130, in *B.P.P.*, vol. 34.

13. George Jackson and Edmund Gabriel, Commissioners at Loanda, to Viscount Palmerston, 30 April 1847, in *Correspondence with the British Commissioners at Sierra Leone, Havana, Rio de Janeiro, Surinam, Cape of Good Hope, Jamaica, Loanda, and Boa Vista, Proceedings of British Vice-Admiralty Courts, and Reports of Naval Officers, Relating to the Slave Trade*, class A, 169, in *B.P.P.*, vol. 34 (noting the Portuguese prosecutor's appeal of an acquittal to Lisbon and stating that "it furnishes proof of the sincerity of the authorities at Lisbon, and consequently holds out some hope that the impunity on which slave-traffickers have hitherto confidently reckoned when brought before the ordinary tribunals, may no longer attend them").

14. See George Jackson and Edmund Gabriel, Commissioners at Loanda, to Viscount Palmerston, 6 February 1847, in *Correspondence with the*

British Commissioners at Sierra Leone, Havana, Rio de Janeiro, Surinam, Cape of Good Hope, Jamaica, Loanda, and Boa Vista, Proceedings of British Vice-Admiralty Courts, and Reports of Naval Officers, Relating to the Slave Trade, class A, 147, in B.P.P., vol. 34 (describing the case of the Flor de Campos, taken by the Portuguese brigantine Tamega, and referring to the Lisbon Decree of 10 September 1846, which directed that "the same system should be followed with respect to vessels condemned by the Prize Court" as those in the mixed commissions).

15. First Report from the Select Committee on Slave Trade; Together with the Minutes of Evidence, and Appendix, House of Commons, 21 (testimony of Captain Joseph Denman), in British Parliamentary Papers, vol. 4 (1847–48; photo. repr., Shannon: Irish University Press, 1968) (hereafter cited as First Commons Report); see also Report from the Select Committee of the House of Lords, Appointed to Consider the Best Means Which Great Britain Can Adopt for the Final Extinction of the African Slave Trade, 1849, 123 (testimony of Commodore Charles Hotham), in British Parliamentary Papers, vol. 6 (1850; photo. repr., Shannon: Irish University Press, 1968).

16. See figure 4.3.

17. The Additional Convention to the Treaty of 22 January 1815 Between His Britannic Majesty and His Most Faithful Majesty, for the Purpose of Preventing Their Subjects from Engaging in Any Illicit Traffic in Slaves, art. VIII, Gr. Brit.–Port., 28 July 1817, in British and Foreign State Papers, vol. 4 (London: James Ridgway and Sons, 1838) (hereafter cited as B.S.P., vol. 4), 85, which was incorporated by the Convention Between Great Britain and Brazil, for the Abolition of the African Slave Trade, Gr. Brit.–Brazil, 23 November 1826, in British and Foreign State Papers, vol. 14 (London: Harrison and Sons, 1854) (hereafter cited as B.S.P., vol. 14), 609, only authorized the mixed courts for a period of fifteen years after abolition; since the Brazilian slave trade had been outlawed in 1830, the fifteen years expired in 1845. See Separate Article to Additional Convention Between Great Britain and Portugal, for the Prevention of Slave Trade, Gr. Brit.–Port., 11 September 1817, B.S.P., vol. 4, 115 (providing a fifteen-year expiration period after complete abolition of the trade).

18. See Bethell, Abolition of the Brazilian Slave Trade, 247–53.

19. Convention Between Great Britain and Brazil, for the Abolition of the African Slave Trade, art. 1, 23 November 1826, Gr. Brit.–Brazil, B.S.P., vol. 14, 610; Wilson, "Some Principal Aspects of British Efforts," 518.

20. See figure 4.3.

21. *Third Report from the Select Committee on Slave Trade, House of Commons, 1848,* 226–29, in *British Parliamentary Papers,* vol. 4 (1847–48; photo. repr., Shannon: Irish University Press, 1968) (hereafter cited as *B.P.P.,* vol. 4).

22. *Second Report from the Select Committee on Slave Trade, 1848,* 37 (testimony of Jose E. Cliffe, MD), in *B.P.P.,* vol. 4 (hereafter cited as *Second Commons Report*).

23. See Bethell, *Abolition of the Brazilian Slave Trade,* 281.

24. See, e.g., *Report from the Select Committee of the House of Lords, Appointed to Consider the Best Means Which Great Britain Can Adopt for the Final Extinction of the African Slave Trade, 1850,* 225 (testimony of Robert Hesketh), in *British Parliamentary Papers,* vol. 6 (1850; photo. repr., Shannon: Irish University Press, 1968).

25. Bethell, *Abolition of the Brazilian Slave Trade,* 325–41; Christopher Lloyd, *The Navy and the Slave Trade* (London: Thomas Nelson, 1968), 142–47.

26. Bethell, *Abolition of the Brazilian Slave Trade,* 313–15.

27. David Eltis, "The Nineteenth-Century Transatlantic Slave Trade: An Annual Time Series of Imports into the Americas Broken Down by Region," *Hispanic American Historical Review* 67, no. 1 (1987): 114–15 table I.

28. Warren S. Howard, *American Slavers and the Federal Law, 1837–1862* (Berkeley: University of California Press, 1963), 47.

29. Ibid. The data on estimated slave imports to Cuba and Brazil are drawn from Eltis, "The Nineteenth-Century Transatlantic Slave Trade," 114–15 table I, 122–23 table II. It includes not only known slave trading voyages, but also imputed imports based on population and census figures.

30. David Eltis, *Economic Growth and the Ending of the Transatlantic Slave Trade* (Oxford: Oxford University Press, 1987), 200.

31. See N. W. Macdonald and John Carr, Commissioners at Sierra Leone, to Viscount Palmerston, 12 December 1846, in *Correspondence with the British Commissioners at Sierra Leone, Havana, Rio de Janeiro, Surinam, Cape of Good Hope, Jamaica, Loanda, and Boa Vista, Proceedings of British Vice-Admiralty Courts, and Reports of Naval Officers, Relating to the Slave Trade,* class A, 37, in *B.P.P.,* vol. 34.

32. Ibid.

33. See J. Kennedy and Campbell J. Dalrymple, Commissioners at Havana, to Viscount Palmerston, 7 January 1847, in *Correspondence with the British Commissioners at Sierra Leone, Havana, Rio de Janeiro, Surinam, Cape of Good Hope, Jamaica, Loanda, and Boa Vista, Proceedings of*

British Vice-Admiralty Courts, and Reports of Naval Officers, Relating to the Slave Trade, class A, 69, in *B.P.P.,* vol. 34 (noting that no slave vessels arrived or departed from Cuba).

34. See *First Commons Report,* 5 (testimony of Viscount Palmerston).
35. Eltis, *Economic Growth,* 201.
36. Ibid., 202.
37. Harral E. Landry, "Slavery and the Slave Trade in Atlantic Diplomacy, 1850–1861," *Journal of Southern History* 27 (1961): 184.
38. Ibid., 196, 201–3.
39. Constitution of the Confederate States of America, art. I, § 9, cl. 1 (1861).
40. President James Buchanan, Speech to the Senate and House of Representatives, 19 May 1860, in *A Compilation of Messages and Papers of the Presidents: 1789–1897,* vol. 5, ed. James D. Richardson (Washington, DC: Government Printing Office, 1898), 593, 595.
41. A. Taylor Milne, "The Lyon-Seward Treaty of 1862," *American Historical Review* 38, no. 3 (1933): 511–14.
42. Eltis, *Economic Growth,* 218–22.
43. Milne, "The Lyon-Seward Treaty," 514 (quoting Russell to Lyons, 26 April and 2 May 1862, Russell MSS; *London Times,* May 24, 1862; *Hansard Parliamentary Debates,* 3rd series (1862), cols. 1957–59, 2179–81).

CHAPTER 8

1. See e.g., Louis Henkin, *The Age of Rights* (New York: Columbia University Press, 1990), 1 ("The contemporary idea of human rights was formulated and given content during the Second World War and its aftermath").
2. See Antonio Cassese, *International Law,* 2nd ed. (London: Oxford University Press, 2003), 281–82; Eric A. Posner and John C. Yoo, "Judicial Independence in International Tribunals," *California Law Review* 93, no. 1 (2005): 1, 9 (describing the Permanent Court of Arbitration in 1899 as one of "the first tentative steps towards the ideal of formal international adjudication").
3. See Cassese, *International Law,* 454.
4. Jan Herman Burgers, "The Road to San Francisco: The Revival of the Human Rights Idea in the Twentieth Century," *Human Rights Quarterly* 14 (1992): 447–48. For examples of this approach, see Lynn Hunt, *Inventing Human Rights* (New York: W. W. Norton, 2007), 181–82, 196, 201–3 (arguing that nationalism, socialism, and communism led to the declining popularity of human rights until the

aftermath of World War II); and Jack Mahoney, *The Challenge of Human Rights: Origin, Development, and Significance* (Malden, MA: Blackwell, 2007), 21–37, 42 (skipping from early nineteenth-century philosophers to the aftermath of World War II, with a brief mention of Karl Marx's criticism of rights as a reason for the "eclipse" of the appeal of human rights as a political concept in the late nineteenth and early twentieth centuries).

5. Burgers, "The Road to San Francisco," 448.

6. See Hunt, *Inventing Human Rights*, 176 ("The long gap in the history of human rights, from their initial formulation in the American and French Revolutions to the United Nations' Universal Declaration in 1948, has to give anyone pause. Rights did not disappear in either thought or action, but the discussions and decrees now transpired almost exclusively within specific national frameworks").

7. Burgers, "The Road to San Francisco," 449–64 (discussing NGOs' advocacy of international human rights standards as well as the League of Nations' treatment of human rights issues in the 1920s and 1930s). Historian Paul Gordon Lauren's book, *The Evolution of International Human Rights: Visions Seen* (Philadelphia: University of Pennsylvania Press, 1998), is a magisterial overview of protection of human rights around the world that includes much pre–World War II history, but his book is not a legal history and does not specifically trace the intellectual and social origins of the use of international law as a mechanism for protecting human rights.

8. Inter-American Commission on Human Rights, "The Situation of the Rights of Women in Ciudad Juárez, Mexico: The Right to Be Free from Violence and Discrimination," OEA/Ser.L/V/II.117, Doc. 44, March 7, 2003, http://www.cidh.oas.org/annualrep/2002eng/chap.vi.juarez.htm.

9. Lawrence Douglas, *The Memory of Judgment: Making Law and History in the Trials of the Holocaust* (New Haven: Yale University Press, 2001), 16–17.

10. Jean-Marie Kamatali, "From the ICTR to ICC: Learning from the ICTR Experience in Bringing Justice to Rwandans," *New England Journal of International and Comparative Law* 12 (2005): 96.

11. See Clark M. Eichelberger, *Organizing for Peace: A Personal History of the United States* (New York: Harper and Row, 1977), 268–72.

12. See Carol Anderson, *Eyes Off the Prize: The United Nations and the African American Struggle for Human Rights, 1944–1955* (Cambridge: Cambridge University Press, 2003), 38–43.

13. See W. E. Burghardt DuBois, *The Suppression of the African Slave-Trade to the United States of America, 1638–1870* (New York: Longmans, Green, 1896).

14. For example, another NGO represented at the UN Convention was the National League of Women Voters. See Dorothy B. Robins, *Experiment in Democracy: The Story of U.S. Citizen Organizations in Forging the Charter of the United Nations* (New York: Parkside Press, 1971), 209. The National League of Women Voters was the offspring of the National American Woman Suffrage Organization; see League of Women Voters, "About Us: Our History," accessed February 28, 2011, http://www.lwv.org/AM/Template.cfm?Section=Our_ History&Template=/TaggedPage/TaggedPageDisplay. cfm&TPLID=36&ContentID=1501, which was in turn a product of the merger of earlier women's suffrage organizations that had close ties to abolitionist organizations. See Judith Resnik, "Sisterhood, Slavery, and Sovereignty: Transnational Antislavery Work and Women's Rights Movements in the United States During the Twentieth Century," in *Women's Rights and Transatlantic Antislavery in the Era of Emancipation*, ed. Kathryn Kish Sklar and James Brewer Stewart (New Haven: Yale University Press, 2007), 19, 22.

15. John Bassett Moore, *International Adjudications Ancient and Modern: History and Documents*, vol. 1 (New York: Oxford University Press, 1929), lxxxi.

16. Manley O. Hudson, *International Tribunals: Past and Future* (Washington, DC: Carnegie Endowment for International Peace and Brookings Institution, 1944).

17. George A. Finch and Harold G. Moulton, foreword to Hudson, *International Tribunals*, v.

18. Hudson, *International Tribunals*, 5.

19. Ibid., 23.

20. Ibid., 181.

21. Ibid.

22. Ibid., 183.

23. Ibid.

24. Ibid., 186.

25. N. Politis, "Y a-t-il lieu d'instituer une juridiction criminelle internationale?" Actes du Premier Congrès International de Droit Pénal 1926 (Paris 1927).

26. See John W. Bridge, "The Case for an International Court of Criminal Justice and the Formulation of International Criminal Law," *International and Comparative Law Quarterly* 13 (1964): 1260–61.

27. Hersch Lauterpacht, "The Law of Nations, the Law of Nature and the Rights of Man," *Transactions of the Grotius Society* 29 (1942): 1–33.

28. Ibid., 1.

29. Charter of the International Military Tribunal, in Agreement for the Prosecution and Punishment of the Major War Criminals of the European Axis Powers, 8 August 1945, 82 U.N.T.S. 280, 59 Stat. 1544.

30. Antonio Sanchez de Bustamante, *The World Court*, trans. Elizabeth F. Read (New York: American Foundation, 1925), 187–88.

31. George Weis, "International Criminal Justice in Time of Peace," *Transactions of the Grotius Society* 28 (1942); see also Manley O. Hudson, Editorial Comments, "The Proposed International Criminal Court," *American Journal of International Law* 32, no. 3 (1938): 549.

32. Vespasian V. Pella, "Towards an International Criminal Court," *American Journal of International Law* 44, no. 1 (1950): 54.

33. Ibid.

34. Ibid.

35. Ibid.

36. Quincy Wright, "Proposal for an International Criminal Court," *American Journal of International Law* 46 (1952): 71. See also T. B. Murray, "The Present Position of International Criminal Justice," *Transactions of the Grotius Society* 36 (1950): 200–201.

CHAPTER 9

1. WorldPublicOpinion.Org, *World Public Opinion and the Universal Declaration of Human Rights* (2008), 11, http://www.worldpublicopinion.org/pipa/pdf/dec08/WPO_UDHR_Dec08_rpt.pdf.

2. President George W. Bush, Proclamation, "Human Rights Day, Bill of Rights Day, and Human Rights Week, 2003, Proclamation 7744," *Federal Register* 68, no. 240 (December 10, 2003): 69,939, http://edocket.access.gpo.gov/cfr_2004/janqtr/pdf/3CFR7745.pdf; also see President George W. Bush, Proclamation, "Human Rights Day, Bill of Rights Day, and Human Rights Week, 2004, Proclamation 7854," *Federal Register* 69, no. 240 (December 10, 2004): 74,947, http://georgewbush-whitehouse.archives.gov/news/releases/2004/12/20041210-17.html.

3. Glenn Beck, "Obama Wants THIS Guy?" Glennbeck.com, March 30, 2009, http://www.glennbeck.com/content/articles/article/198/23372/.

4. Sonia Harris-Short, "International Human Rights Law: Imperialist, Inept and Ineffective? Cultural Relativism and the UN Convention on the Rights of the Child," *Human Rights Quarterly* 25, no. 1 (2003):

130–81. This article does not argue that human rights law is, in fact, imperialist, inept, and ineffective, but its title reflects a common critique.

5. Eric Posner, "Think Again: International Law," *Foreign Policy Online*, September 17, 2009, http://www.foreignpolicy.com/articles/2009/09/17/think_again_international_law?page=0,1.

6. David Kennedy, "The International Human Rights Movement: Part of the Problem?" *Harvard Human Rights Journal* 15 (2002): 101–25.

7. *Sosa v. Alvarez-Machain*, 542 U.S. 692, 749–50 (U.S. 2004) (Scalia, J., concurring) (emphasis in original).

8. See, e.g., Eric A. Posner and John C. Yoo, "Judicial Independence in International Tribunals," *California Law Review* 93, no. 1 (2005): 69 (arguing that prosecutions "will inevitably raise questions about the legality of a decision by a state to use force and the legality of the tactics used by a state").

9. Although there was some initial suggestion that the ICC should have jurisdiction over terrorism, this suggestion was discarded. See Richard J. Goldstone and Janine Simpson, "Evaluating the Role of the International Criminal Court as a Legal Response to Terrorism," *Harvard Human Rights Journal* 16 (2003): 13–15.

10. See Philip Alston, "The 'Not-a-Cat' Syndrome: Can the International Human Rights Regime Accommodate Non-State Actors?" in *Non-State Actors and Human Rights*, ed. Philip Alston (New York: Oxford University Press, 2005), 3, 6.

11. See Kiobel v. Royal Dutch Petroleum, 621 F.3d 111 (2d Cir. 2010).

12. See, e.g., Hugh Thomas, *The Slave Trade* (New York: Simon and Schuster 1997), 196–209.

13. Her Majesty's Judge to Viscount Palmerston, Sierra Leone, May 30, 1838, in *Class A. Correspondence with the British commissioners. At Sierra Leone, the Havana, Rio de Janeiro, and Surinam. Relating to the slave trade. From May 1ˢᵗ, 1838, to Feburary 2ⁿᵈ, 1839, inclusive*, at pp. 43, 44 (describing structure of joint stock company that owned slave vessel *Veloz*), House of Commons Parliamentary Papers Online (2005), ProQuest, http://gateway.proquest.com/openurl?url_ver=Z39.88-2004&res_dat=xri:hcpp-us&rft_dat=xri:hcpp:fulltext:1839-018670:54.

14. The African Company of Merchants, for example, clearly believed it had an obligation not only not to participate in the slave trade after abolition but also to try to suppress the slave trade in the areas of the Gold Coast under its control. See Letter from Mr. Simon Cock, Secretary to the African Company, to the Right Honourable C. Arbuthnot, dated

10th June 1815, in *Papers Relating to the African Company, 20 June 1815,* at p. 3 (noting that "since the abolition of the Slave Trade" the African Company of Merchants' "directions have, upon every occasion, been calculated, according to the best of their judgment, to abolish the Slave Trade and to introduce legitimate commerce"), House of Commons Parliamentary Papers Online (2005), ProQuest, http://gateway. proquest.com/openurl?url_ver=Z39.88-2004&res_dat=xri:hcpp-us&rft_dat=xri:hcpp:rec:1814-004041; *Report from the Select Committee on Papers Relating to the African Forts,* at p.44 ("What orders then were given by the African Committee [of the Company of Merchants] to their servants on the Coast, respecting their conduct since the abolition of the Slave Trade? – The orders given were, to use their utmost power to prevent any Slave Trade being carried on in and near their Settlements."), House of Commons Parliamentary Papers Online (2005), ProQuest, http://gateway.proquest.com/openurl?url_ ver=Z39.88-2004&res_dat=xri:hcpp-us&rft_dat=xri:hcpp:fullt ext:1816-004433:44; Ty M. Reese "'Eating' Luxury: Fante Middlemen, British Goods, and the Changing Dependencies on the Gold Coast, 1750-1821," *William and Mary Quarterly,* vol. LXVI, No. 4, at 867 (October 2009) ("Parliament forbade the new company [the Company of Merchants Trading to Africa, established in 1751], unlike its monopolistic predecessor, from trading in slaves, though its servants could trade in slaves as private individuals"). Although the Company of Merchants was an unusual entity in certain respects, there is no indication whatsoever in the records relating to it that it or other companies were viewed as immune from the slave trade ban. Indeed, one act of the British parliament related to the slave trade took care to exempt from its penalties the transfer of shares in joint stock companies that lawfully owned slaves before the act was passed; by implication, the actions of joint stock companies were otherwise covered by the ban, and liability could even be impossed on shareholders (which is hardly surprising, since corporations did not generally enjoy limited liability until the Limited Liability Act of 1855). See An Act for the more effectual Suppression of the Slave Trade, sect. VI, 6 & 7 Vict. c. 98 (24 August 1843) ("Provided always, and be it enacted, That nothing in this Act contained shall be taken to subject to any Forfeiture, Punishment, or Penalty any Person for transferring or receiving any Share in any Joint Stock Company established before the passing of this Act in respect of any Slave or Slaves in the Possession of such Company before such Time. . . ."). Although this was a domestic statute, it purported to expand upon the earlier Act to amend and consolidate the

Laws relating to the Abolition of the Slave Trade, 5 Geo. IV c. 113 (24 June 1824), which in turn was expressly designed in part to implement the anti–slave trade treaties.

15. See Elisabeth Bumiller, "Evangelicals Sway White House on Human Rights Issues Abroad," *New York Times*, October 26, 2003, A1.

16. See Louis Henkin, Gerald L. Neuman, Diane F. Orentlicher, and David W. Leebron, *Human Rights* (New York: Foundation Press, 1999), 73 (stating, "Until the late 1930's, the international political system, and international law, continued to maintain that how a state treated its own inhabitants was not a matter of legitimate international concern" and describing the Nuremberg Charter's inclusion of *"crimes against humanity"* as "the first formal assertion of an international law of human rights").

17. See, e.g., Peter Singer, "What Should a Billionaire Give—and What Should You?" *New York Times (Magazine)*, December 17, 2006, 60; Noah Feldman, "Cosmopolitan Law?" *Yale Law Journal* 116 (2007): 1022 (discussing contemporary debates over moral, ethical, and legal duties owed "to citizens of other countries who live far away and whose lives barely interact with ours").

18. United Nations, *The Millennium Development Goals Report 2006* (New York: United Nations, 2006), 4, http://mdgs.un.org/unsd/mdg/Resources/Static/Products/Progress2006/MDGReport2006.pdf.

19. Ibid., 5.

20. Ibid., 14.

21. Ibid., 11.

22. Andrew T. Guzman, "A Compliance-Based Theory of International Law," *California Law Review* 90, no. 6 (2002): 1823; Posner and Yoo, "Judicial Independence," 14.

23. Ironically, a similar point was made by Commander Henry Matson of the HMS *Waterwitch* in his testimony before the British Parliament in 1848. Matson explained that the local chiefs in Africa had entered into antislavery treaties with the British in 1841 and 1842 because they had abandoned hope of being able to carry on the trade when the barracoons were destroyed by British warships. "Then of what value is the treaty itself?" a puzzled member of Parliament (clearly taking the realist view) asked Matson. "Because you can enforce it," Matson answered. House of Commons, "First Report from the Select Committee on Slave Trade," in *British Parliamentary Papers*, vol. 4 (1847–48; photo. repr., Shannon: Irish University Press, 1968) (hereinafter referred to as First Commons Report), 85 (testimony of Commander Henry Matson).

24. See generally John Hagan, *Justice in the Balkans: Prosecuting War Crimes in the Hague Tribunal* (Chicago: University of Chicago Press, 2003).

25. For example, Kaufmann and Pape suggest that the British antislavery story does not support constructivist theories of international relations because British abolitionism was mainly a product of domestic religious and social movements, not of the influence of cosmopolitan networks. See Chaim D. Kaufmann and Robert A. Pape, "Explaining Costly International Moral Action: Britain's Sixty-Year Campaign Against the Atlantic Slave Trade," *International Organization* 53 (1999): 631. But they do not consider how it happened that the policy of abolition was eventually adopted by other countries and whether transnational networks or international law played any role in that spread.

26. First Commons Report, 20 (testimony of Viscount Palmerston).

27. Treaty Between Great Britain and Spain for the Abolition of the Slave Trade, preamble, Gr. Brit.–Spain, 23 September 1817, 68 Consol. T.S. 45 (1817–18).

28. Stephen D. Krasner, *Sovereignty: Organized Hypocrisy* (Princeton, NJ: Princeton University Press, 1999), 108.

29. See, e.g., Jack L. Goldsmith and Eric A. Posner, *The Limits of International Law* (New York: Oxford University Press, 2005), 114–17 (discussing the abolition of slavery, though not the antislavery courts, from a rational-choice perspective).

30. See Posner and Yoo, "Judicial Independence," 14–18 (arguing that international adjudication is possible when "states have a surplus to divide," when "the present value of the payoffs from continued cooperation exceeds the short-term gains from cheating," and when "states have imperfect information about whether an action is consistent with a treaty, and the tribunal can help bring that information to light"). Posner and Yoo argue that courts with "dependent" judges are more likely to be successful than those with "independent" judges. The fact that the judges on the mixed courts were not independent of their governments might initially seem to support Posner and Yoo's argument, but in fact the mixed courts do not fit neatly into the category of dependent tribunals based on the criteria that Posner and Yoo propose. The antislavery courts were permanent, rather than created for the duration of a dispute; states consented to them before particular disputes arose; the power to initiate cases rested with individual naval officers seeking prize money; and each court was bilateral, but the network of treaties was multilateral. See ibid., 26 and table 1. The mixed courts also do not fit neatly into the framework for international judicial effectiveness

proposed by Anne-Marie Slaughter and Laurence Helfer. See Laurence R. Helfer and Anne-Marie Slaughter, "Why States Create International Tribunals: A Response to Professors Posner and Yoo," *California Law Review* 93, no. 3 (2005): 899. They were not deeply embedded in national legal systems, like the modern European supranational courts, though there were some connections in both personnel and jurisprudence between the mixed courts and the British vice-admiralty courts. See ibid., 908. They did not exactly allow access by private citizens without the support of a government, but they did create incentives for individual naval captains to initiate cases. See ibid. In many respects, however, they do support Slaughter and Helfer's more general arguments about "constrained independence" of international tribunals. As in the modern courts Slaughter and Helfer examine, there were both political and structural constraints on the mixed courts' actions, such as relatively clear treaty provisions about what was prohibited. See ibid., 945–46. Moreover, the discursive constraints of legal analysis appear to have been real, as demonstrated by the cases like the *Maria da Gloria*, in which British judges voted for acquittal, or in which non-British judges easily voted for condemnation.

31. See Guzman, "Compliance-Based Theory," 1823 (discussing a theory of international law that "explains compliance using a model of rational, self-interested states").

32. For a summary of the various schools and subschools of international relations theory, particularly as applied by international lawyers, see Oona A. Hathaway, "Between Power and Principle: An Integrated Theory of International Law," *University of Chicago Law Review* 72 (2005): 469, 476–86.

33. Peter J. Katzenstein and Nobuo Okawara, "Japan, Asian-Pacific Security, and the Case for Analytical Eclecticism," *International Security* 26 (2001): 153–54 (arguing "against the privileging of parsimony that has become the hallmark of paradigmatic debates" and noting the advantages of "drawing selectively on different [theoretical] paradigms").

34. Leslie Bethell, *The Abolition of the Brazilian Slave Trade* (Cambridge: Cambridge University Press, 1970), 12.

35. Jean-Jacques Rousseau, *The Social Contract*, ed. Susan Dunn (New Haven, CT: Yale University Press, 2002), 156.

INDEX

Anti-Slavery Society, 101
apprenticeships, repeated, 100
arbitrator, 69–70
Argentina, 126, 158
Argentine Confederation, 78
Aristotle, 17, 20
Armenians, 115
Article III, of U.S. Constitution, 47, 191n33
Articles of Confederation, 39
Article VII, of Jay Treaty, 45
Article XII, of Anglo-Portuguese Treaty,
    207n67
Austria, 126, 127
    Congress of Vienna, 29, 32–33, 134
ayuntamiento (city council), 105

Bagot, Charles, 52
"Baptisms of coloured people," 105
barracoons, 220n169
Beck, Glenn, 159
Belgium, 116, 127
bilateral treaties, 28, 196n9
Blackstone, William, 20, 119, 133
Bolivia, 78, 126
Bonaparte, Napoleon, 24, 33–34
Bonny (river), 7, 103
Borneo, 127
Brazil, 32, 74, 85, 88, 92–93
    Anglo-Brazilian convention, 128
    Anglo-Brazilian Treaty, 205n52
    Britain and, 127–29, 142–44
    domestic policies in, 140
    judges of, 70
    Rio de Janeiro, 69, 92, 110
    sugar of, 143
bribery, 31
Brisk (ship), 84
Britain, 9, 16, 67
    abolition policy of, 14–15, 17
    Anglo-American treaty, 131
    Anglo-Brazilian convention, 128
    Anglo-Brazilian Treaty, 205n52
    Anglo-Dutch Treaty, 35, 78
    Anglo-Portuguese Treaty, 35, 75, 78,
        207n67
    Anglo-Spanish Treaty, 35–36, 75, 78,
        188n111
    antislavery policies of, 26
    Anti-Slavery Society, 101

Brazil and, 127–29, 142–44
    court cases of, 26t
    Cuba and, 144–47
    Foreign Office of, 77–78, 96, 103, 108,
        127
    foreign policy of, 169
    France and, 23, 27–30, 45
    laws for the British, 94
    Parliament, 22–23, 29, 63, 82–83, 96,
        126, 128–29, 141, 143, 242n23
    Portugal and, 10, 31, 37, 111–12,
        140–42
    relations of, 78
    Royal Navy, 4, 7, 70, 79, 103, 129
    seizing of slave ships by, 26
    Spain and, 30–31, 144
    U.S. and, 4, 30, 34, 43–44, 46–48, 60,
        62–63, 86–87, 126, 145
Brookings Institution, 152
Brougham, Henry, 146
Brown, John, 41–42
Brown, Moses, 41
Buchanan, James, 145
Buron v. Denman, 220n170
Bush, George W., 158
Butterfield, Edward, 84

Calhoun, John C., 46–47
Canning, Stratford, 28–29, 52–53, 61, 124
capitalism, 13
Caravali, 103
Caribbean colonies, 23
Carnegie Endowment for International
    Peace, 152
Carrillo, Jose Maria, 106
Carrillo, Maria del Carmen, 105
Carrillo, Susanna, 106, 108
Castlereagh (viscount), 28–30, 32, 45, 170,
    185n72
cause of human rights, 134
Chile, 78, 116, 126–27
China, 158
Christianity, 11, 18, 32, 164
Ciudad Juarez, 151
Civil War, 132, 137, 145–46
Clara (ship), 86
classic offenses, 133
Clay, Henry, 46, 49
Collier, George, 67–68, 71

equipment clause, 75, 84, 91–92
erga omnes (against all), 117
Escalera, 109
Esperanca Felix (ship), 7, 9–11
European Court of Human Rights, 150
European Union, 167, 171
Extraordinary Chambers in the Court of
Combodia, 151
extraterritorial jurisdiction, 157

Fantome (ship), 84
FATE variable, 184n58, 206n61, 210n92
Filartiga v. Pena-Irala, 116
final jurisdiction, 58
First Continental Congress, 38
flags
false, 5
foreign-flagged ships, 27, 55, 59
of France, 89
multiple, 216n137
U.S. flagged ships, 44f
Fleeming (admiral), 103
Foreign Office, 77–78, 96, 103, 108, 127
foreign policy, 164, 170
of Britain, 169
of U.S., 60–61
Foreign Slave Trade Act, 22
forfeitures, 3, 41–42
Fourah Bay College, 11
Framers, 160
France, 5, 9, 54–56, 135
Britain and, 23, 27–30, 45
Declaration of the Rights of Man, 149
flag of, 89
French Revolution, 22, 149
mixed courts and, 85
new entry prohibition in, 183n39
ships of, 179n18
Freetown, Sierra Leone, 3, 5–6, 8, 69

Gallinas expedition, 97
Gavino (*emancipado*), 102
Genocide Convention, 148, 150
Gentili, Alberico, 117, 119, 138
Gold Coast, 240n14
Government House, 108
Grasshopper, HMS, 103–4
Grenville (lord), 17
Grotius, Hugo, 17, 65, 118, 138

Grotius Society, 155
Gulf of Mexico, 104

Hague Conventions, 115
on the Laws and Customs of War, 137
Haiti, 23, 127
Harper's Ferry, 41
Havana, Cuba, 7, 69, 72–73, 95, 101, 103–4
courts of, 79
emancipados in, 100, 102, 105–7
judges in, 76, 93
health, 9, 72, 104
AIDS, 164–65
disease, 69, 113, 165
History of the Law of Nations (Wheaton),
115
Holocaust, 154
Holy Alliance, 32
Hope (ship), 41
hostis humani generis (enemies of mankind),
45, 114–15, 119, 135, 149, 154
Hotham, Charles, 82, 211n99
House of Commons, 22, 29, 82, 83, 129
House of Lords, 22, 29, 82
House of Representatives, U.S., 124
Hudson, Manley O., 152–54
humanitarianism, 6, 103, 134
intervention, 118
language of, 134
law, 137–38
humanity, 134–35, 139
crimes against, 6, 13, 114–15, 136, 138,
148, 156
laws of, 116
human rights, 17
abuses, 163
cause of, 134
ideology, 149
protection of, 36
Universal Declaration of Human Rights,
148, 150, 155, 158, 161
violation of, 99, 148
Human Rights Day, 158
human rights law, 13, 116, 138–39, 148
cause of, 134
crimes against humanity and, 114
jurisdiction and, 114
human sacrifice, 118
human trafficking, 163